T0090115

VICTOR WOODS

A
BREED
APART

The True Story of a $40 Million Credit Card
Conspiracy, Betrayal, Prison, and Redemption

Foreword by Ambassador Andrew Young

ATRIA PAPERBACK
New York   London   Toronto   Sydney   New Delhi

ATRIA PAPERBACK
An Imprint of Simon & Schuster, Inc.
1230 Avenue of the Americas
New York, NY 10020

This Atria Paperback edition September 2015

ATRIA PAPERBACK and colophon are trademarks of
Simon & Schuster, Inc.

For information about special discounts for bulk purchases,
please contact Simon & Schuster Special Sales at 1-866-506-1949
or business@simonandschuster.com.

The Simon & Schuster Speakers Bureau can bring authors to your
live event. For more information, or to book an event,
contact the Simon & Schuster Speakers Bureau at 1-866-248-3049
or visit our website at www.simonspeakers.com.

Manufactured in the United States of America

20   19   18   17   16   15

ISBN 978-0-7434-7739-0
ISBN 978-1-4165-9204-4 (ebook)

To God and all the angels watching over me and protecting me every day: thank you for not allowing my enemies to prevail, and thank you for giving me the strength to overcome every obstacle that has been put in my path. I have truly been blessed, and I give all the glory to my heavenly Father.

With love to my grandmother, Mary Louise Martin: you alone revealed my destiny to me as a child. I thank you for your unconditional love and God-given vision for my destiny in life. I will always bask in the sunshine you left, and I am shining it on people who need it all over the world. In my darkest moments you were always there cheering me on, and there is not a day or night that I do not think of you and miss you. I will continue to strive to be the best that I can and be worthy to be called your grandson.

In appreciation and respect for my grandfather, Dr. Anderson Major Martin, for providing a spiritual foundation for me and all of our family members to follow and stand on. Your tireless commitment to God, your family, and your community was unprecedented. Your life and sense of style was legendary. I will always walk in the shadow of your greatness, and I will continue to do my best to keep your legacy and memory alive for new generations. Your powerful spirit has compelled me to resume my proper place in life.

To my parents, Deborah and Irving Woods: thank you for the gift of life. In spite of our many differences I want you to know that there has never been a day that I haven't loved you, and I will always be willing to give my life or anything that is in my power to help you. I thank you for all the positive things that you did to help me in my life.

Victor, my son, never be afraid. Have courage and integrity, and believe in God, and help people whenever you can. There is absolutely nothing that you can't do if you believe in yourself. Always know that I love you. Follow my path, my son, but avoid the pitfalls I fell into. Choose your friends wisely, and seek out not fortune or fame but wisdom, knowledge, and understanding. Remember always and forever that you are a prince and act accordingly.

To my nephew Blake: you are a handsome and gifted young man. Never let those who are uncaring or too ignorant to understand what you have to offer the world frustrate or deter you from your greatness. I recognize who and what you are and, most important, what you have to offer. Never give up. Love, Uncle Victor.

Amira, my daughter born on 7-7-7: you are a special, beautiful, sensitive child of God. What a smart young lady you are: you are destined to become a great woman of substance and value. I expect you to fulfill greatness in your life: you are special. May your life be filled with happiness and all your dreams come true. Never let anyone define your existence or potential. Always put God first. Love, Daddy.

Sasha, my daughter and fierce little warrior: your spirit is great, peppered with drive and energy. You are a beautiful, special child who is destined to do great things. Put God first and no human being before you, and the world will be yours. I love you.

To my daughters Amanda and Alexis Woods: may you find the courage to look in the mirror and change the things that you can, accept the things that you can't, and strive to reach your true potential in life. Life will not always be easy, but if you never give up and continue to try, the world and everything good in it will eventually open up to you.

To my sisters, Valerie and Vanessa: may you obtain peace, joy, and happiness in your lives, and may your children be blessed and your futures bright.

Foreword

My first encounter with Victor Woods was not a meeting by chance. To the contrary. Our paths inevitably crossed in St. Louis, at a speaking engagement where we both addressed the state of our nation's youth. It would be the beginning of a friendship immersed in our mutual concern for humanity, and, in particular, the present state of African Americans as it relates to the criminal justice system, in which a hugely disproportionate number of people of color are incarcerated.

The odyssey of Victor Woods is a complicated journey peppered with peaks and valleys, triumphs and disasters. At the time of his birth, the path to his eventual success had already been set. Born to two college-educated parents, graduates of Morehouse and Spellman Colleges, and with the ever-present guidance of his maternal grandmother, who never stopped believing in his potential and his abilities, Victor Woods was able to achieve greatness in his life. Even in his darkest hours, his grandmother's faith was unmoved and unswayed. Faith is the belief in things unseen, and she maintained her faith in Victor through all his trials and tribulations. He is the grandson of a prominent Baptist minister, the late Reverend Dr. Anderson Major Martin, and Victor's grandmother, Mary Louise Martin, prophesied that Victor would indeed follow in the reverend's footsteps. As fate would have it, this prophecy would eventually become a reality.

Although Victor was afforded every opportunity to achieve success and compete in mainstream society, at an early age it became painfully apparent to those who loved him, particularly his parents and teachers, that his journey to success would take a different, more arduous path toward fulfilling his early promise. However unlikely a candidate for a life of crime, Victor was incarcerated twice, once for a sophisticated armed robbery ring as a teenager, and later for his participation in a multimillion-dollar conspiracy in which he refused to turn in his friends and members of his own family. They would ultimately betray him, justifying their own culpability and responsibility for their criminal behavior. Victor Woods is a man who would not sell out his family and friends to buy his freedom, and that is called integrity.

Victor would begin his incarceration with his head bloodied but unbowed, and, most important, with his integrity intact. As one delves into the unfortunate criminal behavior that led to Victor's downfall, it's worth noting that the intelligence, talent, and brilliance he possessed were remarked upon by any number of people in the criminal justice system. U.S. Attorney Josh Buchman, at the time of Victor's sentencing, would remark: "Mr. Woods is a man of considerable talents. His power of persuasion is remarkable."

If not for Victor's vision, tenacity, determination, and ability to survive, his talents might have been squandered, lost in the criminal justice system like those of so many young African-American males in prisons scattered across the United States. For these young men, surviving and finding a path back to their families and society is a daunting task and, in many cases, almost impossible. In the 1980s, the United States incarcerated 500,000 people. Today that number has ballooned to 2.3 million. Of that number, African Americans, Hispanics, and other minorities make up more than 60 percent. In fact, depending on the geographical location, that number may be even more disturbing and appalling, with an even greater percentage of African Americans in the prison industrial complex. There is a multiplicity of issues standing before this nation in regard to the current state of affairs of the penal system. In the state of Illinois, for example, African Americans make up only 15 percent of the general population but represent 65 percent of the overall prison population, which is incredible and unacceptable. One out of every 10 African-American men is in prison or under the control of the criminal justice system in one way or another, such as probation and/or parole. The United States incarcerates a larger percentage of the African-American population than South Africa did at the height of apartheid. Indeed, there are more African Americans incarcerated in the United States now than during slavery, thus wreaking havoc on the structure of the black family and the community at large. More than 2.7 million children have an incarcerated parent: the ratio of children with a parent incarcerated has increased from 1 in 125 to 1 in 28 in just the last twenty-five years.

These are the circumstances from which Victor Woods would ultimately rise from the ashes like the phoenix, determined on being a beacon of light and forging a road map for those still incarcerated. Moreover, Victor has become a shining light of inspiration for anyone trying to find a way through life with all its trials and tribulations. There is no pain so dire as pain that is constant, and no tragedy so heavy as one seemingly without meaning.

The beginning of Victor Wood's life is a story of reckless youth and unbridled passion and ambition gone wrong. Today, his life, without question, is a testament to the unconquerable human spirit. A gifted orator, Victor speaks with conviction and has become a force for good and a voice for all those lost souls searching for their purpose and rightful place in life. In spite of insurmountable odds, he set out to change the trajectory of his life. Often, like so many people attempting to pull themselves out of the depths of hopelessness and despair, he was met with fierce opposition from those hell-bent on reminding him of his past transgressions, instead of inspiring and encouraging him on his new journey to uplift and motivate the human spirit. At last, he has found his voice, and his purpose in life could not be clearer. His grandmother's vision of him addressing multitudes of people has been manifested. The sum total of his commitment and success is far beyond someone who was simply incarcerated and has made good. Victor's success far exceeds that of most people, who have never been faced with the obstacles he has overcome. Whether he created those obstacles, or overcame those that befell him, he had the character to stay steadfast and ever vigilant on his journey. Clearly, ambition cannot be taught, only nurtured. Victor's ambition is obviously boundless, and his life has now shifted from what might have been to focusing on his current ascension to achieving greatness in his own life. His message is not only for those who are incarcerated or at risk for incarceration; it speaks to all of us who desire to make the best of what's been given to us.

CHAPTER 1

The Sting

It was a lovely Chicago summer day in July 1990. The sun was shining, not a cloud in the sky. My girlfriend and I were cruising down Lake Shore Drive in my Corvette. The convertible top was down, and I could smell the last vestiges of well-seasoned food we'd just eaten from the Taste of Chicago as we passed Grant Park.

The beauty of the sunlight reflecting on Lake Michigan was complemented by a cool breeze from the lake. In a matter of seconds, Soldier Field, home of the Chicago Bears, was behind us. A few minutes later, we passed the Museum of Science and Industry and then onto Stoney Island Avenue. We were on our way to Razor's jewelry store. It was near 69th and Stoney.

When we arrived, Delilah stayed in the car and I went in. I was greeted by Razor's wife, who took my watch and began cleaning it, as she usually did when I visited the store. There was no one else in the store, so we got right down to business.

Razor was a brother in his mid-thirties. I asked him if he had the money as we agreed. His negative reply irritated me. He then asked if I had the merchandise. I told him "No." Obviously, we were both being cautious about the exchange.

I told him the merchandise was nearby, and with a telephone call, it could be dropped off. He said once it was received, we would pick up the money at another location. I was perturbed that we had to alter our original plan. We finally agreed that I would instruct my guy to make the drop, and we would then proceed together to pick up my cash.

I called my guy, Jimmy, and told him to deliver the package to the Holiday Inn in Harvey, Illinois, as Razor requested. Twenty-five minutes later, Razor received a call that the 700 blank Visa Gold credit cards were received, and all was well. I then talked to my guy, and he confirmed that everything was cool.

Razor casually got into his new Thunderbird, and Delilah and I followed him to the drop. Rainbow Beach was also on Chicago's South Side, and not too far from Razor's store. It was afternoon when we arrived at the beach. There were a few cars scattered in the parking lot and several people enjoying the summer day. Razor parked near a Datsun 280Z, and I parked about twenty-five feet away from Razor. Again, I told Delilah to wait in the car.

Everybody got out of their cars simultaneously, looking to the left and to the right, while proceeding toward one another. After we converged, the brother from the 280Z said, "What's up?" He opened a duffel bag he had been carrying on his left shoulder, and showed me the money: $30,000 in 100-dollar bills. He then tried to hand me the duffel bag. I told him no thank you. There was no offense intended, but I didn't know him from Adam. I told him to give the bag to Razor, and Razor would give it to me.

As Razor took the money and reached out to give it to me, the whole parking lot lit up like a Christmas tree. There were undercover agents everywhere. Some were closing in on us in cars, while others were running toward us on foot, guns drawn. It was the most police I had seen in a long time. The United States prosecutor was even in attendance for the show.

All of us were handcuffed and thrown against one of the unmarked police cars. As an agent pressed a shotgun against my head, Razor looked at me and asked if I had set him up. I just looked at him and the other brother in total disgust. On the contrary, I knew I had just been set up. They had Delilah surrounded in my Corvette. She looked over at me and smiled, as if to say it was all some big joke.

I rode downtown in an unmarked car with three Secret Service agents, just as I had three weeks earlier. But then, I knew the game was over. I knew I was headed back to prison. As I was sitting inside the federal building handcuffed to the wall, Lee Seville, the same gray-haired agent who had told me three weeks before to help myself and cooperate with the government, came into the room.

He informed me that my guy Jimmy was telling him so much that I had better start talking before there was nothing left to tell. He said if I didn't talk, I was going to the Metropolitan Correctional Center (MCC) in downtown Chicago. At that moment, I knew what I had to do. I began to reflect on the circumstances that had led me to this place and time—on how I came to find myself in big trouble for the second time.

Well-Bred

My parents never spent much time talking about their parents. However, my father did tell me my great-grandmother was blind and deaf, and she had been raped by an Irishman. As a result, my father's mother was so fair that people thought she was white. I never met my grandfather. They had four children—my father and his three sisters— all with light skin. My father's hair was black, but his sisters all had red hair and freckles.

My father, Irving Woods, grew up in Florida at a time when segregation prevailed, and black people regardless of their complexion were treated like dogs. My grandfather left my grandmother, who was a nurse, when their children were small. My father grew up in a tiny house that rested on a dirt road. There was no toilet, only an outhouse. He grew up like most black people in the South at that time: poor and discriminated against. However, he had a tremendous amount of motivation and inner strength. Attending segregated schools that had only secondhand books, he read all he could. He worked odd jobs, and helped his mother, and prided himself on the fact that he never caused his mother any problems. At high school, where he was chosen to lead the band, he already had a good reputation.

Extremely handsome and intelligent, my father was and always had been a very proud man. He told me about a white instructor who administered the driver's test at a motor vehicles bureau, who insisted my father call him "sir."

"I'm not here to Uncle Tom you," replied my father. It was no surprise that my father failed the driving test.

Dad attended Morehouse College in Atlanta, Georgia, where he met my mother, a striking Spelman woman with beautiful honey-brown skin, big brown eyes, and an arresting smile. She was smart, incredibly talented, and had a good sense of humor.

My mother, Deborah Woods, grew up differently from my father and from most black people in the fifties. Raised in a sprawling home surrounded by beautiful things and wanting for nothing, she was the

daughter of a prominent Detroit minister who had risen from humble beginnings to the very top of his field. Mama was the most popular girl in her high school and was always the center of attention. She
sang and played piano at social gatherings. My mother lived a more
privileged existence than most white people. My mother and grandmother told me many stories about my grandfather and how much he
loved them and the Lord. Most of the important details about my
grandfather were handed down to me by my grandmother.

My maternal grandfather, Rev. Dr. Anderson Major Martin, grew
up in Mississippi, left home at an early age for Chicago and received
his degree from the Moody Bible Institute. He was flamboyant and
always had a new Cadillac. One man who knew my grandfather for
years told me he was the most sharply dressed man he had ever seen.
He had a pair of shoes and a hat to match each tailored suit. But most
importantly, I've been told he was a great family man.

My grandmother, Mary Louise Martin, was a beautiful, extremely
intelligent Christian woman from Brooklyn, New York. She adored
my grandfather. Her whole world was her two girls, her husband, and
the church.

At one time, Rev. Dr. Anderson Major Martin was one of the most
respected ministers in the country. His sermons were said to be spell-
binding. One Sunday morning, before I was born, he died as he
wanted to: preaching in the pulpit to his congregation. Former
President Richard Nixon sent flowers to his funeral. Before my grandfather died, he told my grandmother that if anything ever happened
to him, he didn't want her to remarry because he wouldn't be able to
rest in peace if anybody mistreated her. My grandmother never did
remarry. A selfless person who lived to serve God and take care of her
family, she worked as a math teacher so my mother and aunt could
complete their college educations.

After college, my parents married. It was 1962, and although my
father had a college degree, as a black man he had trouble finding a
job, so they moved in with my mother's mother. My father took a job
at a local grocery store stocking shelves, while continuing to look for a
better job. Eventually he secured a job with a Fortune 500 company,
and was promoted and transferred frequently.

I was born on March 23, 1964. People said I was a beautiful baby.
My mother said that everywhere she took me people would stop her

and ask to look at me. My parents were proud and showered me with attention.

My grandmother and I started loving each other from the first time we laid eyes on each other. Her love remains with me to this day. My grandfather's death had left a tremendous void in her life, so when I was born, she dedicated herself to me. As long as she lived she showered me with love, wisdom and knowledge. My grandmother taught math in Detroit for thirty-five years. I remember always going to school with her when I was a little boy. Before I could even walk or talk, I had already formed a strong spiritual bond with Mary Louise Martin.

Grandma treated me like a prince. She constantly showered me with gifts. I was a hyperactive child; I got into anything and everything. I was also spoiled rotten. I began to get into mischief early on. When I was two years old, I locked the baby-sitter out of the house. I ran around so much that she could barely keep up with me. I was so out of control, my doctor prescribed Thorazine to calm me down. Apparently, it rendered me almost comatose. I sat on the couch in front of the TV like a zombie. After a week, my mother felt sorry for me and took me off the medication. She resigned herself to letting me run wild.

At three, my parents enrolled me in Montessori preschool. I was Dennis the Menace, Chuckie from *Child's Play,* and Damien from *The Omen*—all in one. I wouldn't sit when they told me to sit, nor would I stand when they told me to stand. I followed none of the rules and was so disruptive that my mother was often called to pick me up early. Finally, the teachers gave up and told my parents not to bring me back—by age three, I had been kicked out of school. I had already started to develop a pattern of behavior I would maintain well into my adult life.

I refused to follow rules; it had to be my way or no way. And despite my incorrigible behavior, I could charm people. I had an early grasp of the English language, and people always commented on how well I spoke, how smart I was. Most people thought I was "so cute" and allowed me to get away with just about everything. I recognized that and used it.

When I was three, my mother gave birth to a baby girl. Valerie was a beautiful baby with a head of curly black hair. I used to get my sister into trouble by knocking her food onto the floor while my mother's back was turned. Valerie would cry and my mother would scold her while I sat back, watched, and enjoyed the show. Even though I sometimes got my sister into trouble, we did everything together, and eventually became best friends.

Suburban Life, Jack & Jill and Racism 101

I continued to act the fool in kindergarten. I refused to listen to the teacher or follow the rules. Valerie was the opposite. She was a very quiet child who didn't get into any trouble. My teachers began to tell my parents what they would hear throughout my school experience; I was smart, but didn't listen and wouldn't follow the rules.

My father continued to earn promotions and we were constantly moving. He was successful, and we were comfortable. I never remember wanting for anything during my childhood. My father took excellent care of us, determined to do what his father never tried to do.

Through all the promotions and moves, I maintained an intensely close relationship with my maternal grandmother, Mary Louise Martin. She wrote me loving letters and we talked on the phone. We always spent Christmas at her house in Detroit, or she would visit us. My mother's sister, her husband, and their two children would also gather at my grandmother's house for the holiday festivities.

My grandmother was a fantastic cook. She made cookies and cakes from scratch and the best hot rolls I have ever tasted. I remember sitting at the table watching her make rolls. I would eat the dough, and she'd say, "It's gonna rise in your stomach," and we would burst into laughter.

My grandmother's house seemed like a castle to me. There were two different stairways leading upstairs, five bathrooms, a bar in the basement and an attic as big as most apartments, equipped with a bathroom of its own. My grandfather's study had shelves of books and a handsome desk and chair. A large colored picture of him hung on the wall, and everywhere I moved in that room, my grandfather's eyes would follow.

When we went to see my grandmother, we attended service at Newlight Baptist Church, where my grandfather used to preach. My grandmother was still active in the church and was considered its first lady. The church was so huge that the preacher had to speak through a microphone. There were two choirs and nurses for people who caught the Holy Ghost. When I was growing up, all the people in the church knew and remembered my grandfather, and expressed love and respect for him.

After church service, we were treated like celebrities. People lined up to talk to me and meet the late reverend's grandson. Many old men and women just wanted to kiss me. It used to scare me, but I loved all the attention. I never could begin to imagine that one day I too would find myself in the pulpit, speaking to thousands of people.

My grandmother told me stories about my grandfather so often I felt I knew him personally. Some nights, in bed with my grandmother, I fell asleep in her arms as she talked about him. I was going to preach one day as my grandfather had preached, she said, making sure to keep my grandfather's memory alive. "You're going to talk to large crowds." I disagreed, but she would laugh and say, "You just wait and see."

In the mid-1970s, we moved to Arlington Heights, Illinois, an affluent suburb of Chicago. We were the first black family to move there. A neighbor who befriended my parents told them that others were saying "niggers are moving in" and held a town meeting where they tried to raise enough money for the town to buy the house in order to keep us out. I was in the fourth grade when we moved to Arlington Heights. We had moved from a diverse neighborhood in New York. I knew little about racism. I quickly made friends with a few boys on the block and enjoyed that first summer. But I was going to receive a crash course on racism.

I was unprepared for the first day of school. My sister and I were the first black children to attend Juliette Low Elementary School. I was called "nigger" more times than I care to remember. Although they had never been around anyone black, those white children had been told black people were "niggers." When they saw me, they pointed and called me a "nigger." It was like a child seeing a giraffe in a book for years, then finally going to a zoo and seeing a real one. Racism is taught and learned.

Being the only black in my class was horrible. I hated it. I especially hated it when the teacher would talk about slavery. Each of those white children in class one by one turned to look at me, as the teacher explained the little bit that American public schools share with students about black people and our history.

One day in Social Studies class, we discussed the subject of welfare. One boy in class said his father told him all black people were on welfare. Everybody turned around and looked at me. The teacher admonished him, but the damage was already done. I don't think my parents considered all the cruelties that would be inflicted upon their children when they thrust us in an all-white environment. They had been raised in segregated black environments.

The never-ending battle with my parents remained constant with regard to my behavior at home. I was determined to do things the only way I knew how—my way. Despite the madness at school, I had a normal childhood. I played baseball, rode my bicycle, and watched TV. *Kung Fu* was my favorite show; I was a karate man. My grandmother even bought me a karate uniform. I was fascinated with Bruce Lee. I watched his movies and read any book about him I could find.

My second sister was born when I was in the fourth grade. It was an exciting time. After my parents brought my baby sister home, Valerie and I ran home from school and rushed in to see her lying in her crib. I held her, under the watchful eye of my parents.

Vanessa was a beautiful baby and had the Woods's trademark head of hair. She was happy and athletic—crawling within months and walking early. She would go on to become a track star in junior high and high school.

In addition to sports, my parents involved us in Jack & Jill of America, an exclusive black social organization whose goal was to bring black children from good backgrounds together. At the time its members were mostly upper middle class and wealthy families, but recently they have reached out to less fortunate blacks for membership. Jack & Jill has chapters across the country, and membership is by invitation. Through Jack & Jill, I was able to meet black children from the other suburbs and other cities who were the only blacks in their schools, too, experiencing similar trials and tribulations.

Jack & Jill had local, regional and national politics, with children seeking offices, and mothers trying to get them elected. Annual regional and national conventions allowed us to meet black children from across the country. The only black people I interacted with were those we met when we visited my grandmother in Detroit or through Jack & Jill.

I had a deep hunger in my heart to meet and understand all kinds of black people, not just the black bourgeoisie.

As most years went by, most of the children in my neighborhood grew to accept me, and by junior high school, I was one of the most popular kids in school. *Saturday Night Fever,* starring John Travolta, was a hit movie and one of my other friends and I put together a routine, tried out for a school talent show, and won. After that, I was invited to all the parties, and the girls always wanted to dance with me.

My grades were always a mess. If I got a C, my parents were happy. I refused to study and couldn't concentrate. I was the class clown and enjoyed making the other children laugh. Being the lone black student I quickly adopted the philosophy: Better to make them laugh with you, than at you.

School was one big party. White kids asked me stupid questions like: What do you do with your hair? Or, do you wear suntan lotion in the summer? I hated the questions, but I knew most of them didn't mean any harm, they were simply ignorant.

The morning after Jimmy Carter had won the presidential election, I was waiting at the bus stop to go to school. My parents had felt good about the election and although I didn't know a thing about politics, I felt good about it, too. I made the mistake of sharing that joy with one of the white boys at the bus stop. "The only reason President Carter won was because all the niggers voted for him," he said. The others started laughing at me. Hurt and disgusted, I retaliated in the way I knew best—fighting. Hearing the word "nigger" was like pulling the trigger for an ass-kicking from me. In spite of my popularity, I still constantly had to deal with insensitive comments from other students.

On 1950s-day in school, a day everybody dressed up in fifties' attire, one white girl asked me why I bothered to dress up, since there were no black people in the fifties! She never saw any black people on TV show reruns of the era, so we must not have existed.

The irony, however, was all of those white kids were bobbing and hopping to music created and performed by black people. The truly scary thing, though, was that the girl really believed there were no black people in the 1950s. I had to deal with ignorance every day.

I had a few girlfriends in junior high school. All we did was hold hands—no big deal. In eighth grade being black in an all-white environment became even worse. One night at a party, we started playing spin the bottle. None of the girls wanted to kiss me when the bottle landed on me. When it came to kissing, I was no longer the cute little black kid. I left the party hurt and disturbed. That night marked the beginning of my education on how truly unaccepted I really was in white America.

Freshman Year, High School

Poor grades aside, somehow I graduated from junior high and entered Rolling Meadows High School in 1978. Other than being the class clown and getting poor grades, I was a good kid. I had never stolen anything, nor had I ever tried drugs or alcohol. I was excited about going to high school, but worried at the same time. I knew I would probably be the only black child in the school—again. There was the threat of upper classmen who were bound to give me a hard time.

Also, there would be an influx of new freshmen from several different junior high schools. That meant having to deal with unfamiliar white kids who probably never went to school with a black kid before. The mere thought sickened me.

I spent the night before my first day of high school worrying about what I was going to wear. I was a simple dresser. I wore what the white kids wore: blue jeans, Colorado boots, and a long-sleeve shirt with the sleeves rolled up.

My first day, I was surprised to see a black girl—Teresa—in the freshman class. It was nice to see some more color. I considered my first day of high school good, because nobody called me nigger. (By high school, most white kids knew they shouldn't call blacks niggers, at least not to their face.)

As the year moved on, I settled into being the constantly tardy class clown and throwing things in the classroom. Then I decided to try out for the freshman basketball team. I had spent the summer on the court. My favorite player was Julius Erving, more affectionately known as Dr. J.

Happily, I made the team. My jump shot was only fair, but I had excellent ball-handling skills. I wanted to play like Dr. J., and did exactly that whenever I got the chance. I didn't play much, however, because the coach wanted me to play within the team concept. But I was on the team, and that gave me status.

Then some of my white friends began to make derogatory remarks about black people in my presence. When I took offense and told them so, they would smile and say, "Victor, you're not like one of them, you're one of us."

All I could see was white. I didn't know much about black people, but I knew I wasn't white.

The "spin-the-bottle" incident had assured me I wasn't one of them, and could never be one of them. I didn't *want* to be one of them. Surrounded by whites, I never wanted to trade my beautiful brown skin and curly black hair for their pale skin and straight hair. I was always proud of who I was.

Midway through the year, *Roots* by Alex Haley came on TV. Every day at school, students were calling me Kunta Kinte. I hated sitting in history class when we talked about slavery, and black people being less than human. I also disliked civil rights' lessons. When a white person in a classroom movie used the word "nigger," everyone in the class, including the teacher, would look for my reaction. I hated all of that; it made me extremely uncomfortable. Yet, the suburban environment seemed natural, and every other black child I knew in Jack & Jill was going through the same stuff. I just dealt with it the best way I could.

I kept my grades just high enough that I could continue to play basketball. I was obsessed and thought about going pro. I got my first revelation that I wasn't good enough to play pro ball when I went to my grandmother's house for the holiday. I went to the MacKenzie High School gym with one of my cousins who lived in Detroit.

I had only played with kids at my high school. I had never been exposed to a gym full of brothers playing ball. I got on the court and I couldn't keep up. Some brothers, not much bigger than myself, were slamming. I had the unfortunate task of guarding one brother who not only clearly outplayed me, but dunked on me, too. It was a humbling, eye-opening experience.

"Which pro team you want to play for?" I asked that brother after the game.

"I'm not good enough to play pro ball," he replied. At that moment I knew I wasn't going to the NBA.

The rest of my freshman year was uneventful. I continued to be the class clown and my grades were barely above average. I continued to stay clear of any real behavioral problems. I still didn't drink, smoke, take drugs, or steal. That summer, my grandmother came to visit us and I had my first brush with the law.

CHAPTER 2

Grandmother Is Nobody's Fool

A couple of kids and I had made a sport of throwing objects at cars that were being driven down the street. After dark, we would hide in the bushes off a busy street and wait until a car approached. At the right moment, we would barrage the car with mud balls or tree bark. The driver would usually slam on the brakes, look for the culprit, and then drive away, frustrated. Hidden in the bushes, we would laugh until our sides hurt and tears ran down our cheeks.

Our house was at the corner of a street that had plenty of passing cars. My best friend at the time was a Polish kid named Tim. I devised a plan where we could stand in my yard, shielded by the garden and fence that surrounded my house, and still be in perfect position to mud bomb cars. We tried to outdo each other with the force with which we hit the cars.

One day, we set up shop on the side of my house, next to my little sister's swing set, and waited for dark. My mother and grandmother came home from shopping and asked what we were doing.

"Just talking," I lied.

Grandmother lingered a bit and said, "I know you are up to something!" While my grandmother was a sweet woman, she was nobody's fool. Plus, she could read me like a book, and could sense something was in the air.

The sun went down, the fun began, and we were having a field day. It seemed like we hit every car that passed by. None of them could tell where the mud balls were coming from, until they were well beyond us. They were going too fast to see what actually happened. We were so successful, that I started collecting rocks instead of dried mud. Tim thought I had gone crazy when I suggested we throw rocks. "Cars can't stop on the busy road, anyway, so why not throw rocks and put some dents in them?"

I convinced Tim and we started throwing rocks. Tim threw a rock that hit a car so hard it made a piercing thud as it hit. The car tried to stop but couldn't because of the traffic. We laughed at how hard the rock had hit. About ten minutes later, a car pulled into my driveway. We each took off running like bats out of hell. As we scampered through my neighbor's backyard, Tim ran into a barbecue grill that was cemented into the ground. I helped him up and we made it to his house.

We hid in his backyard for ten minutes. When I thought about it, I realized we didn't know who was in the car that pulled into my drive-way. It could have been one of my mother's friends. I decided we should go back to my house. Tim was scared, and I had to talk him into walking back with me.

The first thing that caught my eye was that all the lights were on inside my house. In my driveway sat a big new gray car; it looked like a Mercedes. I told Tim that it was cool, because my mother had a friend who owned a Mercedes. We decided to go in. The front door was locked, so I rang the doorbell.

My sister Valerie answered the door. "Here they are, both of them."

As I walked into the house, a million lies and excuses were running through my mind. A white man, about forty-five years old, stared at us with a disgusted and angry look on his face.

I heard my mother coming downstairs and I was prepared to give her the "It wasn't us" speech. Then I saw her face; she was crying.

"Victor, why did you hit this man's car?"

Totally disarmed, I just put my head down. "It was just like a TV show," I said lamely.

". . . but you can't turn this show off." The man was a doctor and had just bought a new BMW. He had used our phone to call the police. The only upside to the situation was that my dad was out of town on business. Otherwise, I would have gotten a good whippin', on the spot.

My mother called Tim's parents, who got out of bed to join us at my house. Tim looked crazy and scared throughout the whole fiasco.

Finally, the man agreed not to press charges, as long as our parents paid for the damage to his car.

The next day, my father called and said simply, "When I get home, your ass is mine!" I spent the next few days scared to death. The day my father returned I was a nervous wreck. I sat in my room and waited for him to make good on his promise.

Somewhere between him coming home and finding his way to my room, my grandmother intercepted him. To this day, I don't know what she said. He came to my room and I received a long lecture. All the while, I was waiting for him to take that belt off and commence beating my ass. But that never happened. I found out later that both Tim's parents and my parents paid for the damage.

My mother was teaching, and my father had become a big-time Fortune 500 company executive. That summer, we took our family vacation in the Virgin Islands. I stayed out of trouble for the rest of the summer.

I wasn't looking forward to my sophomore year, because I would again be the only black male in school.

CHAPTER 3

My First Real Black Experience

On the first day of my sophomore year, my eyes focused on a beautiful sight walking down the hallway toward me. Among the sea of white faces were two black faces. Upon eye contact, we instantly came to one another, just like magnets, and started talking. It was too good to be true—two brothers to take some of the pressure off of me.

Robert, a senior, and Greg, a junior, were natural brothers. They had just moved into the area from Cleveland, Ohio. They also had a younger and older sister. I noticed something different about them; they were not like the Jack & Jill black kids I was used to. They were more like the black kids in my grandmother's neighborhood in Detroit, the ones I never really got a chance to know. They talked and acted differently.

Robert and Greg had grown up and gone to school with black people all of their lives. They couldn't get over the fact that there were no blacks in the high school other than the three of us and Teresa, who came in with me.

Robert and Greg spent hours telling me about the black girls at their former school. Also, many of their teachers were black. I was fascinated with the idea of an all-black classroom. I was starting to see that what I had perceived as a completely normal situation, was not normal for every black teenager.

Although Robert and Greg were brothers, they were nothing alike. Robert was studious and responsible. Greg was the opposite. He smoked cigarettes, drank beer and acted crazy. He hated our school, and flat-out refused to deal with an all-white student population. At first, I spent more time with Robert. He ran track and loved playing basketball. We played ball together a lot and became best friends.

Robert came over and met my family, and I went to their apartment and met his mother, who was beautiful and looked like a model.

Recently divorced, she worked as a flight attendant and had relocated to the area with her airline.

Robert's family wasn't involved in Jack & Jill, but sought black folks in places I never thought to look. They liked to roller-skate, so they began going to the Axle Roller Skating Rink in a nearby suburb. Robert and Greg told me what a great time they had skating and that beautiful black girls were there. I asked my mother if I could go, but she always said no. I talked Robert's mother into meeting and talking with my mother, which was no small feat, because Robert's mother was out of town so much. She finally came by, and talked my mother into letting me go.

Before the big occasion, Greg told me the girls were going to go crazy when they saw me. I couldn't understand why. I knew I wasn't ugly, but I couldn't imagine girls screaming over me either. White girls thought I was cute, but treated me like a mascot.

The roller rink was huge and filled with people, mostly black. I was shocked. Girls pointed and screamed looking in my direction. I looked behind me, but Greg was quick to tell me the girls were looking at *me*. Those girls were showing me a kind of attention I had never experienced before. I was overwhelmed. I loved every minute of it. I started going there every weekend. I told Cliff and Earl and some other Jack & Jillers about the roller rink. They fell in love with the place, just like I did. I loved being around my own people. I was fifteen years old.

Clifford and Earl fell in love with the roller rink for the same reason I did: because of all the bench girls. We all went there every weekend, after having spent the week before planning what we would wear and what new girl we could hook up with.

Now there were two black families in our neighborhood. My sisters didn't have nearly as bad a time as I did going to school because I fought their battles. If anybody made a racial remark to either of them, I immediately dealt with it. Most of their classmates knew they were my little sisters and left them alone. When some junior high school students chased Vanessa away from the park, called her "nigger," and threatened to hit her with their baseball bats on her way home from elementary school, she came home crying. I couldn't get my shoes on quick enough. I marched my baby sister back to the park. When the boys saw me, they started running. I ran down the biggest one, hit him a few times and made him apologize to my sister. She had some fun and told him to kneel in the mud and say he was sorry, to which he gladly complied.

Everything was going great that year, until I got cut from the sophomore basketball team. My mother called the coach to ask why. He said I didn't follow directions, that I was a selfish player. I was devastated. My only real connection to school was through basketball. Without that, I didn't belong.

Now I had a lot of time on my hands. As I look back, it was during that period that I developed my first real conspiracy. I had a natural ability to speak and convey thoughts on paper, so I decided to start my own underground newsletter—the first of many times I would use my talents in the wrong way.

Angry about getting cut from the basketball team, I wrote rude remarks about the coach and the team, the poor cafeteria food, the school, as well as some teachers in my *J. B. Winway Report*. I wrote as J. B. Winway, a distinguished, older-looking white man. I searched magazines to find a picture to match my vision, then convinced my friend Tim to type the report for me and got another friend to copy it in his father's office. I distributed the reports to key locations throughout the school, available to all students.

The response was better than I had expected. Students read the report, laughed and passed it to a friend. I even saw some teachers laughing as they read it. In fact, some of my teachers read it out loud to the class. Of course, nobody suspected me—a derelict, with poor grades—of writing the reports.

In the second *J. B. Winway Report,* I promised that J. B. Winway would come to the Rolling Meadows High School and meet with the students. Obviously, I couldn't do that, so I decided to create a spin similar to a popular television series at the time, *Dallas*. On *Dallas*, the main character, J. R. Ewing, played by Larry Hagman, had been mysteriously shot. The cliff-hanger for the season was "Who Shot J.R.?" I found a blurry picture of somebody being shot, and ran the headline "Who Shot J. B. Winway?" The copy said that J. B. Winway was shot on his way to our school, attempting to bring truth and justice to the students.

In *Dallas,* the question "Who Shot J.R.?" was played over several episodes. So, in the third issue, I copied pictures of the principal, the dean of students and some teachers from the yearbook and wrote a possible motive each one of them would have for killing J. B. Winway.

One day before I printed that issue, I noticed the vice principal and the dean of students carrying past issues of the *J. B. Winway Report*. They looked disgusted, but I didn't realize how serious they were.

I was sitting in algebra class when the vice principal called me from class. As we walked to his office, he searched my folders. Unbeknownst to me, the police were called and a detective was assigned to figure out who was publishing the newsletters. Tim had been caught, and he had told them everything. When I arrived, the principal, the detective, and Tim were already there.

"What's this all about?" I bluffed.

The principal, upset with my cavalier attitude, started yelling and immediately threatened to expel me, not only from school, but from the entire school system. He suggested that whoever I had used as the face of J. B. Winway, could even file a lawsuit against me.

I agreed to stop printing the reports and the upside was that they didn't call my parents. It also felt good to see all the commotion from my little newspaper.

Meanwhile, Greg was cutting school just about every day to go to Evanston Township High School, which was and still is a high school with a significant black student population. He would ride the bus for two hours each way. He had been bugging me to go with him, constantly telling me about the fun he was having. I had always refused Greg's request because I couldn't ditch school and remain on the basketball team.

I met a girl from Evanston at the roller rink. I was absolutely crazy about Tracey, and wanted to see more of her, but Evanston was about thirty miles from my house. The thought of seeing Tracey, and the fact that there was a large black population, made the prospect of a trip enticing. And since I wasn't playing on the team, what did I have to lose? Greg said he would call my school and pretend to be my father, and excuse my absence. I was both nervous and excited.

When we arrived at Evanston Township High School, I was shocked. There were black people everywhere—students and even some teachers! Our girlfriends had arranged for us to get visitor passes. I spent the day going to all of Tracey's classes.

It was strange sitting in a classroom full of black teenagers like myself and I marveled that they did not receive the verbal racial abuse that I did, being one of four black people in a high school of more than 2,000 students. As I sat there in peace, I became angry with my parents. I was furious with them for subjecting me to all the grief I had put up with for years. Black children who grow up being the only black, or one of only a few blacks in a white neighborhood or school respond in one of two ways. The first group begin to believe that they are white. They completely assimilate. They lose their cultural identity and think they are white. It's a sorry sight. They are not proud to be black.

The second group understands they are in a hostile environment, deals with racial tensions as best they can, and flees to a black college for cultural and emotional rehabilitation. My sister Valerie, Cliff, and Earl are among these blacks. Perhaps it would have been better for me to deal with the pain I felt in a similar manner. However, fate had something else in store for Victor Woods.

I went to Evanston Township High School every chance I got. I started talking and dressing differently. I began imitating the black kids I was meeting from Evanston. I got a part-time job at a restaurant as a busboy, so I could buy some hipper clothes and spent all my money buying clothing. I stopped wearing blue jeans and started wearing baggy pants. I replaced my old Levi's jean jacket with a Members Only jacket. I even bought a dress hat with a feather in it, like my grandfather, the good Reverend, used to wear. My parents had a fit. They didn't understand their son was desperately trying to find himself, his black self.

My parents' reaction to my new behavior was to attempt to alienate me from my new friends. They were indifferent to my feelings. They simply could not realize why I wouldn't embrace my suburban lifestyle.

I didn't know what being black was about. I thought dressing up like all the brothers was being black. Dress doesn't make anyone more or less black. But, back then, I didn't know that. I was trying to do the opposite of what my white friends did. I became fascinated with black culture.

Even though my grades were still bad and I was ditching school, I had never smoked or used drugs. I never even thought about stealing or committing crimes. One night, as I cleaned a table at the restaurant

I noticed that a man had accidentally left his wallet. I grabbed it and went running after him to give it back. I caught him in the parking lot. He was a white man, with his family. He thanked me and gave me five dollars. It never occurred to me to just keep the wallet. I was an honest kid back then, without any larceny in my heart. I never even looked in the wallet.

The more time I spent in Evanston and the roller rink, the more I hated living in Arlington Heights. I told my parents I resented them for subjecting me to all the madness I had endured over the years. My parents simply dismissed what I was feeling. They said I should have been happy to live in such a nice neighborhood and attend good schools.

I told my grandmother, Mary Louise Martin, and my aunt in Detroit how I felt. They both offered to let me move in with them. They understood how I was feeling. My parents had attended black schools all of their lives, so I guess they couldn't empathize with me. My father's good friend Dennis Archer (who in 1998 became the mayor of Detroit, and in 2003 was voted in as president of the National Bar Association, the first black man in history to do so) tried to discourage me from wanting to go to an all-black school. He said I was lucky to be living where I was. He said I couldn't make it in that type of environment. I might get hurt, or worse. I knew my Uncle Dennis and my parents meant well and were just trying to protect me, but I was insulted.

What kind of black person would I become if I couldn't relate to my people? What kind of person didn't want to get to know and feel comfortable with his own people? Whoever that kind of person was, I knew I didn't want to be like that.

When they refused to let me move in with my grandmother or aunt, I was devastated. My mother was too proud to let someone else raise her son, even her own mother.

That was a turning point in my life. With my dress and behavior becoming more drastically different every day, my parents stopped me from going to the roller rink, as well as hanging out with Robert and Greg. They were bad influences. My parents tried to completely cut me off from my new life. But they were beginning to lose control of me. Once I realized that I could just run away from home and go where I wanted to and do what I wanted to, my parents lost total control. We had many ugly fights, which usually ended with my parents giving me an ultimatum, and I, in turn, having total disregard for their rules and regulations. Even though I was only a teenager, I felt so strongly about wanting to be around my own people that I was willing to fight my parents or anybody else.

My parents sent me to a black psychiatrist and much to my parents' dismay, he told them he understood how I felt, and there was nothing wrong with me. Unwilling to pay for him to essentially side with me and against them, my parents eventually settled on a white psychiatrist who, for $100 an hour, told my parents what they wanted to hear—I was crazy. I never saw the black psychiatrist again.

My parents felt my sisters and their friends' children were dealing with their suburban environment. Why couldn't I? They did not understand I was different.

School had become unbearable. With my new clothes and new attitude, I *really* didn't fit in. Black people accepted me with open arms. Soon after, another young brother found himself at our high school. His name was Calvin. He was a little shorter than me and he hated being there as much as me and we became friends fast.

One day in school, the vice principal called me to the dean's office. He and the dean feigned concern. "Victor, why are you wearing different clothes? Why the feathered hat? We liked the old you. We're wondering why there is such a drastic change in your appearance." I was only fifteen, but I understood exactly what they were saying. The dean and vice principal were comfortable when I acted like I was white.

In the midst of my chameleonlike change, things at home were coming to a head. I completely stopped doing my schoolwork. My parents grounded me and took away my telephone privileges. Every parent and teenager knows that can be devastating to a teenager. And it was to me.

One day Tracey made the long trip to see me because I couldn't call her or leave my house. She was worried since she hadn't seen or heard from me. She went to Robert's apartment and he came to my house. As luck would have it, I answered the door before my parents did. Robert quickly explained to me that Tracey was at his place waiting for me. I asked my parents if I could go to Robert's to see her. They refused. I asked if Tracey could come over, sit in our living room, and visit with me. Again, they refused.

I was at a crossroads in my life. Either I could respect my parents' wishes or I could defy them. I opted for the latter. I waited a couple of hours, packed some things, put on my coat and just walked out the front door. I ran away from home.

Running Away from Home

It was a bold move. I was nervous and scared. But the excitement was thrilling, and in my heart I knew my parents were wrong for not allowing Tracey to visit under their supervision. "They are simply determined to stifle my black experience," I said to myself.

Initially, I stayed with Robert and Greg because, during the week, their mother was flying. On weekends, when she was home, I would hide in Robert and Greg's closet at night. Their mother never suspected a thing. Robert and Greg's sisters were cool and never told their mother that I was hiding there.

Every day I took the long bus ride to Evanston to see Tracey. Tracey and I never had intercourse. However, we spent hours on her mother's couch with me mostly sucking her beautiful black breasts while trying to get her so excited that she would allow me to creep into her pants. I'm sorry to say that never happened. I quit going to school. I was happy.

After a few days, my parents had called the police and had me put on the runaway list. When I had been gone a few weeks, I needed more of my clothes. My plan was to sneak back home and retrieve my things. I surprised my sister Valerie at the bus stop and convinced her to give me her keys to the house. I had forgotten mine in haste when I left. She reluctantly gave them to me.

I waited until the time I knew my father would have left for work. When I arrived, the car was not in the driveway. I walked right into the house, just like I had walked out.

I started to close the door and my father finished it—slamming it shut. He grabbed me and held me down, while he telephoned the police. He forced me to his car in the garage and drove me to the police station. I guess this was supposed to scare me. As I sat in a jail cell for the first time in my life, I felt no fear. I did not know I would eventually spend almost a decade of my life in prison.

After about an hour, my father looked through a little window at me. An officer let me out and I was taken to a different officer who, with my dad, lectured me. The officer said he could send me to a terrible foster home in the city, or I could go back home with my father. He and my father expected me to beg to go home. I looked my father and that officer right in their eyes, and told them I wanted to go to the foster home.

Until I met Robert and Greg, my only black friends were from Jack & Jill families or other upper-middle-class or rich people my parents knew. Most had forgotten or didn't care to remember where they came from and their children were isolated from the realities of the majority of black America; they didn't have a clue about the condition of most black people in this country or our culture.

Black people in America can ill afford to forget where we come from—especially those fortunate blacks who slipped through the narrow crack of success. It's not enough to look back and reflect on the difficult days. Those who can, have to reach back and help those who need help.

Many peoples have come to this country, and make up this huge melting pot called America, but blacks are the only ones to have arrived in chains, the only ones uprooted, and brought here unwillingly. That has been an excuse for not supporting one another, for not gathering knowledge and resources, and moving our race forward as a community.

We need to start by making the preservation and development of our children our top priority. No other race in this country is going to save black children from being cut down in our streets. The responsibility falls where it deserves to be: in the hands of black people.

It's not a bad thing to network through Jack & Jill or any other organization designed to uplift black people, but exclusion and not knowing about *all* of your people, regardless of their social or economic status, is wrong. I knew black people who talked about other black people as if they, themselves, were not black and look down on their less fortunate brothers and sisters. Only by the grace of God were they born into a family that could afford to live in the suburbs, or in a nice home, or be sent to college.

There are too many black people in this country who get a little something and spend all their spare time trying to feel good about themselves, at the expense of less fortunate brothers and sisters, when, in reality, many of those people are a paycheck or two from that level themselves. I guess that, even at a young age, I could see through all of that bullshit.

Growing up in bourgeois black America, I'd heard the backroom conversations. I'd heard fortunate black parents and children refer to less fortunate black people as "niggers." It made no sense, because white people who use that word do not distinguish whether or not you have an education or are economically well off. Simply being black qualifies you as a "nigger."

When that officer said the foster home was really bad, that it was in a bad neighborhood, he was saying it was in a black environment, talking about black people, my people.

Why should I be scared of being with my own people? I chose to go to the foster home that night because I knew it was a journey I should not only take, but one I should embrace.

Reverend Watkins came to the police station and drove me to my new home in Chicago. I sat in the car in silence as we made the forty-minute drive into the city. Approaching our destination, the houses looked far different from the larger new ones I had grown accustomed to in Arlington Heights.

We finally stopped in front of a tiny house, with a small yard. Mrs. Johnson, a black woman about sixty-eight or seventy, met me at the front door. I was directed to the bedrooms in the back of the house. I lay on my bed, taking in the new environment. I sensed something moving as I stared at the ceilings and walls. As I sharpened my focus, the walls and ceiling appeared to be moving. The cockroaches that covered the surfaces of the room created the illusion of movement.

It was the first time I had ever seen roaches. I heard scurrying sounds on the floor—mice had infested the room. I pulled the sheets over my head, not knowing what else might appear while I tried to sleep.

The next day, the young brother who shared my room told me he was abandoned as a child.

The house was old and small. It had a musty smell to it and was definitely not clean. The furniture was old, too, and covered in plastic. The other children there seemed wild and unkempt. Yet there was a calmness to it all. Despite the bizarre situation, I got the feeling that it was all business as usual in this place called the foster home.

As I sat down to eat breakfast in Mrs. Johnson's home, roaches ran across the kitchen walls, floors, and even the table. No one in the house tried to kill or push the roaches away. In the light of day, I could see mice darting from place to place in the house. My mother would have a fit if a fly was in the house. I accepted that living with vermin was the reality for some.

In spite of the severe change in environment, I adjusted well. If roaches and mice were what the average black person had to endure, then I would, too. As the days turned into weeks, I began to earn the trust of Mrs. Johnson and the friendship of her daughter, Maggie. She was in her forties and helped her mother run the foster home. I ran errands for Mrs. Johnson—taking her clothes to the laundry, and doing her grocery shopping. I also played basketball with the brothers in the neighborhood park.

The community was completely black. So, in a sense, I had arrived exactly where I wanted to be. The children assigned to Mrs. Johnson's foster home were usually only there for a few days. She had a curfew for the children who stayed in her house, but because we got along so well and she trusted my judgment, I didn't have one. That freed me to take the bus out to Evanston to see Tracey. I was even given a key to the house.

While living with Mrs. Johnson, I found interesting ways to amuse myself. Before I went to sleep, I baited mousetraps with cheese, and placed them around my bed. The next morning, I anxiously awoke to check my traps. I had done better than adjust; I fit right in and considered Mrs. Johnson's place my new home.

My parents wanted to scare me, make me appreciate my bourgeois lifestyle, by placing me in the foster home. They had no idea I had turned my stay into a vacation from cultural isolation and white racism. That was the first time my special gift—my survival skills— would surface. It certainly would not be the last.

It had been a month since I had seen my parents. Mrs. Johnson informed me they would be coming to see me with a social worker at week's end. I wasn't worried about their arrival, because I believed I could stay with Mrs. Johnson as long as I wished.

I greeted my parents and the social worker in Mrs. Johnson's tiny living room. I didn't as much as hug my parents. I just sat down. The social worker asked, "Mrs. Johnson, how has Victor been doing?"

That old black woman told them in her tired, sincere voice, "He's helped me so much since he got here."

"Are you ready to return home with your family?" the social worker asked me.

"I want to stay with Mrs. Johnson." I planned to register for school in the neighborhood.

My parents were appalled. That was more than they could take. My parents and I were having a war, and I was clearly winning that battle. They ordered me to gather my things and snatched me right out of that foster home. I cried as I hugged Mrs. Johnson good-bye. I waved good-bye from the car. I would never see Mrs. Johnson again.

My mother celebrated my homecoming by beating me—with her hands and anything else she could find. She was disgusted that I wanted to stay in Mrs. Johnson's humble home; she did not see that it offered me a cultural environment that my lovely Arlington Heights home never could.

The racial makeup at Rolling Meadows High School slowly began to change; a few more blacks were attending. Some hardworking black families moved into low-rent apartments in a neighboring suburb, in the hope of exchanging inner-city madness for suburban serenity.

One day in school, I saw a beautiful black girl. Our eyes mutually locked and I walked up to her and introduced myself. Saundra was a freshman. She had smooth, beautiful, dark skin, along with a budding body. Tracey and I had broken up, and she became my next girlfriend. We made out in school and after school. She kept telling me she wanted us to be alone so we could have sex. We both lived at home, and I didn't even have a driver's license. Not to mention, I was permanently grounded. Being alone with her would be no easy task; however, a fifteen-year-old boy's libido will make him go to drastic lengths.

My father had just purchased a new Lincoln Mark V. My parents planned to have dinner with friends during that upcoming weekend. The friends would drive to our house, and they would all leave together in my father's new Mark V.

My plan was to hide the car keys, forcing my parents' friends to drive, leaving the Mark V for me to pick up Saundra and bring her to the house.

Several weeks earlier, Valerie had skipped school and accompanied me to Evanston High School. I called our school in my deepest voice and pretended to be my father excusing her for the day. I threatened to tell on her if she told on me; I thought I could count on her to keep the secret from my parents.

I needed her help. Someone had to baby-sit Vanessa and keep her out of the way, because she would surely tell my parents.

Saturday arrived and my father's car keys were in their usual place on the mantel above the fireplace. While my parents were upstairs getting ready to go, I took the keys and hid them in my bedroom. The stage had been set.

My father was always ready before my mother. They were planning to leave around 8:00 for an 8:30 dinner reservation. About 7:45, my father began looking for his keys. Soon my mother was finished dressing and assisted in the search. I sat in the family room watching TV. Moments before my parents' friends arrived, my father asked me if I had seen his keys. I looked him right in the eye and said "No."

My parents left in their friends' car, and armed with very little driver's education or experience, I used my father's Mark V to pick up Saundra. I drove right back to my house. Valerie had successfully diverted Vanessa's attention, and we went right to my bedroom.

Somehow in the midst of fumbling and bumbling, we managed to have sex. Saundra was not as experienced in bed as she pretended to be. Neither was I, so it worked out fine. I took her home and returned without little Vanessa suspecting a thing. Valerie had done a good job of keeping her occupied. My plan was a complete success. Even the keys turned up when my parents returned.

The next morning, Sunday, as I slept soundly, Valerie went for confession at the breakfast table instead of at church. She told my parents about her misdeeds, and mine, too.

They were livid and at the end of their rope with me. Still unwilling to let me move to Detroit with our relatives, my parents sent me to a mental institution for problem teenagers from well-to-do families.

There were about forty other youths, and one other black teen. I had a brief talk with a psychiatrist and my father, before I was admitted. Instead of remaining composed, I ranted and raved about how my parents wouldn't allow me to be with my girlfriend, so I took my dad's car so I could have sex with my girlfriend. This time, my parents were winning the battle. The good doctor didn't hesitate to admit me.

The program was designed for rich people's children who had problems. Most of the teenagers were there for drug addiction, although there was one kid there for molesting his little sister. It was completely bizarre.

I was unable to use the telephone, and I was locked in my room at night. I refused to cooperate in any of the group sessions, or even talk to any of the psychiatrists on staff.

Eventually, I was befriended by a black man who worked there as an orderly. He didn't understand why I was there. When I explained my story to him, he felt sorry for me: my crime was trying to have sex with a girl. I was sure that my parents were keeping my whereabouts secret. I talked him into calling my grandmother in Detroit, and giving her the details of my plight. After my grandmother and aunt received the news, they put pressure on them. I was released after two weeks, and returned to the madness: home.

Things continued to be really bad at home and I faded into my own world. I began staying up late watching TV. After midnight, a miniseries called *The Gangster Chronicles*, about Charles "Lucky" Luciano and his childhood friends, Bennie "Bugsy" Siegel and Meyer Lansky, was aired.

The series started off with Lucky Luciano as a teenager in New York City. It detailed his rise from a small-time criminal to his position in the Mafia syndicate. I became obsessed with his story. I looked for any information I could find on his life. I found his autobiography in the library, *The Last Testament of Lucky Luciano*.

I was also fascinated with *The Thief*, a movie that starred James Caan as a master thief. After I watched *The Godfather*, I fantasized about living a life of crime. I wanted to move out of my house so badly. But, at fifteen going on sixteen years old, where could I go? Becoming a gangster would give me the money I would need to live on my own and away from my parents and the hated white suburbs.

One evening, my father came to my room for a badly needed father-to-son talk. "Son, you wanted so badly to be around black people that you wanted to move away from home. Let me explain some hard facts that I've learned in my life growing up in an all-black environment."

He detailed his life as a child growing up without a father, in the South, with segregation and the Ku Klux Klan in full bloom. He had grown up with some down-home black people, not the college-educated blacks that the suburbs had provided me. My father went on to say that just because we had the same skin color didn't mean that all black people were my friends. He told me about how some black people behaved like crabs in a bucket: when one crab tried to climb out, the others would pull him back down. He said that was how some people were with him while he was growing up.

He explained that everybody who looks black isn't black. Some black people were "niggers," and "niggers" would kill you over a quarter. Some black people would call you brother, to put you at ease, before they fucked you over. Then he went on to tell me how the majority of white people feel about black people, about those who smile in your face, while they are calling you "nigger" behind your back. He discussed the negative aspects of society that he thought he had so effectively shielded me from all of my life, not understanding I'd lived these realities daily in school and on the playgrounds.

Lastly, my father said, "There isn't one black-owned Fortune 500 company in America. If you want to succeed, you have to know how to deal with white people."

My parents were trying to protect me and my sisters from the discrimination and negative circumstances that they had endured and prepare me for success in a white world. I comprehended some of what my father said but other points would not become clear until years later.

CHAPTER 4

Introduction to *the Game*

I left home after another blowup with my parents over my curfew. My friend Robert had graduated high school and was attending Harper Community College, a local junior college. Robert met a football player named Dontae, who was about six-four and weighed 250 pounds. Dontae had a two-bedroom apartment and was looking for a roommate. After a brief introduction from Robert, Dontae and I hit it off right away. I moved in with Dontae, and he became a big brother to me. He was like a big teddy bear.

My bedroom furniture consisted of a mattress on the floor and a dresser, but I had my freedom. Without my parents' money and the benefits that went along with it, I had to get a job that was a step up from busboy. I found a job at Burger King, but I wasn't making enough to pay rent and eat.

One of my duties at Burger King was taking out the trash. The manager would often leave the refrigerator unlocked, with all the frozen meat inside. I told Dontae to come by one afternoon and I would leave two cases of hamburger meat in the trash. We decided to have a cookout, and sold hamburgers for seventy-five cents each to our neighbors in the complex.

That was my first conspiracy, my first real score. It felt good. I went back to work like nothing ever happened. I was eventually fired because I was just plain lazy. I didn't like physical work. I never have. I never will.

As a matter of fact, my friend Earl was a factor in my getting fired from Winchell Donuts. I had worked my way up to the point that the store manager would let me run the place by myself. One day Earl came by to help me kill some of the downtime. We talked as he sat at the counter drinking some pop, while I cleaned.

I'm not exactly sure how it started, but Earl and I got into a full-fledged doughnut and pop fight in that Winchell Donuts. Jelly doughnuts, long johns and Coke were flying everywhere. The floor was completely soaked because we each had a fountain gun and were shooting at the other. By the time we finished, the store was a mess, and the next day I was looking for another job.

I would lose three more jobs at fast-food restaurants for laziness or not showing up. Eventually, I was forced to call my grandmother for money. She was happy to help and never questioned me. She only asked me to be careful; she worried about me. Living on my own was fun. I drank, had sex at home, and didn't go to school if I didn't want to.

One of the few days I *was* in school, I had to go to the principal's office to provide a letter from my parents explaining why I had not been there. I told him that I had been sick and stayed home. He wanted to call my father and I calmly told him that I didn't live with my parents, that I had my own apartment. The look on his face reminded me I was winning the war without my parents.

When school was out for the summer, Dontae moved back to Chicago. I either had to move back home, or find another place to live. Teresa, the black girl who started high school with me, had just moved into an apartment in the same complex with her boyfriend, Ernest. I just moved my mattress and dresser in with them. I had a roof over my head, but I was broke. Looking for another job was out of the question. I was in search of fast money.

A Mexican man in the apartment complex said he would pay me twenty-five dollars for every ten-speed bicycle I stole. I waited for white kids to park their bikes at the 7-Eleven right across the street from the apartment complex. When they were inside, I would hop on, ride off, drop off the bikes, and get my cash. I also stole from the grocery store as I hustled for my daily bread.

Hustling every day was too much like work. I needed real money, cash, so I could lie back and relax. I had watched enough robberies on TV; to commit one was the next logical step. My first armed robbery was a carefully selected restaurant that was poorly lit and a good distance from the street. I picked it because it sat by itself. There was a field for me to hide in. Those were the two main things I looked for in an armed robbery.

In movies, some young punk rushes into a store, holds it up and gets himself killed. There would be none of that mess for me. I sat out every night for hours and watched the manager close the restaurant. I would lie in that field and watch that place like a female lion watching her prey.

Every night at midnight a police car would pass the restaurant; another one wouldn't pass for hours. The manager came out around 12:30 A.M. and locked up by himself. It was a strange excitement, knowing I was going to do something that no one else knew about. It was especially exciting to watch the people that I was about to rob.

After watching the restaurant for two weeks, I told Ernest what I planned, and asked him to join me. I estimated that there would be anywhere from $2,000 to $5,000. Then I took Ernest out and showed him "the score." After seeing the layout, he agreed to join me.

On a warm summer night, with two stolen BB guns in tow, we set out for the prey that I had so carefully hunted. As we sat in that field with the stars above us and feeling the gentle breeze, I was a little nervous. My adrenaline was in overdrive. I had watched the place and I knew it inside and out. It was mine.

Ernest was a nervous wreck. He was sweating and babbling about getting caught. It was about to be show time, and he pulled out a picture of his mother. "Man, my mother would roll over in her grave if she saw what I'm about to do."

His reaction didn't have a damn thing to do with his mother. He was just plain scared. He was a punk. It takes a lot of balls and a lot of heart to rob a place. You've got to have nerve. Ernest wouldn't be the last person I would see buckle under pressure. While in the process of reassuring Ernest, I looked up and saw the manager coming out of the restaurant, right on schedule. The manager's back was toward me and he was locking the doors to the restaurant, just like the other nights when I had cased the place. Like a panther about to pounce on its prey, I took off from the field, and yelled "Freeze!" and drew my BB gun.

I had never pulled a gun on a person. I had absolutely no idea how that man was going to react. He started hollering and screaming, and pleaded with me not to shoot him. I then realized the power of a gun—even if it wasn't real. With darkness providing shadow, no one could tell it was fake. A strange calmness moved over me as I realized I was in total control. I was no longer nervous. I proceeded with my plan. After warning him about not hitting any alarms, we went inside.

Through the narrow slits of my ski mask, I watched the manager closely, careful not to give him the chance to wrestle the BB gun from me. By keeping a distance, I created the illusion that I could shoot him if he tried to do anything stupid.

The manager went down to the floor, which I thought was strange at first. Then I realized it was a floor safe. He was so nervous, it took him three attempts to open it. I asked him how much was in the safe. He said $2,800. I smiled under my ski mask. That was a lot of money for a high school teenager.

I locked the manager in the storeroom and took my ski mask off. I looked out the window into the street. It was dark and desolate. I walked out of the restaurant calmly and went back to the apartment. I checked my watch and only twenty minutes had elapsed. I liked the thought of $2,800 for twenty minutes of work.

I walked in proud, with a bagful of money and there was punk-ass Ernest, sitting on the couch. Even though he didn't have my back, I gave him a couple hundred dollars. I was on cloud nine. I got the criminal bug that night. That something-for-nothing feeling was intoxicating.

I didn't even think about getting caught, let alone going to prison. It never occurred to me that what I was doing was wrong. I never even worried about the police. I knew I had done my homework, cased that restaurant well. I had gotten away with it, and it felt good. I had just entered into *the game,* with no education other than what I had read or seen on TV about the Mafia. And I had broken one of the cardinal rules of *the game.* The criminal game has to be taught. Somebody with experience needs to teach and educate a beginner, like anything else. I was a kid, and I had no idea of the danger involved with *the game.*

The first thing a criminal must do is hide his money. I had never had to hide my money in my own house. I just put the money into the closet, and went out every day blowing money at the video arcade and buying pizza—one of my favorite meals.

A week later, as I approached the apartment, Ernest met me on the sidewalk. He cursed me, and Teresa had to get between us. He accused one of my white friends from school of stealing from the apartment. He said I had to move out of the apartment immediately.

When I walked into the apartment, tables and chairs were overturned. It looked like a tornado had gone through the entire place.

There were broken dishes all over the floor. The clothes in the house were strewn everywhere.

I stood there in shock. My money was gone. Teresa stood there crying, while Ernest continued to blame me for his apartment being robbed. I had nowhere to go, and even if I did, I had no money to get me there. I broke down and cried.

I just needed a place to lay my head and think. I called my friend Cliff from Jack & Jill. His family lived in the neighboring suburb of Palatine. They had a beautiful home and they welcomed me. Cliff's mother was and still is one of the most beautiful parents I know. She was lenient with Cliff, and as long as we weren't in trouble, we could do what we pleased.

Cliff's mother was friends with Teresa's mother. One night during their conversation, Teresa's mother mentioned that her daughter had just bought an expensive waterbed and bedroom set for her apartment. Neither Teresa nor Ernest had jobs. They could barely afford rent and food. I had been ripped off. Ernest was one of those guys my father had tried to protect me from all my life. Ernest was a "nigger," a smiling-in-your-face, shaking-your-hand, and then stabbing-you-in-the-back "nigger." But he was jealous afterward because I had the money and he didn't. He just sat around and tripped in his head until he could come up with a way to take my money.

A "nigger" doesn't look to create for himself. Oh no, that's too hard. He would rather just take what you have. That's why he wanted me out immediately.

Let me explain how I feel about the word "nigger." There is a difference between a black man and a "nigger." A "nigger" can be white or black. I know a lot of white "niggers" too. Being a "nigger" is a behavior, not a skin color.

Ernest had all the characteristics of a full-fledged "nigger." He just wanted to bask in all my money. Friendship and brotherhood didn't matter to him. Like my father said, a "nigger" will kill you over a quarter. Well, I had $2,800, so I guess I was lucky that I didn't get killed in my sleep.

A real player would have peeped the play right away. A player could have picked through that bullshit with his eyes closed. Me, on the other hand, all I could do was cry. I didn't know anything about *the game*. Remember, *the game* should be passed on like a father passes a trade on to his son. You don't go looking for it. If it doesn't find you, then don't go looking. Crime isn't a game you want to learn as you go along.

So as I cried, Ernest laughed inside. He and Teresa bought a waterbed and bedroom set, and drank and partied without a care in the world about me. Ernest was a "nigger," like my father had warned me about, but like so many things he told me as a child, I just couldn't grasp the concept at that time.

Once I figured out that Ernest had robbed me, I had a couple of options. I could forget about the whole thing, or go after my money. I couldn't sleep knowing that punk had my money. He didn't have the balls to rob the restaurant. He didn't even wait for me when I went inside. The more I thought about his cleverly orchestrated ploy, the angrier I got.

Hoping to retrieve some of my money, I confronted Ernest outside of the apartment complex. I accused him of stealing my money. My direct approach caught him off guard, because he came right out and said he was sorry. He had the gall to say that he was planning to tell me about the whole thing. The money was now completely spent, he confessed.

That was the beginning of my journey into the life of crime. My informal education in *the game* had begun. The summer was at its end, and it was time for my junior year in high school.

CHAPTER 5

Learning How to Play *the Game*

B roke again, I had no alternatives; I went back home. My parents received me with an attitude that said: We told you you couldn't make it out there on your own. My sisters were too young to really pay any real attention to my activities. With many thefts and a successful armed robbery under my belt, I was becoming well-grounded in criminal life. I had had a taste of fast money, and I loved it. It was intoxicating. It was addictive. I hated every minute of being confined at home. But it was a good place to plan my next big "score."

In school I still made everybody laugh. I loved talking to people and people loved talking to me—the jocks, nerds, druggies whom we called stonies back then, and of course, women. I had everyone's ear—in particular, Ken's, our blond, overweight class president. Ken was smart, did well in school, and was so trusted that the administration gave him keys to the school.

Ken's voice was heard every morning giving the daily announcements over the school intercom system. Every parent wanted a son like Ken. He was the all-American boy. But to me, Ken was just the guy with the key to the audio-visual department, where there were seven or eight video recorders.

I wanted to steal the video recorders from the school and in order to pull that off, I needed help. I talked to Ken. Judges, detectives, and the Secret Service agents thirteen years later were baffled by my ability to convince apparently law-abiding people to commit crimes. Most people like the idea of getting something for nothing. If I show a person how they can get away with a crime, they will choose the reward of easy money over their sense of right or wrong. I explained to Ken that all I wanted him to do was give me the keys, and drive me home from school after I stole the video recorders. I didn't have a driver's license or a car to drive. I told Ken I would split the money with him.

By the time the plan was fully developed, Ken was actually going inside with me, acting as a lookout. I instructed Ken to drive back to school around 7:00 P.M., and meet me at a side door. It was fall, so it was good and dark by that time.

I decided to stay after school and just hang out. With my strict parents, there was a chance they wouldn't let me back out if I went home. After school was a busy time with basketball, gymnastics, band and modern jazz practices; I walked around the school socializing until Ken showed up right at 7:00 P.M. The way I had planned it, we could steal the video recorders and be out of the school in thirty minutes.

Ken and I put on Halloween masks and went up the stairs, through the library to the room where video recorders were stored. My heart was pumping and adrenaline was flowing. It was the same feeling I had when I did the armed robbery. I loved to steal; it made me feel good. Ken opened the door to the audio-visual department with his keys, and one by one we snatched those video recorders.

In 1980, recorders were big and bulky. Lined up neatly on carts, they looked beautiful. We took them down to Ken's father's car parked at the side of the school. We left the building through a side door. "The score" went perfectly.

As we sat in the car, I relished in the moment. I figured we would sell them for about $250 apiece. I was feeling good.

I told Ken, "We should go to school early, and sit in the audio-visual study hall so we can see the expression on the supervisor's face." I could barely contain my excitement, but the whole experience was having the opposite effect on Ken. He wanted no part of that. He was a nervous wreck, and scared to death.

The next morning, I practically ran through the school to get to the audio-visual department. As I walked up the stairs and finally into the department, the lady who worked there looked upset. She was standing there talking with another teacher. I got close enough to hear them, although I already knew what they were talking about.

Then, Ken walked in. Apparently, he couldn't stay away either. But, he was nervous and had a worried look on his face. I said "Look man, just relax, it's almost over, we're cool." Ken sat down and we were talking when his face turned white. I turned around and two uniformed police officers were slowly walking toward us. They moved past us and went over to the teacher who was in charge of the department.

The video equipment was kept in a glass room. As the teacher and the police officers walked inside the glass room, I watched one of the officers taking down notes. Ken was about to shit in his pants. I couldn't stop laughing. I wasn't worried because I knew I had worn gloves, so there were no fingerprints, and a mask, so no one could see me. I knew they didn't have a clue. I loved the attention my crimes caused. That would be part of my undoing in years to come. That day, it was fun.

The bell rang and I had to go to class, although I hated leaving the show. I was on top of the world.

We were supposed to watch a video that day in my human development class. I was eager to hear what my teacher was going to say. He walked in and told us we wouldn't be watching the movie because someone broke into the school and stole all the video equipment. The whole class was groaning but I sat in the back laughing.

About ten minutes later, Mr. West, the tall, matter-of-fact assistant principal, came into the classroom and called me out to the hallway. The class was ooing and awing.

"Do you know anything about the stolen video equipment?"

"All I know is what I just heard in class."

I was always in trouble in school and I could tell he was fishing. "Why are you singling me out?" I asked.

"You were seen after school, and I'm questioning all of those students, since the theft occurred after school. And, Victor, you were the only one hanging around after school who didn't have a specific after-school activity."

I didn't know enough about *the game* to know that I should have been out of sight before the score went down. I became a little nervous. The assistant principal was acting like he had some idea that I did it. I didn't panic; I tried to stay cool. Ken was scared. When I saw him I couldn't let on to him that I was worried because I was the glue holding him together. The rest of the day went along quietly. If I had understood *the game* I would have known that the mess was just beginning to unfold.

I sat next to Ken on the bus, on our way home from school. Ken hadn't been questioned by Mr. West. I assured him that if the police knew something, we would have already been arrested.

As I walked through the door, the telephone was ringing. I picked it up and was greeted by a calm, almost friendly voice, who asked for Victor

Woods. After I said, "Speaking," the person introduced himself as Detective Finley of the Rolling Meadows Police Department. Detective Finley told me he wanted to ask me some questions at the police station.

I fought through my nervousness to maintain my composure as I agreed to go to the police station. I could feel that he believed I did it.

I called Ken and told him about my conversation with the police. I told him to pick me up before my parents came home, otherwise I couldn't leave.

My stomach was jumping and my heart was pounding as I walked up to the front desk and asked for Detective Finley. He came out to greet me with his hand extended. We shook hands, and I followed him back to his tiny office.

I sat in a chair directly across from his desk. He asked me why I was at school that evening. I told him I was collecting notes for an upcoming test. It was obvious to me that I was the main suspect, and he was trying to catch me in a lie. I felt his eyes studying me, and watching my every move. After about thirty minutes I was permitted to leave. I knew I would be talking to Detective Finley again.

Ken was waiting for me in the car, his face paler than it had been when the police arrived at school that morning. As he drove me home, I told him what was said and calmed him down.

The next day I got another call from the detective. In that same calm, almost friendly voice, he asked me to take a lie detector test. I flatly refused. My parents weren't aware of the police calling the house, and I wanted to keep it that way. I needed a lawyer. Richard Cohen, a Jewish neighbor, about eight years older than me, had just started law school. I called him and explained my situation. Richard explained to me that once a lawyer informed the police a suspect was represented by counsel, the attorney had to be present for any subsequent meetings. I asked him to call Detective Finley and tell him he was my attorney. After Richard's telephone call, I never heard from Detective Finley again.

As I continued in *the game,* there would be occasions when law enforcement suspected that I had committed a crime, but couldn't prove it. Those times would be almost more enjoyable than the money I was stealing. Almost.

I sold the video recorders for $100 apiece. I kept $500 and gave Ken $200. Being the leader had its advantages. In my criminal career, I never committed a crime in which I wasn't the leader.

CHAPTER 6

My Only Burglary

All I could think about was crime. I was sure I wanted to be a gangster. I wanted nothing else but to be involved in a life of crime. With my successes, there was no downside. You rob, you steal, you get paid and you spend money. It would have taken me months of working full-time at Burger King to make the money I made in thirty minutes stealing those video recorders. I was hooked and you couldn't convince me that I wasn't right. But, like an addict, I needed another score.

School became a meeting place for me to daydream and plan crimes. There was a new black girl in school. Tasha was tall, with long legs and a model's body. We quickly became an item and spent a lot of time together. She was sexy and wanted to have sex all the time—in school, in the park, or at her home. Tasha and her mother, who was equally beautiful, had moved into the neighborhood about a mile from my house. They lived with her mother's boyfriend, an Italian guy named Antonio.

Tasha's mother and Antonio would go to the opera every Wednesday night. I spent many Wednesday nights having sex and watching movies with Tasha. Antonio's house had the latest TV and stereo equipment: it looked like an electronics store. There had to be $10,000 worth of electronics and stereo equipment in his house.

A few months later, Tasha's mother and Antonio broke up. I was hungry for my next score, and their breakup presented a prime opportunity. I knew the layout of the house and Antonio's personal habits. It was an inside job.

I needed help. I called Ken, who had gotten the bug to make some fast money. In *The Thief*, James Caan had a team of criminals using walkie-talkies and police scanners. I was fascinated with their sophistication. Ken wanted to become an FBI agent, and already had walkie-talkies and a police scanner. To operate a police scanner, you needed certain crystals to pick up the proper frequency of outgoing police calls. We picked up the crystals at a local RadioShack. It was about time for us to become high-tech for that score.

A police scanner was important for the score. If by chance a neighbor suspected something fishy and called the police, we would have heard the police officers being dispatched the moment they received the call. That would allow us to get away before the police arrived.

It occurred to me early on, that if I thought out my crimes thoroughly and executed them properly, I would have successful results. I enjoyed the security of knowing I could protect myself during my jobs, and thus feel at ease while I was committing them.

One important piece was missing—a van. I talked another friend, Chris, into letting me use his parents' van. He also committed to helping me take the equipment from the house to his parents' van.

We would hit Antonio's house on a Wednesday. I told my parents I was playing basketball. Chris picked me up and Ken followed in his father's car.

Antonio usually left at 7:00 P.M. I called at 6:30 P.M. When he picked up, I hung up. I called again at 7:15 P.M. to make sure he had gone. I called one last time at 8:00 P.M. to make sure he hadn't returned for some unexpected reason.

At eight o'clock the coast was clear on that cool and dark October night. Ken took his position at the end of the block. Chris and I drove into Antonio's driveway. Before we exited the van, we checked with Ken to make sure the walkie-talkies worked. As Ken spoke, I sat back and enjoyed myself for a moment.

Chris and I proceeded, with gloves on, to the back of the house and to the basement window well. We put electrical tape on the window, to keep the glass from shattering after the window broke—another tip I learned from criminal movies.

In no time, we were in. I knew my way around, since I had been there so many times, and we ran up the stairs. I talked to Ken on the walkie-talkie to make sure everything was all right. We opened the garage door, and Chris pulled the van inside.

We took everything we could fit into the van: TVs, stereo, microwave oven, alarm clocks, video recorders, jewelry, anything we thought we could sell. We tried to stuff the big-screen TV into the van, but it wouldn't fit. I couldn't stand the fact that I had to leave it, but it just wouldn't fit.

We checked with Ken on the walkie-talkie to see if the coast was clear, and pulled out of the garage. I was laughing to myself and telling Chris to get us outta there as we drove away into the night.

I had planned and executed another perfect heist. We stored the merchandise at Ken's house. I returned home around 9:30 P.M., and told my parents we went to McDonald's after playing basketball. I took a shower and was off to bed. The next day I woke up with a huge smile on my face and a satisfied feeling of a job well done.

I now went to school for the sole purpose of selling off the stolen electronics. Chris and Ken were serious about school. I was serious about making money. I figured we had about $5,000 worth of goodies. I was already spending my share.

What I didn't know was that nobody buys stolen merchandise for what it's worth. You're lucky to get half, and if you get 25 percent of a stolen item's value, you are doing good.

The people I knew were interested in buying a quality item, but nobody wanted to pay top dollar. We sat on that stuff for at least a month, trying to find a buyer to pay top dollar for the merchandise. One day, I was in a shoe store and a white salesman in his early twenties was showing me a new pair of gym shoes. I cracked on him about buying some TVs, stereos, or electronic equipment. He was interested. He was eager to buy everything, but he only wanted to give me $1,000 for all of it. It was the best offer I had gotten, so one night Chris, Ken and I moved the equipment from Ken's garage to the guy's house.

That was my first and last burglary; I was so disgusted that I didn't even get a quarter of what all that stuff was worth. I did learn an important lesson: so-called "legitimate" people are often interested in getting something for nothing, too. Without Joe Citizen, a criminal can't exist. The criminal needs someone to rip off, but he also needs another Joe Citizen who'll sell the stolen stuff.

I was having success in my criminal life but life at home was worse than ever. When it finally became too much, I moved in with Earl, in the spring of 1981. He explained my situation to his parents, and they agreed to let me move in. Earl and I had been best friends since we had met in Jack & Jill. Earl was like a big brother to me. He had access to a car; I didn't even have my driver's license. He had a quiet maturity about him. Earl was, and still is, a great listener. We would stay up all night, talking. We also played basketball together and horsed around.

There is one guy in every group who is cool; that person was Earl. I didn't think he had a curfew, and he seemed to have no rules to follow, but after living with the brother, I saw he had many of the same rules that I had. He simply knew how to handle them. He was never in trouble or even grounded.

Earl is a quietly handsome brown-skinned brother, with baby smooth skin and curly hair. He was the only brother I knew who didn't have acne. I always looked up to him. He knew how to say the right things to people. Earl's personality captivates people. Even the mothers of the girls he dated loved him. I got my fair share of women, but I couldn't even begin to compete with Earl. At parties, he would spend more time talking to parents than to the kids his age.

Earl's father, Dr. Caldwell, is a handsome, dark man with smooth skin. His mother was a beautiful woman who was smart, gentle and kind to me. Earl's older brother, Dwayne, is tall, smart, and cool. His sisters, Barbara and Andrea, are both older than Earl. Although I got along with both his sisters, as far as they were concerned, I was just one of Earl's friends.

While I lived with Earl, a sense of peace and tranquillity came into my life. I didn't think about crime. After about a month of living in bliss at Earl's house, I needed to get some more clothes. In my haste to leave home, I left with very little clothing. I was particularly upset about leaving my favorite Ralph Lauren Polo shirt.

Earl agreed to drive me to my house one day after school. His main concern was that my parents not be home. My parents disliked Earl and his whole family, because they allowed me to stay in their home.

The ride from Highland Park to Arlington Heights was about thirty-five or forty minutes. It was early evening when we arrived. I used my key and walked right in the front door. It felt strange to be back inside my home. As I walked through the house reveling in my parents' and sisters' absence, Earl quickly admonished me to get my clothes, so we could leave undetected, and without incident.

I quickly went downstairs to the basement to get a suitcase, and then up to my room. I packed shirts, blue jeans, shoes and socks. As we were about to leave, I remembered that I hadn't retrieved my favorite Polo shirt. I must have overlooked it in the basement.

"Don't go back downstairs. We have to leave," Earl said. "We've been here too long already."

"I have to have that Polo shirt."

He said, "Hell, no, we've got to get out of here."

"I can't leave my favorite Polo shirt."

I went back downstairs. After finally finding my shirt, I walked up the stairs only to hear my family's voices. The last thing I wanted was a confrontation. Earl had eased himself between the door that separated the kitchen and the living room. When my family stepped in, he could leave unnoticed. They went straight to the family room, on the opposite side of the kitchen from Earl's position. He tried to time it so that, as they walked into the kitchen, he was walking out the opposite end, through the living room and out the front door without being caught.

It almost worked but as Earl was about to walk out the door, Valerie yelled, "There's Earl!" I climbed the rest of the stairs and ran like a bat out of hell out of the house, as Valerie yelled, "And there's Victor, too!"

Earl had already started the car and was pulling it around. My parents came outside just in time to see Earl and me turning onto the street where Tim and I threw mud and rocks at passing cars.

In June or July 1981, our Jack & Jill chapter hosted the Midwest Teen Regional. Since I was in and out of my parents' house, I had stopped participating in Jack & Jill events, even though my family was still active. Hosting the Regional was a big thing for the North Shore Chapter. While the kids participated in the planning and organizing, it was really the mothers who did most of the work.

My parents didn't register me for the conference. I had been instructed that I was not invited and could not participate at the Regional. That was disappointing because it would have been a chance to see my old friends from other cities. Plus, there were hundreds of new girls. I had resigned myself to the fact that I wasn't going to be involved with the Regional, the last that Cliff, Earl, and I would participate in together. They were a year older than me and on their way to Morehouse College in the fall.

I didn't know Earl was behind the scenes working on my behalf. He was vice president of the North Shore Chapter, and worked on the Conference Coordinating Committee which, among other things, determined room assignments and issued registration passes. He worked it out so that I not only shared a room with Cliff, but had an identification badge for access to the entire event. Needless to say, that was the best Teen Regional we had ever attended.

Earl's mother was and still is a mother's mother. During that tumultuous time in high school, I never wanted to go home. Mrs. Caldwell treated me like her own son. She opened her home to me, rather than allow me to live as a runaway. I might have been on the streets or worse. But when Earl left for college, I was forced to move back home with my family.

Missing Graduation

I was back at home for my senior year of high school. Instead of thinking about college, I turned my attention to committing more crime. I was after big bucks. My biggest score was the armed robbery I had pulled about a year and a half before, but I devised another scheme before I would eventually return to armed robbery.

A young black kid in school talked about stealing cars. I decided that if I could find someone to buy the cars, I could make big money. I brought the idea to another friend named Doug, a white kid who, like most teenagers, was trying to find himself. We became partners. The only thing I needed was a chop shop.

I was so green, I thought all we had to do was go to auto body shops in Chicago, and ask if the managers were interested in buying stolen cars. I didn't realize the only way to meet people who bought stolen cars was to be introduced to them in *the game*.

We drove into the city with the yellow pages in tow, and called on auto body shops and used car lots that were listed. Doug waited in the car while I walked in and asked for the manager. I introduced myself and asked to speak to him in private. Then I asked him point blank if he wanted to purchase stolen cars. Every manager looked at me in disbelief, and politely said no.

The managers probably thought I was sent by the police. That mistaken belief was probably the only reason that I didn't get my ass kicked or worse. I know now that the way I approached them was insane. But, back then, I didn't know any better.

People in *the game* only talk to other people in their circle about business. The only exception is when someone in your circle introduces you to someone else outside your circle, and vouches for their character. Even then, you have to be careful. Just because someone in your circle introduces you, doesn't mean their judgment is any good. In the legitimate world, that is called *networking*.

I went home truly perplexed. We had visited 100 auto shops. I abandoned the idea. I was not getting this game.

Almost a Morehouse Man

I had missed so much school that I only had enough credits to be a junior, making it impossible for me to graduate with my class.

I should have graduated from high school in June 1982. My parents were disgusted with me as they watched the neighborhood kids, and many of their friends' children move on to college. My parents rarely failed to remind me that if I had graduated from high school, they would have paid for the college of my choice. They took every opportunity to point out that everyone else from Jack & Jill had managed to graduate from high school and go on to college in spite of their suburban upbringing.

On the day of my high school graduation, I was planning a bank robbery. I was considering robbing a bank four blocks away from my house.

One of our neighbors worked at the bank. I milked as much information from him as I could. He volunteered information about the number of silent alarms, and how the tellers could reach them. I planned to rob the bank with a BB gun and get away on my bicycle. But, after I went in to case the bank, I couldn't figure out how to rob it without a teller sounding one of the silent alarms.

The war with my parents, the unending struggle over where I would live, where I would go to school, what time I would come in at night, who I would associate with, and how I was to behave, had made our home a battlefield instead of a nurturing environment. I had become a worthy adversary for my parents, but my mother and father ceased to be parents and I ceased to be a son. Our family ultimately lost the war.

My parents were part of the civil rights movement of the sixties. They took advantage of the new opportunities afforded blacks. My parents acted out of love for their children by moving to the suburbs and were brave in their quest for our family to be the first blacks to integrate Arlington Heights. Our family made it a little easier for the next black family. I love and will always love my parents for trying to provide the best for me and my sisters, even though their efforts were a personal challenge for me.

My parents wanted me to go to night school for two years to get my diploma. I couldn't bear the thought of another two years of anguish in the suburbs. They constantly reminded me that I had blown my chance to go to Morehouse College, where Cliff and Earl were having a ball in a positive black environment, with support from teachers and the administration. They talked about being among the most beautiful black women in the world, the richness and unique aspects of their college experience. My friends sounded different. They spoke with more assuredness and authority. They were becoming young men.

Talking to them ignited a light in me. I desperately wanted to join them, and I needed a high school diploma. I could never complete two years of night school while living at home. If I stole in order to have my own place, I wouldn't be able to concentrate on night school. I needed to find another way.

I had heard of a test called the General Equivalency Diploma (GED), similar to a high school diploma. I called Harper Community College to see about taking a GED course. Since the GED stands in place of a high school diploma when applying for college, if I could get a GED, I could attend Morehouse and move on with my life.

I would need assistance in preparing for the GED exam, especially in math, my worst subject. When I thought about a teacher to help me, there was only one logical choice—my grandmother.

She had taught math in Detroit for more than thirty-five years. My plan was to take a Greyhound bus to Detroit and, once there, have my grandmother tutor me for the GED exam.

When I told my parents my plan, they were against it. My mother felt that I should go to night school. She was also totally against my going to Detroit; I would worry her mother to death. She said I couldn't pass the GED exam, and added that I had no chance of going to college.

I arrived in Detroit after the six-hour bus ride. My anticipation grew with each minute, as I rode in the taxicab to my grandmother's house. When I finally arrived, relief and excitement shot through my body all at once. My grandmother had a sweet and gentle smile on her face, and I immediately felt calmed. She hugged and kissed me as I walked into her house.

That time with my grandmother was magical. I never remotely thought about breaking the law. My grandmother, Mary Louise Martin, created a loving and nurturing environment. I couldn't even contemplate any kind of negative behavior in her presence. She loved me so much, I could do no wrong in her eyes. She believed in me and only saw the best in me. She knew in her heart what I would eventually become, despite my turbulent teenage years.

My grandmother's house had so much history. She kept my grandfather's spirit alive in her house. I could feel his presence everywhere. I felt wonderful, as if my life had some special purpose.

My grandmother was familiar with the GED exam, and had already acquired the necessary books for me to study. It had sections in math, science, English and history. Over time, I did well in all the sections except math. In order to pass, you must earn a certain percentage in each section.

After a month of preparation, my grandmother felt I was ready. I was concerned about the math section because algebra and geometry seemed to elude me. My parents thought I was going to fail and while that motivated me, my will to prove my parents wrong didn't affect my understanding of math.

The night before the test, my grandmother and I got on our knees and asked God to not only bless me, but everybody in need, and our family.

I drifted off to sleep and awoke the next morning to the smell of bacon and eggs. After breakfast, we prayed again.

While I had butterflies in my stomach, my grandmother was calm and sure that I would pass. The exam was at Ruth Ruff Adult School (which is now Malcolm X Elementary School), about twenty minutes from my grandmother's house. She gave me cab fare, a hug and a kiss, and assured me that I would do well. She told me to hurry home after the test.

The day was rainy, dark, and gloomy. The sun was nowhere to be found. I registered and found my seat. As I sat there, I thought about all that was at stake. I didn't want to disappoint my grandmother, the one person in the world who thought I was great. I didn't want to make my parents right, by failing the test.

As I began, the hours my grandmother spent tutoring me were paying off. I knew just about everything on the test. Things were moving along splendidly, until I started the math section.

The ease in understanding the questions and my rhythm quickly disappeared. The numbers weren't adding up. I became frustrated and started guessing. My confidence was slipping, as were my hopes of passing the exam. Then out of nowhere, a ray of sunlight shone through the window, beaming down directly on my paper. I was startled, because it was a completely overcast, dreary, gloomy day.

The energy from the sun relieved me of all the anxiety. Without thinking, I began to follow the light on my paper. I used it to guide me to select the answer for each question. I'm not saying God gave me the answers. But that light guided me to the answers.

I not only passed the GED exam that day, but scored in the 95th percentile. A chart listed career choices based on the score received on the test. My score on the chart indicated that college was an option for me. I was told that my score was the second highest score ever at Ruth Ruff. I felt proud as I rode in the backseat of the taxicab, on my way back to my grandmother's house.

I decided I would try to fool my grandmother when she opened the door. I was greeted with a smile, but I came in dejected and sad. "I failed."

"No you didn't, I know you passed." There was no fooling that very righteous woman.

I immediately called my parents with the good news. They were shocked.

My grandmother once said that God talked to her when she was a child. I believed her when she told me that. The ray of sunshine that shone on me that day has been shining on me all my life. It has protected me, and protects me now. The prayers of my grandmother and the will of God are the only reasons that I am alive today. An angel has watched over me. Many more times God intervened, to allow me to reach my destiny.

Armed with my GED, I was ready to return home and go away to college with Cliff and Earl at Morehouse. But my parents wanted me to go to junior college to prove that I was worthy of going away to college. My dad said he wasn't going to pay for me to go away to school and flunk out. He even refused to help me get accepted to Morehouse. "You're not going to my alma mater and flunk out and embarrass me!"

I asked Cliff to send me an application. When I got it, I filled it out by myself. On the application, a section asked if any of your family members went to school there. I indicated that my father had and it must have helped, because within a few weeks of mailing the application, I was accepted to Morehouse College. My dad was more help than he knew.

My parents were completely shocked. But they still weren't budging. They refused to pay for me to go to Morehouse. Pissed, looking for a way out, wanting to hurt my parents, I signed up for the Marines. I walked into a recruiter's office and signed up. My parents didn't know what to do with me, and didn't really try to stand in my way. A heart murmur just like my father's delayed my acceptance in the Marines, pending more tests. It turned out that my murmur was functional—I could do anything that anyone else could do, without fear of heart failure. I was then given clearance to join the Marines.

By that time, I was no longer interested. Soon war broke out in Beirut. In fact, a friend from high school died in a hotel bombing in Beirut. I might have been a casualty, too.

But I had come up with another plan.

CHAPTER 7

Armed Robbery Ring

I decided to organize a string of armed robberies to raise money for college tuition. In my mind, this was reasonable. I recruited a few new and old associates: Ken, who was attending junior college, would be the scanner man and getaway driver; Scott, a white kid who was always in trouble, and who would fit in wherever I needed him; and Calvin, another black friend from high school, who would sit in on a few jobs for moral support.

Armed robbery was the smartest move to make because I hadn't been caught and it yielded my biggest score. Large grocery stores probably had $80,000 to $100,000 in their safes, more than enough for four years at Morehouse.

I began to case a large grocery store chain in my neighborhood, as I did the restaurant two years previously.

One of my neighbors was a stock boy at the grocery store, so I got as much information as I could from him. My sidekick on the job was Scott. He was five-five and skinny. But he had balls. I didn't want to use real guns or bullets. If I planned it right, I wouldn't need them. I didn't want to take a chance of killing anyone: it just wasn't that serious. I knew the store managers didn't carry guns.

Scott's father had an old World War II gun replica that looked like a machine gun. I had two BB guns that looked like real guns. Only a gun expert could tell the difference; in the dark, there was no way to know.

Even though I had cased the place, Scott and I sat in Scott's father's car together for a couple weeks and watched the staff close the store; we went in and looked around, and every night we marked down all the license plate numbers of the cars that belonged to the employees.

By doing that, on any given night, we knew who would be inside when we robbed it. I wanted to know how many men and women were inside when we hit. I recorded the times the police went by the store.

According to my neighbor, the stock boy, all the money was handled by three cashiers. One of them was the head cashier. She put all the night's revenues into the safe. They usually finished around 11:00 P.M. The manager was the last to leave, around midnight. That was perfect. I would confront him when he walked out and turned his back to lock the door, and make him open the door, go back inside, and open the safe.

That job was a learning experience. It took us three weeks to pull it off, after casing the place. The first weekend, the manager left early with five people. Everybody scattered in different directions making it impossible to surprise everyone and corral them all back into the store.

The second weekend, as the manager was walking out alone, the police stopped a car for a traffic violation, with the lights flashing, right across the street from the grocery store. Scott and I were hidden behind the shopping carts, wearing ski masks, gloves, and army coats. The manager walked right past us. I was sick.

The third weekend everything was on track, except we changed the job from Friday to Saturday night. Ken was in the car with the police scanner and walkie-talkies. Scott and I were waiting for the manager to come out. Everybody left when they were supposed to, the way I had seen them do at least twenty times before. As usual, right before an armed robbery, my adrenaline was flowing. Scott and I sat there waiting, which is part of the thrill.

A lot of guys tell you they're never scared. That's bullshit. Every human being gets scared. However, it's what you do when you're scared that distinguishes a man from a boy. Do you control and harness your fear, and use it to your advantage? Or do you allow it to consume and control you, and render you helpless?

As we were mentally prepared, I heard a bang and felt a sting. Scott, playing with my BB gun, had pulled the trigger by accident and shot my arm. I had forgotten to make sure the BB gun was not loaded. It shot clear through the coat and ripped into my flesh. BB guns have power! I was about to open my jacket and look at the wound when the manager came out of the front door.

He was about six-two, 240 pounds, with dark hair and looked Italian. I popped out on him with my ski mask on and a BB gun pointed at his head and yelled, "Freeze." The manager was cocky and didn't look terribly scared. His look said, "Is this for real?" He looked hard at my smaller size, but looked even harder at the gun. I told him to open the door. He wasn't moving fast, as if he might try to challenge me. He began to move real fast to open the door when Scott, crouching on the ground, pointed the fake machine gun at his face.

I calmed down once we were inside. I had done my homework; I felt right at home. I asked the manager who else was inside. There were some cleaning people in the back. The manager and I went to the back of the grocery store and up a flight of stairs, with the manager leading the way.

When I burst into the room, I saw five white men; they looked like Polish immigrants. I ordered them all to walk downstairs and I said if they even slightly moved in the wrong way, I would blow their heads off. Scott made all the guys lie facedown on the floor with their hands behind their backs, and I took the manager behind the counter, to the safe.

I threatened to shoot them, but I also let them know that if they cooperated, we would not hurt them. A guy who thought you were going to kill him might panic and do anything.

The manager told me he couldn't open the safe because it was on a time lock. I had never heard of such a thing. I said, "You're full of shit," and he explained that once the safe was closed, it wouldn't open again until the morning.

I couldn't believe that. "How much money is in there?" When he said about $75,000, I put the gun to his head, to be sure he was telling the truth. He began crying and nervously told me that he couldn't open it. "I am going to count down from ten to one, and if you don't open the safe by the time I get to one, I am going to blow your head off."

As I counted, he cried like a baby. By number four, I realized he didn't know how to open the safe. At one, I accidentally pulled the trigger, without thinking. If I had had a real gun, I would have killed him. It would have been a stickup murder. I could have gotten the death penalty.

The manager was so scared, he didn't notice that I had pulled the trigger. He continued to beg for his life as I contemplated what to do next.

I decided to quit while I was ahead. I thanked them all for their cooperation, and bid them a good evening. My first big robbery, and I walked out with nothing. For all of my hard work, I was rewarded with a hole in my arm and a headache. I went home disgusted and went to sleep. I awoke to an oozing wound where the BB had pierced my arm.

The next day, Sunday morning, my dad made a big family breakfast. We usually went to church, but that weekend we skipped it. My mother called me down to breakfast and when my flesh wound raised a few eyebrows, my family asked about my arm. I told them a friend accidentally shot me with a BB gun.

Midway through the meal one of my mother's friends called. "Oh my God!" Mother said. She told my dad to go outside and get the paper. The attempted robbery of the grocery store was on the front page.

My mother sat down and started her "What's the world coming to?" rhetoric. She used to shop there every week. My father read the paper. I thought, *you all don't know the half of it. That should have read $75,000 taken in an armed robbery.*

A doctor said it would cause more damage to take the BB out than to leave it in. To this day, that bead is in my arm and the scar remains.

My home life was a mess. My parents were all over me about getting a job. It was time to move on for good. So I did what every red-blooded American suburban kid would do when angry and upset with his parents—I stole their checkbook, took the third family car (a Buick Electra 225), packed my clothes, and left. I cashed a check for $1,500 and moved into the Holiday Inn.

Clockwork

In the Holiday Inn, not more than two miles from my parents' house, I ordered dinner and drinks from room service, had parties for my friends, and conceived an armed robbery ring that to this day is unprecedented in the northwest suburbs of Chicago. That string of robberies would baffle local law enforcement and would eventually land me in one of the worst state prisons in the country.

I was spending my newfound freedom hanging out at night in

clubs for people twenty-one and older. I had an older friend from the days when I was a lifeguard at a swinging apartment complex. You had to live in the complex to go to the pool. It was a hangout for the many airline flight attendants who lived in the complex because it was close to O'Hare airport.

I used to let a guy named Rick into the pool, even though he didn't live in the complex; he would, in turn, take me out with him at night. He had a Corvette and a condo. We became friends and started hanging out together. He was white, in good shape and good-looking. He used to date a lot of women. He and I would hang out at all the clubs where he knew all the bouncers. They would let us in for free, without checking my ID.

My money quickly got short. I decided to rob something easy, like a fast-food restaurant, so I could do the actual robbery myself and make around $5,000. I would only need a getaway driver.

There wasn't enough money to split with anyone, so I used a young white teenager named Bob as my getaway man. I was introduced to Bob, who was itching to make some fast money, by Scott. After I robbed the restaurant, I planned to hide in the trunk of his mother's car, and ride back to the hotel. The police would be looking for a black guy, Bob's mother had a big Cadillac. The trunk would be perfect for me to hide in.

The restaurant was located off by itself on a big hill and had an enclosed garbage area, a perfect place to hide. There was very little light. You couldn't see the main street from the restaurant and vice versa. Bob would wait on the side of the road leading up to the restaurant.

We only cased the place one time. I was a little cocky, and didn't even use a police scanner.

On the night of the robbery, I waited for the manager and two female employees to come out and sprang out on them. I wore a ski mask and gloves, and carried two BB guns. I yelled, "Freeze!" and the manager screamed and tossed the bag he'd been carrying up in the air.

I took them back inside, and said I wouldn't shoot them if they just cooperated, and instructed the girls to lie facedown on the ground. The manager opened the safe—another floor safe—and pulled out all the money, a couple hundred dollars. I looked closer and saw that there was a safe within the safe. When I told the manager to open it he told me only Brinks had the key.

To make sure he was telling me the truth, I used the old "I'm going to count down from ten to one" routine. I began counting down, and at around five, I even put the gun right on his head. One of the girls screamed, "Joel, open the safe, just open it."

I got down to two and he yelled "Okay!" He reached under a shelf in the safe and opened the other compartment. Bingo! There was $3,500. I took the money, put the employees into a back room and told them I was going to stay in the restaurant for a while and count the money, and if they moved, I would kill them.

I pulled out all the telephone cords, so they couldn't call the police. I walked out to Bob's mother's Cadillac and climbed into the trunk.

It went perfectly, without a hitch. We parked at the hotel and I gave Bob $500. It was Friday night, and I had just gotten paid. I took a shower and headed out for a night of clubbing. I had done my job to perfection, and was ready to enjoy the fruits of my labor.

On my way to the club, I stopped by a Denny's for a bite to eat. It was minutes from the armed robbery I had just committed. As I ate my burger, three Cook County sheriffs walked in and sat down directly across from me. They were in heavy conversation. I attempted to listen, but the noise from the other patrons prevented me from hearing the specifics. I definitely heard about an armed robbery that had recently occurred. The young man sitting there in a sports coat, tie and top-sider—looking like a college kid—had just turned in his armed robbery costume. I wasn't at all nervous. As I left the restaurant, I wished the officers a good night. They offered me the same in response.

I went to one of my favorite clubs and since I was only eighteen, I was happy to be with the older crowd. When I came out, my car had been towed. I had parked in a no parking zone. I had to get a ride back to the Holiday Inn. But worse, the towing company called my dad, since the car was registered to him.

By the time I found the towing company's address, my dad had retrieved his car. I was pissed, even though it was his car. My financial situation had just gotten tighter.

I decided to call my parents and assess their mood. I hadn't talked to them for a few weeks.

My mother was quick to speak. "The money you stole from our checking account surely has to be running out, Victor. And what are you going to do about transportation?"

I had to pull another job. It never occurred to me to get an apartment. I paid my $50 a night and ordered room service at the Holiday
Inn. To this day, I still love hotels. There's something cool and refreshing about going to a nice hotel. I ordered some daiquiris and relaxed
as I contemplated my next move. I looked farther west to another suburb, for a place that looked like it was doing a lot of business and was
situated in a way that I could rob it easily.

I didn't think of the people who worked there as victims. They were
merely tools for me to get to the money I wanted. I felt I was giving
them a gift by not threatening their lives with a real gun. Armed with
this strange sense of wrong and right, I set my eyes on another fast-
food restaurant. It sat off from the main road and was poorly lit. It
even had trees in the parking lot. Other businesses were a good distance away. The place was screaming, "Rob me."

I cased the place for a few days. I ate there; it was a fun-looking place
with video games and a carnival atmosphere. I laughed to myself thinking about the uproar my handiwork would cause a short week later.

I probably should have waited an extra week to study it more, but I
thought I could do it with no problem. I was tired of not having a car.
I contacted Scott and also decided to use Bob again as the getaway
driver. We decided to pull the job on a Sunday. I expected to get
Friday's, Saturday's and Sunday's proceeds—$20,000 to $25,000.

The night of the robbery was calm, clear, and summery. Bob
parked in the back, about seventy yards from the building, in another
store parking lot. Scott and I, dressed in army jackets, ski masks, and
gloves, carried BB guns. I put Band-Aids on my fingertips in case my
gloves came off. I still wouldn't leave any fingerprints.

We waited beside some bushes on the side of the restaurant. We sat
there quietly watchful. There is no need for talk between partners in
that situation. A man thinks about the unexpected things that can
happen when he's crouched down waiting to do an armed robbery.
Each man climbs into himself to harness the fear of the unknown,
and experience his adrenaline.

Three men walked out together and I sprung on them: "Freeze."
Scott had my back but I always led in an armed robbery. That first
moment you confront a person is always the riskiest, most difficult,
and most important moment. By showing authority and strength in
your voice and movements, the people are less likely to panic. Someone

losing their cool could have exposed me as not having a real gun. That was why the initial confrontation was so important. If I was believable, the gun would be believable, too.

I knew from casing the restaurant that there was an alarm code that had to be inputted before reentering the restaurant. When the manager put the key into the door, I stopped him and said I knew the alarm had to be turned off. "If you enter the wrong code, and the police come, you'll be the very first person shot. You'll be the first to go." He used the correct code and we went in, with a toy BB gun at the manager's back.

The two employees were kids my age who were understandably scared to death. Facedown on the ground, one kid kept looking at me. I didn't want him looking at that gun too hard. He might notice that it wasn't real. "Facedown!" I commanded.

This safe was a big old one, about half the size of a refrigerator. When I saw it, I couldn't help but ask how much was inside. The manager said, "$10,000." I was disappointed, expecting around $20,000. The manager opened the safe and there was close to $11,000. I handed him a duffel bag and made him fill it.

I didn't know that one of the employee's parents had come to pick him up. They suspected foul play. Fortunately, it was the age before cellular phones and they went to a pay phone and called the police. As the police were making their way to the scene, we were wrapping up. When I came out, Scott was trying to steal about $400 in change from the cash register. I told him to let it go, twice, before he relented. We ran out, got into the car with Bob, and drove off.

I would later find out that the police missed us by seconds.

When we got back to the hotel, I gave Bob about $800, and Scott about $3,000. Scott and Bob were still in high school. So that was big money for those guys. I kept nearly $7,000 for myself. I always enjoyed counting the money, dumped onto the bed.

I was feeling remarkably good about my biggest score to date. It was midsummer and I was piling up a nice sum of money for tuition and living expenses in Atlanta while I attended school. I called Cliff, who was home from his first year at Morehouse, and he invited me out. Some rich white friends were throwing a party. It was a typically white suburban summer party: plenty of beer and plenty of smoke. Cliff introduced me to everyone there, including Antonio "Tony"

Pappas, a well-built, good-looking Greek kid. Cliff told me that Tony had been busted for doing burglaries. I didn't think much of that stuff. Especially with the distaste of my one burglary experience.

I also met the kid who was throwing the party. It turned out that his father was selling one of his cars. Cliff knew I was looking for a car and suggested I take a look. We went out to the garage and saw a Corvette, a Cadillac and a little sports car I had never seen before.

The boy's father explained to me that it was a Fiat X-19. It was a beautiful bright red, with a removable top. It looked great and I wanted it. Problem was, I didn't know how to drive a stick. The kid's dad took me out that night and started teaching me. He wanted $2,800 and the next day I bought it, instead of saving all of my money for college. I thought the party would go on forever. I bought a bunch of Polo shirts and shorts, new gym shoes and a JVC radio. I must have spent $1,500 in Woodfield Mall that day. I ran into one of my mother's friends, whose husband was an FBI agent, and whose daughters had been in Jack & Jill with me. Sometime later, after I was busted, she would recall seeing me coming out of Mark Shale with shopping bags full of clothes.

It felt great to be able to buy whatever I wanted and not look at the price tags, or have to put it on layaway. I was living high on the hog at the hotel. I felt sensational and decided it was time to pay my parents a visit. I put on a brand new Polo shirt, shorts, and new topsiders. I took the top off of the sports car and drove over. I had just washed the car and it looked brand-new. I intended to offer my father the towing fee he had to pay when his car was towed from the club.

Everybody Plays the Fool

When I pulled into my parents' driveway, my sisters ran to the window and called my parents. The first thing my mother said was, "Oh God, he's stolen someone's car." I had to apply for license plates, so there were none on the car, just a little green sticker on the back window. My dad appeared while I was explaining that to my mother. I said I wanted to pay him back for the towing charges. I pulled out a wad of about $2,000 cash, and asked him how much it was. I truly enjoyed the look of disbelief on their faces.

My father got angry and tried to hit me but I ducked. "Irving, cool it, the neighbors," my mother begged. "Get the hell away from our house," he shouted, and I was careful to stay at least an arm's length away from my father's reach. At six-one and a fit 190 pounds, he could have easily kicked my ass.

In midst of the commotion, I felt great. My parents and I had been at war for three years, and I felt victorious.

I returned to the Holiday Inn. Things were going well, but I still worried about running out of money. Spending fifty dollars per night was killing me, not to mention room service. I needed to move from the hotel.

I called my friend Rick, a college-educated salesman, who wanted more adventure and excitement in his life. He let me move in with him. That move saved me about $500 a week. He knew nothing of the armed robberies. He just thought that I was down on my luck.

My little crew and I pulled a few more jobs that summer. Because I was new to *the game*, I didn't understand that my easy money would not go on forever. Before we would pull our final job that summer, we decided another fast-food restaurant was necessary practice.

The job was like the rest of the jobs, but after I got the money from the safe, I took the manager and the employees to the walk-in freezer. When I opened the freezer door, there were two big truck drivers. Unbeknownst to me, a truck had pulled up for a late-night delivery. Scott walked out to the truck, pulled his BB gun and escorted them into the freezer. He took their wallets, which I made him give back. Those wallets weren't our business. We left with about $3,000.

That was my summer in 1982: I hung out, partied and lived like an outlaw. It was one big adventure. However, nothing in *the game* lasts forever. You have to know when to quit and step back.

The police had been investigating each armed robbery. They knew that the robberies weren't random because of the methodical way each one was done. In fact, police reports would later indicate the robberies had been committed by professionals. Teenagers were not capable of organized, polished, precision crime, time after time.

Our next target was another grocery store, a store with big money. We planned to pull it on a Saturday night. It had been about two weeks since our last job. We were to meet at 10:30 P.M. I went to a well-known nightclub called the Snuggery. I was drinking, spending money and feeling pretty good.

In the trunk of my car was a briefcase containing a notebook with the names of everybody involved in the robberies, ski masks, BB guns, and newspaper articles of jobs I pulled. While speeding on the highway to meet everyone, I was stopped by a state trooper. I had several unpaid traffic tickets and had to post money for bond. The officer agreed to follow me over to Rick's condo so I could give him the $150 cash and avoid going to jail.

By the time I posted bond, it was too late, and we agreed to pull the job on the next weekend. Then I went to Thumpers, another joint, but they were checking IDs, so I couldn't get in. I decided to go to a club in Elgin, a black suburb about thirty-five minutes away. Some guy at the bar told me about a house party a few blocks away. I went and the party was jumping. People were inside and out, fine women, loud music—the whole nine yards.

I was looking good, with my hair too curly, and driving my exotic sports car. My presence got the attention of a lot of the ladies. I didn't know the danger I was in, going to a black neighborhood alone, where I knew no one. Many brothers have been killed, stepping into somebody else's territory, by some jealous fool trying to eliminate the competition. I was a homicide waiting to happen.

I met a sister at the party, and we went to Dunkin' Donuts before returning to my car to fool around a little bit. I left there around 5:30 A.M., drunk and tired. I drove for about thirty-five minutes before I finally got near the expressway that would take me home. There was a stoplight just before the expressway. I was so tired that I fell asleep at that light. I can still remember a white man's face as I woke up behind the steering wheel. He looked at me and shook his head. I gave him a defiant look and got on the expressway, driving to the tune of Michael Jackson's "PYT" (Pretty Young Thing).

On the same expressway where I had gotten a ticket not more than eight hours before, I was again speeding. But I wasn't stopped by the police. I stopped *myself*—by falling asleep behind the wheel. I woke up just before my car slammed into the guardrail. I had just enough time to see that I was about to crash and brace myself before impact. A split second more sleep, and I would have broken my neck on impact.

The engine in a Fiat X-19 is in the back, and the trunk in the front. The car was smashed like an accordion. I had only minor facial injuries. I jumped out of the car, to make sure I still could. The expressway was deserted. Finally, a guy in a Trans Am stopped and offered me a ride home. I forgot to grab my briefcase out of the trunk. I left it there, with my BB guns, ski masks and newspaper articles. The truth of the matter was that I really should have left that stuff at the condo when I ran in and got the money for the speeding ticket the night before. Any player knows what can go wrong, may very well go wrong. Of course, back then I was hardly a player, and I had no idea about such things.

By the time I got back to Rick's condo I knew I'd erred and called Robert, my friend from high school, and asked him to go to the accident site and pick up my briefcase.

Robert rolled past and saw that the police had the briefcase open. They drew their guns on him and asked who owned the car. Robert told them he didn't know my whereabouts, then called me and relayed the unfortunate circumstances.

Had I known how the police work, I would have packed my things and gotten the hell out of Dodge. I would have known the detectives would find out that a state trooper had stopped me the night before and knew where I was living.

I didn't even think about it. I was ordering pizza and drinking beer, while the police were surrounding the apartment complex. They buzzed the front door and identified themselves. A detective told me they wanted me to come down to the station and fill out some papers about the accident. I had no idea that I was a suspect. I got in an unmarked car with them.

When we got to the station, they left me in a small white room for about an hour. I sat waiting to answer questions about the accident, when two detectives walked in. One stated, as soon as he walked in, that he wanted to talk to me about the armed robberies I had committed.

"I don't know what you're talking about."

"We know everything—the ski masks, BB guns, newspaper articles, the names in your notebook."

I should have known that they really didn't have any hard evidence against me, but I panicked. I had not been schooled on the golden rule of *the game,* which is: Say nothing to the police. Never talk to the police without a lawyer. Let your lawyer be your mouthpiece and do all the talking on your behalf. If you just shut your mouth, you have a chance of getting your ass out of trouble. I didn't have a lawyer, or even a clue about how to deal with the situation.

That evidence, my briefcase full of newspaper articles of all the robberies, ski masks, BB guns, and notes with names and addresses of my partners, in a court of law would have been circumstantial. The items in my briefcase were perfectly legal for anyone to have, unusual, but perfectly legal. Those detectives played me like a fool.

As the evening progressed, they brought in the other guys who were just as ignorant as I was. We gave them their case on a silver platter. I didn't even have sense enough to ask for a lawyer. I would later be arrested on numerous other charges, but I never again said a word. I learned my lesson well.

I called my parents that night from jail and told them the serious trouble I was in. I stayed in lockup, my first experience in a jail cell overnight. I wasn't scared, but I did know that jail was a place I didn't want to spend a lot of time. The judge set our bonds at $1 million.

The next day, we were front page news. "Armed Robbery Ring Broken Up." That morning, they brought us some food to eat, and we were off to bond court: Scott, Bob, Ken, Calvin (who'd done one small job with us), and me, along with all our parents. I turned around and looked at my parents. They had a look of disgust, anger, disbelief and embarrassment on their faces. Then I turned back and looked at the stone-faced judge. I couldn't decide which face looked more menacing: my mother's, my father's, or the judge's.

The judge lowered our bonds to $100,000 each. You needed 10 percent to get out of jail. All of our parents made bond for us that day, and we were set free.

As soon as I got into the car with my parents, my mother started beating the hell out of me. I couldn't blame her. My father just drove. But I could read the disgust and disappointment on his face. The days and weeks that followed were just awful. My parents had my ass in the house on lockdown. I couldn't go anywhere. I was back at home, miserable. My life had become a full-blown mess.

My parents found an attorney through a good friend. Charles Jenkins was a black Chicago lawyer out to make as much money as possible, with the least amount of work. Slightly bald, bearded, fivenine, and about 170 pounds, he drove a green Lincoln Continental

Town Car out to my parents' house for an initial meeting. I was sure he saw the dollar signs when he parked at our suburban dwelling.

I was the first Woods for at least three generations of the family on both sides to get into trouble. No one could remember anyone being in trouble with the law.

Mr. Jenkins said he needed a $20,000 retainer to provide a proper defense, and almost guaranteed that I wouldn't go to jail. "They never send white kids, with no records, to jail. You're lucky you're with them, because the way you look, you wouldn't make it in prison," he said, implying that if I did go to prison, I would be so badly maimed and injured by the time I got out, I wouldn't be of any use.

He scared us to death to justify his big retainer. My parents hired him, and we began the long legal process. Fortunately for Ken, his family was spared this experience. As fate would have it, charges against Ken were dropped for lack of evidence.

CHAPTER 8

Recruiting

Morehouse College was now out of the question. I enrolled at Harper Community College. At least it got me out of the house. My lawyer wanted me in school to make a good impression on the judge. I was expected to get probation. Harper Community College was one big party to me. I made friends easily, as I always did. My old friend Robert went there before he transferred to the University of Kansas on a track scholarship. Life for me got back into the normal bad routine, except I had to go to court once a month. My parents gave me a 1:00 A.M. curfew. They were tripping about everything I did and I wanted out badly. I needed money to buy me some freedom.

One day while I was sitting at a table full of girls in study hall, Tony Pappas walked up to us. We recognized each other from the summer party. He had a presence, a cockiness that said, "You better not mess with me." But he also had class, the kind of class you get from being exposed to a lot of money. He had good manners, but his arrogant demeanor implied that he was better than everybody else.

I didn't know much about Tony, but I did know that his father had been a big-time real estate developer, and a multimillionaire who had been shot to death at his office. According to Cliff, who went to high school with Tony, his father had been subpoenaed to testify to a grand jury. Rumor had it that he wouldn't disclose what he was or wasn't going to say to the grand jury, so somebody killed him. His father was found sitting in his Mercedes-Benz with three bullet holes in his head. After hearing the news, Tony drove from school to the scene, where he fought through the police, only to see his father slouched over the steering wheel. The death of his father really shook him up. He began pulling burglaries, even though his father had left the family a beautiful debt-free home in an exclusive upper-crust neighborhood. Each child was left an individual million-dollar trust fund, but had to wait until he was in his twenties to receive money from his trust. Tony had an all-black Trans Am with personalized license plates. His mother drove a Jaguar. They still had his father's Mercedes. Tony didn't need money; he was looking for power. He was always fighting in bars and knocking people out.

I pulled Tony to the side that day and told him I had a plan that I wanted to bounce off his head. I wanted to go into the city and recruit teenagers from the projects. They would commit armed robberies with our guidance. We would train them, case the places, and coordinate the details. He listened to my words with great interest; he loved the idea. But he questioned whether we would get those teenagers to actually participate. I suggested that we get dressed to a T and drive his father's four-door Mercedes to the city.

We went to the Cabrini Green housing project. For anyone not from Chicago, Cabrini Green was the housing project displayed in the TV show *Good Times*, and considered one of the worst projects in the country. The plan was simply to drive around in the Mercedes, and get names of teenagers interested in pulling some stickups for money. I never imagined how easy it was to get young people to approach us. Hundreds of young men ran up to the Mercedes. They were hungry. They came to the car in droves. I explained that I was working for some people who wanted me to find young men to do setup jobs. We took names and phone numbers. I asked how much criminal experience they had and heard stories from armed robbery to murder.

We left that day with about seventy names of teenagers we thought might be viable candidates to train. I was excited and anxious to pull our first job, so I could move out of my parents' house for good. Tony brought in one of his friends, Stuart, to be the getaway man for our new recruits. I also brought in a friend named Jose, a small-time Mexican coke dealer I had met in high school. Jose was looking to expand his cocaine business with revenue from the armed robberies.

Tony's friend Stuart was white, fat and a little sloppy. Stuart's brother had made the mistake of falling asleep while Tony was driving home from a bar in Wisconsin. He never woke up. Tony wrapped the car around a tree and the kid was thrown from the car and died. I never slept when Tony drove.

We ripped off a fast-food restaurant one night, with Jose as the getaway man. We quickly cased the restaurant, robbed it, and took about

$5,000. I had always been the lead guy, but Tony had balls. When he was the lead guy, he never got any complaints from me. It was nice to follow someone else for a change. Tony carried a real gun. He insisted on it. After his father's death, he wasn't taking any chances.

I had a real partner for the first time, in Tony. I loved him for that.

My mother had been taking the phone receiver to work with her, so I couldn't talk on the phone. While robbing the fast-food restaurant, Tony had the presence of mind to steal a phone receiver for me. He was in total control of his emotions during the robbery; I liked that in a partner.

We went to his house to split the money three ways, and headed to my house, about fifteen minutes away, driving in Jose's Camaro. As we pulled into my driveway, two squad cars and one unmarked car pulled up behind us with their lights flashing. One of the detectives, who arrested me last summer, jumped out of his car, walked toward us, and hollered, "Victor, what have you been up to?"

I said, "I was at my friend's house." One of the officers picked up the phone and asked about it. Jose was quick on his feet, and said, "I used to work for the phone company, and make extra money fixing phones." He even had his old employee ID card in his wallet.

They split, and I went inside. Fortunately, my parents slept through the whole thing.

If those cops had done their homework, they would have known that a telephone was taken during the robbery, and we would have been busted. The phone number from the restaurant was even on the phone.

I played Joe Student for a few months at Harper.

A couple of months later, the shit hit the fan at home, once again. A friend of mine had tickets to a Chicago Bulls basketball game, and I wanted to go. After an argument with my parents, my dad said that if I went to the game, I was not to come back home. I said, "Fuck you," packed my clothes, and left. I moved in with Tony for a few days, and it wasn't long before we were back at work again.

Our next score was a family restaurant. Tony, Jose and I went in to eat and case the place. We robbed it without a glitch and got about $3,000. With my share of the money, I moved into the Sheraton Hotel to plan my next move. Meanwhile, I was still going to court once a month for the other armed robberies from the previous summer.

We began to case places we thought would be good first-time hits for our teenage recruits. We selected three of the teenagers and brought them from Chicago to the suburbs, to rob a grocery store on a Sunday, when it would have the most money.

Tony and I would sit up long nights casing places. He would talk about his dad and how he died. He loved his father; you could feel it. We often used the very car that his father had been murdered in, the gray four-door Mercedes, to case places. We even hatched a plot to question the mayor of the town where Tony's father was murdered. Tony felt the mayor was crooked and may have had some knowledge about his father's killer. The case surrounding Tony's father's death was unsolved.

After weeks of planning, we were ready to pull our first job with the teenagers. The store was situated away from the street, across from a busy gas station, where we could park and watch. We took pictures of the place and made notes.

The day before the robbery, we checked into a room at the Holiday Inn, and sent for the teenagers. Stuart picked them up in a Ford Bronco. We fed them and let them go swimming. It was like one big adventure to them. We picked them up on Friday night and let them party. On Saturday, it was all business, and time to learn the details of the robbery.

I spent most of the time explaining to the three of them what to do, and how to handle problems during an armed robbery. One teenager, Cedric, stood out. I made him the floor manager. Cedric seemed to be more mature and stronger than the other two. He was smart. During an armed robbery, you have to be able to think quickly or it could cost you your life.

Tony didn't believe in using BB guns. Since I wasn't actually going inside, I let Tony call the show. He gave each teenager a gun and showed them how to use it.

On the night of the robbery, my stomach was jumping with antici-pation. Stuart dropped the young brothers off at the grocery store, and they hid in some bushes off to the side of the building. Tony and I were parked across the street at the gas station. From there, we watched the scene unfold with binoculars. We kept in contact with Stuart and the teenagers with walkie-talkies.

Tony and I were waiting to see if the teenagers could do it. I believed they could, but I wouldn't be sure until I actually saw them rob the store. Then, right on cue, through my binoculars I watched the manager come out. Those teenagers charged him like a pack of hungry dogs going for steak. They grabbed the manager and forced him back inside. I watched those young men like a proud parent. It was fun watching something actually happen that I had planned and trained people to do. But a part of me wanted to be there with them. They were doing a great job, and Tony and I were eating it up. We were laughing and celebrating.

The teenagers made a successful getaway. They quickly got into Stuart's Bronco and we all met at the Holiday Inn. Once we were in the safe confines of the hotel room it became clear that we had celebrated too soon. The manager only gave them the petty cash box that contained about $1,200. The teenagers left behind about $60,000. I was sick and upset. Tony was too disgusted to speak. We quickly consoled ourselves with the thought that we had completed a successful job with the teenagers.

Money or no money, the main thing was they did it, and didn't get caught. There would be many more operations.

Stuart drove them back to Chicago, giving them $150 each for their efforts. I went back to the Sheraton, about eight blocks from Tony's house.

We took a few days off to regroup, then decided to rob another grocery store in the area. I was determined to get it right.

The grocery store the teenagers robbed was in Buffalo Grove. The lead detective for that suburb was Lester Aradi, later the commander of the Buffalo Grove Police Department. Detective Aradi made it his business to solve the armed robberies in his town and bring the perpetrators to justice. He solicited help from detectives in the surrounding suburbs and compared evidence and notes.

The first clue came from Scott's fingerprint on a can of beer from one of our previous jobs. Detective Aradi compared the fingerprint with information about armed robberies from the Arlington Heights Police Department. That included me. Detective Aradi began going through the garbage at my parents' house, and they found two things of interest: several Sheraton Hotel receipts and a discarded newspaper from which the recent armed robbery article had been cut.

Detective Aradi assembled a task force and unbeknownst to me, I was the primary focus of that task force. In organizing the task force, both law enforcement and the community came together. Because the police didn't know how sophisticated the armed robbery ring was, they borrowed radios and equipment from a downstate police force. They also borrowed vehicles from local dealerships to track our movements.

They were still unsure if I was their man when they set up shop at the Sheraton hotel, since I had registered under another name. They staked out the Sheraton with plainclothes detectives in the hotel and teams outside in vehicles.

The search had been going on for a while, and still the task force hadn't confirmed that I was in the Sheraton. They suspected someone on the sixth floor was me, but couldn't confirm it.

One night during the stakeout, one of the detectives intercepted a pizza delivery man, pretending he had ordered the pizza. The delivery guy asked what floor he was on. The detective named a sixth-floor room. While the actual room number was incorrect, the floor wasn't. So the pizza delivery guy sold the pizza to the detective. The detective noticed the pizza was to be delivered to room 608. The person who ordered the pizza was Victor Woods. Sometimes luck is more effective than diligence and hard work. The order not only confirmed that I was in the hotel, but gave them my room number, too.

The police didn't want to raise my suspicions by not delivering the pizza, so they scrambled to dress a detective as a delivery guy, got some change together, and proceeded to deliver my pizza. I even tipped the guy.

The task force then put me under twenty-four-hour surveillance. Continuing to do armed robberies in the same general area was the height of stupidity. I wasn't smart enough to read the signs. The first came about a week after the teenagers robbed the grocery store. My father called me at the Sheraton after he read about the armed robbery in the newspaper. He said, "I know you did it." If my father knew I was active again, the cops certainly did, too, but I couldn't see it.

The detectives checked into both rooms on either side of mine at the Sheraton. One night, heading out to a new bar for a night of drinking and girl-chasing, I recognized a man sitting in the lobby as I walked by the front desk. I remembered that he was one of the detectives who had busted me before. Tony dismissed it, saying the detective was moonlighting as hotel security for extra money, as many cops did. That was the second sign I missed. I should have abandoned ship immediately. There were just too many coincidences.

It was Saturday night and the job was planned for Sunday. Stuart picked up the teenagers and took them to a nearby hotel for the night. That night, Tony and I briefed the kids for a few hours and left them to mentally prepare themselves.

The third sign came that night when I was ordering some strawberry daiquiris from room service. The woman who took the order said, "You guys be careful up there."

"What are you talking about?" I asked her.

"I can't say anything else." And she hung up. I was worried, but couldn't put it together.

Sunday came and we were ready. We expected to get over $75,000. Tony was running late. He didn't get to the hotel until 8:45 P.M. It was a cold Chicago March night and the "hawk" was out. We met Tony downstairs; we hopped into his Mercedes and sped off. Stuart had already taken the teenagers to the grocery store and dropped them off. The store was in a strip mall; the parking lot was huge. Parked in the lot about a 100 yards away, we were able to see the action clearly with the aid of binoculars. Tony started talking to Stuart on the Motorola walkie-talkie.

The plan was for Cedric to grab one of the employees gathering shopping carts in the parking lot, then walk in with him—a gun to his head—while the cashiers were counting the money and the safe was open.We'd get the money before it was time-locked in the safe. After 10:00 P.M., the safe would be closed. We sent the teenagers in around 9:20. We watched as they approached the employee who was gathering carts.

The teenagers confronted the employee and walked him, at gunpoint, to the front door, but he refused to open it. The teenagers, not knowing what to do, panicked and ran for our car, the only familiar thing. I told Tony to take off. We couldn't have the teenagers jumping into the Mercedes with ski masks on and carrying guns. He called Stuart on the walkie-talkie and told him to pick up the teenagers and take them back to Chicago. A car boldly cut behind us. Tony recognized we were being tailed and asked if I thought he should lose them. *They have nothing on us. We shouldn't panic. We didn't actually participate in the robbery.* "Let's go to dinner," I replied.

As we approached a four-way intersection, every car in front of us, in back of us, beside us and even across the street was an unmarked police car.

Officers jumped out of their vehicles with their guns drawn. Police were everywhere—more than sixty, in uniform and plainclothes. They yelled, "Put your hands up!" They snatched open all the car doors and threw us down onto the cold hard asphalt, right in the middle of the street. A policeman pressed a shotgun to my head as I lay on the ground. I can still feel that cold steel on my face. I'll never forget it. Another officer hit me in my groin with a shotgun as I lay helpless. Finally they picked me up and leaned me against the car. Traffic was stopped, police were everywhere. Looking at the spectacle was like being in another dimension. I almost forgot that I was in the middle of the madness. In all the excitement, I didn't hear the officer say, "Look straight ahead." When I didn't respond, he slammed my face on the top of the police car. The impact split my front tooth in half. I tasted blood and the metal of the police car hood. They handcuffed everybody, and sped us away in separate cars to the police station.

CHAPTER 9

Surviving Jail 101

The officer who slammed my head down on the police car showed off his handiwork on my mouth.

"Not so pretty anymore," one officer commented.

They put us all in separate rooms. When they came in to question me, I told them nothing. One of the detectives said, "I guess you're too smart for that now."

They said Tony was telling them everything. I knew that was a lie.

Then came Stuart and the teenagers, and they put all of us in a lineup and had everyone say, separately: "This is a stickup, get back inside." I couldn't see the people behind the glass, but I knew they were all white. I also knew the teenagers spoke broken English. I did my best to speak proper English when it was my turn. I spoke like a typical suburban white boy. I articulated the Queen's English for the victims of the robbery. None of them identified me. My bourgeois background paid off for me.

The store that we attempted to rob was on the border between Lake County and Cook County, Illinois. Because of that, we might be transferred to the infamous Cook County jail—one of the toughest and meanest jails in the country that housed around 10,000 inmates. The police sent us to Lake County jail, a kiddie camp by comparison. We all went into the lockup until the bond hearing. The younger teenagers were taken to the juvenile lockup.

The episode made front-page news, "Suburban Armed Robbery Ring Broken Up," with footnotes about gangs moving from Chicago to the suburbs. Unbeknownst to me, and to my surprise, all the teenagers were Gangster Disciples. The Gangster Disciples were founded by Larry Hoover. They are the largest street organization in Chicago and can be found in most major cities. It was my first encounter with the Disciples, and not my last.

That night we were kept in individual cells. In the morning we were transferred to the courthouse. An inmate, Phil Leonardi, a good-looking Italian guy, short but well-built, had court that morning, too. He was about twenty-eight, a seasoned criminal, and had already experienced prison. He looked at us and asked what crime we had committed and was impressed when he learned that we performed the armed robberies with a police scanner and walkie-talkies. We instantly gained his respect.

Everybody's family was in court, including mine. I could hardly look at my parents. They were sick with disbelief. My lawyer was there as the prosecutor made his case to the judge. The prosecutor had to convince the judge that there was enough evidence to suggest that I did the crime. With fifty to sixty detectives present, and several witnesses taking the stand, there was little doubt. Bond was set at $100,000 for each of us. Everybody made bail that day, except me. My parents left me in jail.

Parents, never leave your child in jail with the hope of teaching him a lesson. There are better ways to teach a lesson. Leaving a child in jail might allow that child to be murdered, like the eighteen-year-old kid I saw refuse to give gang members his breakfast. He was repeatedly stabbed, until he died a brutal, miserable death, while the prison staff, other inmates, and I watched.

Nobody on the case, except Tony and me, had ever been in trouble with the law, so their parents were eager to get them out. Tony's mother never let her son spend one night in jail if she could help it. I was already out on bond from the previous summer, so my situation was shit. One by one, my friends were all bonded out. I was taken back to Lake County jail until the previous summer's case came to its conclusion. I was no longer in a holding cell. I was taken upstairs with the other criminals. I was scared to death as they brought me upstairs. It was the kind of fear where you can't feel your legs anymore. The floors in that jail were like dormitories, which meant you had about 100 guys all caged up inside one large room with beds on the floor. Jail was a completely new and different world. There were rules, governors, presidents, drug dealers, police, pimps, gamblers, players, whores and wolves. The wolves in prison were just waiting for a young, good-looking kid like me to come in. I was a suburban black kid who sounded white. Had it not been for my brown skin, one would have thought I was white. With my good looks, perfect brown skin, and wavy black hair, I stuck out like a sore thumb.

They opened the gate and I walked in with my bedroll—blanket, sheets, and a toothbrush. The wolves watched as I came in. They could tell I was new, green, and had never been locked down before. I didn't even know I was being watched. I didn't know what I had to be afraid of, but I was scared when I walked into the dormitory. Wolves can sense fear. The wolves will either rape you, extort you for money, or sell you for packs of cigarettes.

They watched and wondered if I already knew Phil; if so, they had to step back.

Most inmates were from broken homes, child abuse cases, or in drug-infested households. They were hard. They didn't steal for adventure like me. They stole because they had to eat, because their fathers and brothers stole. It was all they knew. They were hungry, bored, angry, and often looked to take it out on a young brother's ass, just like mine. I was a lamb locked up with a pack of wolves.

Of all the floors I could have been assigned to, I was placed on the one with Phil Leonardi. As I entered, he immediately greeted me, surprised to see I hadn't made bond. He took me to my bunk bed and helped me make it. He offered me food, and asked all about my case. Phil was a player, not a wolf. He was in on drug charges. He genuinely liked me and wasn't looking for the opportunity to take advantage of me.

He immediately schooled me about jail. He was well-respected in Lake County jail, and I was his friend. Just like in life, in jail, everything is who you know. That angel who had been watching over me all my life was there again, working through Phil Leonardi.

That night I called my parents, and begged them to get me out. They said, "Jail is the best place for you." I had enough sense not to cry, because everyone would see. But I pleaded for them to get me out. With or without Phil, I figured jail would have its way with me sooner or later. I wouldn't make it.

The jail itself was nasty. There were two commodes attached to the wall and one sink for 100 inmates. You had no privacy when you used the bathroom. Three days passed before I finally worked up the nerve to sit down on the toilet. I waited until just about everybody went to sleep, so I could have a modicum of privacy.

The first morning I only had on my Fruit-of-the-Loom underwear as I was bending over the sink to brush my teeth. They call briefs "come get me shorts" in jail. Phil called me over, and said, "Put some pants on. Can't you see all the guys looking at your ass?" I looked and saw the wolves. I was a fast learner; it was a course for my survival. My life depended on getting an A in Jail 101.

I got some boxer shorts from the laundry and proceeded to learn the ropes from Phil.

My love for the criminal life bonded me with most men there. I was funny and good-natured and as inmates got to know me, they liked me. I blended with my fellow jail mates. I began smoking Pall Malls. The packs were red, my favorite color, so I started smoking that brand. Pall Malls don't have filters. I was trying to kill myself, without knowing it.

Lighting up with the guys, swapping stories about girls, and listening to Phil, I would stay up until the wee hours of the morning. Phil had been where I was going—to Cook County jail and to prison.

A lot of guys had trouble writing and asked me for help. I had a reputation for being pretty smart, so I began to write love letters for the guys. I'd asked for a picture of the girlfriend for inspiration, and read the smooth lines back to them. They loved it.

On the days I had court, the guards would cuff me and drive me out to the Lake County Courthouse. I appeared before the judge who was hearing the first set of armed robberies. The lone black person with two white kids, I looked like the bad apple, especially with my bond revoked for a new set of armed robberies. My lawyer told me I would go to prison. I had already resolved myself to that ugly, inevitable fact. I was a survivor. I got into the role of prisoner.

Although my parents would not get me out of jail, they were good about sending me money for cigarettes and snacks, and coming to court. Around that time, an old Latina girlfriend named Tomasa started looking for me through my parents. She had fallen in love with me, and I had pushed her away.

It was my understanding that she had gotten pregnant during the only time we had sex. I was sixteen at the time. A year later, she said that she had given birth to my baby. I tried to talk to my parents about the matter. They simply said that her claim was ridiculous in light of all the time that had elapsed since I had last seen or heard from her. Without any real support, I had no idea how to resolve the issue. Tomasa and I decided to put the baby up for adoption.

Tomasa got my whereabouts from my parents, and began to visit. She and my parents, together, would come to see me. She loved me, and my imprisonment was her chance to show me. In prison, you cling to the outside world. So I clung to her. She was pretty, had long thick beautiful hair, and was a little overweight.

I began praying a lot. Many prisoners think that they can pray their way out of jail. All you can do is ask God to forgive you and protect you. I thought I could pray and tell God I wouldn't do it anymore, and somehow get lifted out of that mess. I was praying so much that my jail mates started calling me "Preach." It's funny: when things are at their worst in people's lives is, unfortunately, when most folks turn to religion. I was no different. With no one else to turn to, I figured prayer was my way out as well.

While reading the Bible, I came across a passage, Matthew 18:6: "But if anyone causes one of those little ones who believe in me to sin, it would be better for him to have a large millstone hung around his neck and to be drowned in the depths of the sea." I led those teenagers to do wrong. I wasn't going anywhere anytime soon. I started praying for other things—my health and strength to get me through my time in prison.

My final court date came in Lake County, with all the evidence pointing at me. I pled guilty to one count of attempted armed rob- bery. When the judge asked if I had anything to say before sentencing, I stood up and said that Mark Dellums was sleeping in the car at the time of the armed robbery, and he had no prior knowledge of what took place that night. The judge duly noted that, and the case against Mark was eventually dismissed. Mark had really just been in the wrong place at the wrong time.

I was always trying to live down that first time I was in police cus- tody and opened my big mouth. I always wanted to show people that I was a hard-core criminal with balls, and could do it right. The judge sentenced me to four years in the department of corrections. In Illinois, at that time, you did half of your sentence, give or take three or four months. The most time I would actually serve behind bars was two years.

I was off to real jail, in Cook County. Phil had been a good teacher, and I had been a good student. But up to that point, it was all talk. I had yet to put the boat into the water and sail. We said our good-byes a week after I was sentenced. Phil left me with some important words of wisdom. He said, "One of two things will happen when you get to Cook County jail. Either you're going to grab a shield and a sword, or a scarf and a skirt. There are no two ways about it. If you let a prisoner steal your food, the next thing will be your ass. Above all, do page four in your prison survival manual—*mind your own business*. Don't gamble and don't mess around with homosexuals."

I went off with two Cook County sheriffs who came to transport me. They cuffed me and brought me armed with my game plan from Phil, to Cook County jail, aka "the County."

CHAPTER 10

"The County"

From the outside, Cook County jail looked huge, with many buildings attached to one another, forming a complex. A great concrete wall surrounded the building that housed the most dangerous inmates, the maximum security part of the jail. It wasn't a bad-looking building from the outside, not sinister. But it was sinister inside, and worse. The sheriff took me through several halls, down a tunnel, and left me in my new home, handing my paperwork to a guard. I began the all-day affair of being processed.

Easily, 800 men were getting processed that day. They had to fingerprint us, take our picture, and give us a medical exam. Men were lined up everywhere. Some were like me—transfers from other jails. Others had been just arrested. Those who had committed crimes as simple as shoplifting, or as serious as murder, were being processed together. There were twenty pay phones along the wall, with men waiting in long lines to use them. It was pandemonium—noisy and filthy.

It seemed that most already knew somebody there and loudly called out names. The noise was deafening.

I knew nobody. I kept quiet and observed.

While in line waiting for my physical, I heard wincing sounds. The doctor was sticking a Q-Tip in everyone's penis to check for venereal disease. The thought made me cringe. When my turn came, I told the doctor, "I just came from Lake County. I don't need that test." He checked my chart and moved me through.

Your crime determined where you would be housed. For petty crimes, like shoplifting or car theft, you went to the house of corrections. If you had a high bond—$100,000 or more—you'd be in Division 5 or 6. My bond for armed robbery was $100,000, so I was sent to one of the worst divisions, number 6, with murderers and serious criminals. On paper, I was a dangerous criminal.

I was given a pair of tan khaki pants and a shirt that said DOC—department of corrections—and a bedroll, a toothbrush, soap, and a towel. Like a herd of cattle, they moved us from here to there all day and into the night. But, apparently, there was a method to the madness. We were being separated and put into numbered cages that represented the housing units where we would be eventually housed.

The officers asked point blank, "Are you homosexual?" They had a special floor for them and transvestites. Dressed up like women, with makeup, long hair and breasts, several fresh from the previous night's roundup, they looked at me, winking. I turned away—into some of the biggest, blackest, toughest faces I had ever seen.

It felt like a TV show and I was the star. Unlike TV, however, I couldn't turn the show off. I knew others were watching me. I did my best to look cool, smoking my cigarettes off in the corner by myself. I focused on all the advice Phil had given me.

The parts of the jail were attached by tunnels. You could move to any part of the jail without having to go outside. Division 6 was like a big quad with many tiers, labeled with a letter and a number. I was sent to L1; they buzzed me through a metal door. Each cell was for two men. One phone and one TV served about 100 people. An officer sat outside in a glass booth.

Inmates were playing cards, talking and watching TV. It seemed like everything and everyone stopped to watch the new people come in. All eyes were on me as I walked onto the deck—as Phil had explained to me they would be. I was carrying all the things I had been given, plus a sack lunch—a bologna sandwich, milk, and a cookie. It was all I had. I must have been a sight for the wolves: a fresh face and weighing in at 150 pounds. As I looked at the hundreds of eyes staring at me, I knew no one, not a soul.

On my way up the stairs to my cell, I was stopped by a black brother who asked for my lunch. It was just like Phil said it would be. I told him "No," that I needed it. I knew everybody was watching me, looking to see what I was going to do. That was the moment I had to grab my shield and sword.

The guy reached for my bag. I threw down my bedroll and lunch and started swinging. Fast and naturally good with my hands, I started clocking him. It was the last thing he expected; I had caught him off guard. He lunged at me, and we wrestled on the ground until a couple of other brothers broke it up.

I picked up my bedroll and lunch and went to my cell, bruised, but respected. That night I had chosen my shield and my sword. I had followed Phil Leonardi's teachings to the letter. In prison, you were always being tested, and I had passed my first test with flying colors.

The guy in my cell was an older black man, around fifty years old. Mr. Winslow was a nice fellow and welcomed me. Most older people in jail are trying to stay out of bullshit's way. He told me he was in because he shot somebody in self-defense. I took the top bunk. There wasn't much room. The cell was a very small space with a metal sink and toilet.

Breakfast was cold, and far worse than at Lake County jail. It was always cereal. There were too many inmates at the County to get a hot breakfast.

The gangs ran everything. Two main groups, the Gangster Disciples and the Vice Lords, issued the food trays and drinks, and regulated the phones and TV. Each gang was like a family. They watched out for each other and shared what they had. Whichever gang had the most members on a floor, controlled everything. If you weren't in a gang, you could expect to use the phone for only five minutes a day, that was it. I wasn't a Gangster Disciple nor a Vice Lord. So I was basically ass-out. After a few days, I began to piece together the social structure. The Disciples are called "Folks" and the Vice Lords are called "People."

Guys were curious about where I was from and what I did, because I was different. Most were impressed with my crime, especially the use of walkie-talkies and police scanners.

My family came the first day I was allowed to have visitors. Tomasa was with them. We talked for thirty-five minutes through glass on a phone that smelled like shit.

Later in the week, I went to the recreation yard. There were weights and three full basketball courts. Each court had a different level of play—one for the best, the middle court for the OK players, the last court for the scrubs. I went to the best court and watched the action. I loved the game of basketball and I still do. I had the skills to play college basketball, even though I was only five-seven. I had good ball-handling skills, and I was lightning fast.

I called the next game on the "best" court. When it was my game, I walked out on the court and picked my team. I had no gym shoes, so I just took off my prison shoes. The brothers looked at my bare feet and one asked, "How you gonna play with no shoes?"

I said, "Don't worry about it, it's my game." They looked at me like I was crazy. My dad had always told me when I was a kid pestering him for new gym shoes, that a good basketball player could play in his bare feet. That day, I put that theory to the test.

Even without shoes, I was the quickest person on the court. I was passing the ball, dribbling between and around guys. I was too quick for them. I was scoring with ease, as well as stealing the ball. Nobody expected the little brown-skinned, good-looking kid to play great basketball. I was hooping with the best ballers in Cook County jail, without any shoes on. A brother named L.A. stopped the game, and gave me a pair of gym shoes that belonged to a brother on the sidelines. When the game was over, I was accepted. I was in. If you can play sports well, people respect and treat you better—in prison, jail, and society.

Back inside, I had a new set of friends. One guy gave me a soda pop, and I got to know the names of the brothers with whom I had been balling. Some of those guys were six-eight and six-ten. After a couple of weeks, my mother sent me some gym shoes. Every day I dazzled the brothers with my moves. At eighteen, I was at my prime. Even at thirty-three, I was still about the fastest guy on the court. But when I was eighteen, there was no one even close. Around me others were being raped, beaten, or extorted. There was none of that for me. I was even allowed to talk on the telephone longer.

I adjusted to life in jail much the way I had to the foster home. I went from being scared to enjoying my new adventure. I reveled in the fact that I was surviving so well.

One day I was visited in my cell by a couple of brothers I had been playing basketball with in the yard, Too Tall and L.A., who had handed me gym shoes my first day on the jail court. They asked me if I wanted to become an aide and assistant to the Gangster Disciples. Most of the guys I had become cool with were Disciples. They explained that occasionally they meet a brother whom they like and respect, and invite him to aid and assist the gang in good and bad times. I had seen the brothers hanging together: watching TV, playing basketball, eating together, and watching each other's back. And I was somewhat familiar with the Gangster Disciples because most of the guys I had met in the projects were Disciples.

I told them I wanted to think about it, that it would be a big step

for me. I said I was honored to have been asked and shook both of
their hands as they left my cell.

I decided to ask my father and get his opinion. My dad said, "When
in Rome, do as the Romans do." So I decided to join. I would get extra
food and more phone time. I would make friends. The gangs ran
everything, and they were on top of the social hierarchy in jail. I was
always used to being on top. That was my opportunity to get involved
in an organization and try to rise to the top.

I approached L.A. the next day and told him that I proudly accepted
the invitation. I was then formally introduced to all the members.
Each week we all paid dues of two dollars with which we bought soap,
chips, or cookies. Our supplies were kept in a box if any member
needed anything. On weekends, one or two of the members would
make a lunch meat and mayonnaise dip for all the brothers to eat with
Fritos. It all seemed like the Boy Scouts until one night, all hell broke
loose—a fight between the Gangster Disciples and the Vice Lords.

It happened as I walked out of the bathroom. Guys were fighting and
throwing chairs, grabbing mops and mop ringers for weapons. A Vice
Lord whom I didn't know, had never spoken to before, was about to do
me some serious bodily harm. The idea of beating or killing someone,
because they were a part of another group, was all new to me.

I had no time to philosophize. The Vice Lord was moving toward
me with one purpose—to take me out. I sidestepped him and hit him
on the side of the head. Then I moved in for an uppercut. It connected
and he fell. Ordinarily, that would have been a time for jubilation, but
in a gang fight they just keep coming.

Two Vice Lords were coming in my direction. During this madness,
I noticed that those who weren't in gangs, the Neutrons, were sitting
back watching the action. They didn't get to use the phone, or turn
the TV to the channel of their choice, but neither did they have to
fight somebody else's battle for some unknown reason.

I noticed one of the two guys was carrying a shiny metal object—a
prison knife called a shank. I had to deal with the guy with the shank
first, and be open to whatever the other guy did to me. In the movies
there is always a superhero kicking three people's asses all at once.
Real life is vastly different.

In that instant, Six-One comes in, a tactical unit of special guards
equipped with helmets, billy clubs and shit-kicking, metal-toed boots.

Those officers averaged 250 pounds and they come in when a deck goes up. Six-One didn't ask any questions. They just started kicking everybody's ass, Neutrons included. When Six-One entered the picture, it was everybody against the police. The two brothers who were moving toward me immediately turned their attention to Six-One, and so did I. Somehow I was able to maneuver and run back to my cell, staying clear of Six-One. That angel was protecting me because I came out of it unscathed. Being a Gangster Disciple was a hell of a lot different than being in Jack & Jill.

It turned out the whole thing jumped off over a Vice Lord not getting off the phone in time for a Disciple to make his call. Lives were often lost in jail over something that simple. After the incident, we were locked in our cells for two days. Brothers who saw me during the fight said I had heart. That was the highest compliment a Gangster could give you. Many of the so-called hard-core members were hiding and seeking cover. Some even ran away from the action.

The next day I was asked to be a Disciple. I accepted. L.A. gave me lessons on exactly what it meant to be a Gangster Disciple. A dark-skinned brother, he was the leader in our cell house. There were rules, laws, literature, secret handshakes and signs. You had to pursue your education, maintain proper hygiene, exercise, and weren't allowed to disrespect or rape anyone. I took in the information like I did from Phil Leonardi.

Our chairman was Larry Hoover. I knew he had to be a hell of a man to have all those brothers following him to the death, if necessary. When I first heard about him, he had already been locked up for ten years. The more I learned about his teachings, the more I wanted to meet him. His laws and policies were intelligently put together. It wasn't his fault that many of the brothers who followed him were unable to grasp his meaning. From my understanding, he was a small man in size, and soft-spoken. People who knew him said we were similar, except for the soft-spoken part. I was fascinated with the man, having grown to respect him and his words of brotherhood. I studied everything I could about the organization, and soon knew more than other members who had been Disciples for years. Some of the guys couldn't comprehend or think critically or analytically.

The events of the big fight weighed heavily on my mind. After learning our laws, I knew there was a chain of command. The Disciple brother who wanted the phone should have taken his complaint to a higher-up in the Vice Lords organization rather than taken matters into his own hands. He compromised the safety and lives of every Disciple, Vice Lord, and Neutron. I pointed that out at our next meeting. I asked L.A., or the First C (short for coordinator), if I could arrange a meeting with the head of the Vice Lords, to clear the air. If I was going to be in a gang, then I was going to lead. The challenge was I would have to go inside the cell of the Vice Lords' leader and be surrounded by about fifteen of them *by myself.* Anything could happen. But, day after day of Disciples and Vice Lords exchanging ugly glances back and forth wasn't the answer. We thought the Vice Lords were planning an attack on us. Most of the Disciples were talking about getting them first. The last thing I wanted was to be in the middle of another gang fight.

With the prior approval of L.A., I walked up the stairs to the top gallery of cells and then down to the end cell. The long path was soldiered by Vice Lords. I was halfway into the wing before one of their security people stopped me. Coming by myself and walking as if I was on a mission, caught them by surprise. When he stopped me, I told him that I came in peace, and had a message for their chief. I waited five minutes and they motioned me into the cell and patted me down—checking to see if I had any shanks.

Once inside, I let my natural instincts take over. I relaxed and explained that we all wanted peace on the deck. I assured the Vice Lord chief that we wanted no animosity. I suggested that we hold our own members accountable for any disrespect to another organization. That way, we could avoid an all-out war.

The Vice Lords were opposed to an all-out war themselves. I wanted to continue our talk; however, I remembered telling the brothers that if I wasn't back in fifteen minutes, to come and get me. So I cut the conversation short, and returned with a message of peace for L.A. I had again won the respect of my fellow Disciple brothers in the month since I'd joined.

I had conquered Cook County jail in grand fashion, and I was becoming surprisingly relaxed there. I was not at ease in court. I was in serious trouble for the second set of armed robberies. Charles Jenkins, my money-hungry lawyer, was incompetent, made promises he knew he couldn't keep, and was always late.

On the day I was to be sentenced, he was going to argue before the judge a motion to suppress the confessions I had given on the first set of armed robberies, so it couldn't be used against me. He said I should have been allowed to call a lawyer. All my other codefendants separated themselves from me. The guys involved in my original set of armed robberies were white, and had never been in trouble before. When I got busted a second time, I looked like the black child who had gotten those white children into trouble.

Before oral arguments for the motion to suppress began, my lawyer came to the lockup. "We're not going to challenge the evidence," he said. "I talked to your family, cut a deal with the state's attorney. You can plead guilty to simple robbery, instead of armed robbery. Simple robbery carries four years minimum and twelve years maximum in prison. Armed robbery carries six years minimum and thirty years maximum. You'll get a four-year minimum sentence that runs concurrent with your sentence from Lake County. That means you'll be serving time for all the charges at the same time. Since the sentences in both Lake and Cook Counties are the same, you're still looking to be released in about two years, give or take a few months."

For all the armed robberies I did, I thought I had gotten a good deal. I asked my lawyer only one question, "What did my father say?"

"Your father agreed it's a good deal."

Wearing a blue church suit, I stepped in front of the judge. My parents and sisters were there. I looked at them, smiled and then turned my attention to the judge, who asked a lot of dumb questions, like: "Are you being forced to plead guilty? Were you promised anything?" I pled guilty, and the judge announced my sentence. "You will be placed in the custody of the State of Illinois Bureau of Prisons, for a term of four years for simple robbery."

I stood with a blank expression. My family left for a vacation in Hawaii, and I went back to Cook County jail.

All around me guys were facing twenty-plus years or life sentences, so I didn't let anyone know I wasn't pleased with my sentence. Twenty-one months was a long time to an eighteen-year-old. A month was a long time to me. But I was painfully aware that the only way I was going to get through prison alive was to blend in and do the time. It was the life I had chosen, so I was going to have to live with it.

Once you get sentenced, you are taken to the maximum security building. It had real cells instead of cubicles with metal doors. Enclosed by a fifty-foot concrete wall, it was filthy, and infested with roaches and mice. It was summer, and the heat was sweltering. Everybody there had already been sentenced or their charge was so serious—murder, rape—they had to be housed in maximum security.

Division 6 was bad, but guys were still going to court. Nobody wanted to get into more serious trouble while their case was still pending. In Division 6, a guy might think twice before trying to kill you. In Division 1, everybody had already been sentenced and didn't give a damn about taking someone out. I said my good-byes to the brothers and packed my meager belongings.

I had wanted to be a big-time criminal. Jail and prison are among the hazards of being a criminal, much like an accident is to a race-car driver. If the prison system was baseball, I was now drafted into the major leagues.

My arrival in Division 1 was exactly like my arrival in Division 6. When they opened the gate to let me in, everybody looked up at me. A few of my Disciple brothers who had already been sentenced were waiting to be shipped to their final destination. They greeted me and helped me with my things. The usual snakes and wolves had to look the other way because I was a Disciple. To mess with me was to mess with all of us. The Gangster Disciples, at that time, were the most powerful street organization in Chicago. It boasted over 100,000 members. Disciples ran the majority of the state prison system, including most of the staff.

My cellmate was T Bird, a tall, thin brother, with a perm, thick mustache, and a great sense of humor. We hit it off immediately. He started calling me Billy Dee. That eventually became my nickname. T Bird was the Disciples's first commander of the deck.

The Vice Lords in Division 1 were run by a big brother named Conan. He was muscular, weighed about 240 pounds and had an ugly scar running from the top of his chest to his belly button. He looked like a frog that you cut open and sewed shut in biology class. He was always posing in front of his cell mirror with two big knives—like Conan the Barbarian in the movies. Knives are made in prison by sharpening any straight metal object to a point. They could be as small as a pen or as big as a lawnmower blade. The most common shanks were the size of kitchen knives. The metal could be pulled out of mop bucket handles, nails, or pieces of metal that enclosed the mirrors on our cell walls.

Most of the guys passed their time playing chess, cards, and going to the gym. Others spent theirs raping, extorting, and using drugs. Rapes and extortion were more prevalent in Division 1, since everybody was on their way to prison anyway. I was now talking and walking like a gangster—nothing like the suburban kid from Arlington Heights. I was blending in and out-gangstering the gangsters. But it wasn't a game. Many of the guys were really crazy, hard-core killers who didn't give a damn. One, charged with murder, told me that he had broken into a house and killed a man and his wife. Afterward, he calmly made a peanut butter and jelly sandwich and sat down and drank a glass of milk. Another car-jacked a couple in broad daylight. He made them take him to their home, then tied the husband to a chair and repeatedly raped his wife in front of him. The husband was making so much noise in protest that he placed a pillowcase over his face. He laughed about it while telling us the story. Another cut off his girlfriend's head and put it in a plastic bag in his car trunk. He was stopped for a traffic violation and the head was discovered.

These were now my neighbors, and I had to make them believe they were my friends. My survival depended upon it. I never showed them I was appalled by their stories. In my book, you only killed to protect your family, friends, or yourself. Those guys weren't players. They were sick. Money was never serious enough to me to kill for. But Division 1 was their world, and I was in it.

We were only allowed outside to the recreation yard twice a week. The remaining days we were caged up together like dogs. In order to survive, I had to get into their heads and understand them. I became hard and detached.

After I stopped a guy from trying to sucker punch T Bird one day, I was promoted from soldier to second-in-command, my first official title since joining the Disciples. Finally, after seven months, I was giving orders. I had security around me at all times, shank-toting brothers who would cut your eyes out for just about anything.

T Bird was sent to prison and I become first in command of the deck, back in a familiar position of leading. Tension was high and Conan, head of the Vice Lords, kept the heat at a boiling point. He was a bully, a regular psycho. He constantly moved on and attacked anyone who wasn't hooked up in a gang. He beat one kid so badly that he broke his jaw. They had to wire the kid's mouth shut.

Many of the Disciples left the deck bound for the penitentiary, changing the complexion of the deck from mostly Gangster Disciples to Vice Lords. Slowly but surely, Conan turned his attention to me.

One day as I was coming out of the shower, Conan noticed that I was real hairy, and commented, "I like hairy men. They got hairy ass-holes, and when I fuck them, it feels like a pussy."

I knew he was talking about me, and so did the other brothers. I knew one day Conan and I would have a confrontation. It was inevitable.

After what seemed like forever in Cook County jail but was only seven months from my arrival, I finally got designated to go to prison on a Friday. The Thursday before my departure, my family paid their final visit to the jail. Looking back, I feel sorry for what I put my family through, especially my parents.

Before I went out for my visit with my family, I had planned to leave my toiletries and other things I couldn't take with friends, which is prison etiquette when you leave one jail or prison to go to another one. I closed my cell and it locked. While I was gone, Conan and some of his Vice Lords found a way to get into my things. They probably used a mop handle to knock over the box I had used as a makeshift shelf, and then used it to pull my stuff out of my cell.

I came back from my visit feeling up. I was glad to be leaving the County. It had become a living hell. I asked the officer to open my cell and when I entered, I saw all my things were gone. I was genuinely upset, cursing. Instinctively, I knew Conan was responsible. It reminded me of Ernest stealing the money I'd stolen.

All evening before 11:00 P.M. lockdown, I kept thinking about what had happened. The more I thought about it, the madder I got. After lockdown, I lay on my bunk, and tried to prepare myself for my next test, a maximum security prison.

As I was drifting off to sleep, Conan called, "Billy Dee. You OK? They took yo stuff?" He was fucking with me. I knew it, and everyone else knew it. That son of a bitch stole my stuff, and now he wanted to rub it in. He was the kind of guy my father tried to keep me away from all of my life. I just should have answered him by telling him every-thing was OK, but I decided to bad-mouth the thief in front of every-body.

"Whoever the punk, cocksucking bitch was who stole my shit, fuck 'em. The bitch who took my stuff would probably steal from his own mother." I kept on going, and guys were laughing. Conan was quiet. I knew he was angry, but I just kept goading him. "Yeah, the hoe could keep my stuff because he ain't nothin' and his momma ain't nothin'."

I went to sleep knowing I had gone too far, but I was pissed and didn't care. I got a small measure of satisfaction.

The next morning the doors opened at 6:00 A.M. for breakfast. I was already up and dressed and ready to move on to prison. Plus, I wanted to be ready to deal with any negative ramifications for the previous night's remarks. When I got to the day room, I could sense the tension. It was thick. Most of the Vice Lords were up, but there was no sign of Conan. I sat eating at a table with only two Disciple brothers. If you have ever watched zebras or deer as they were being hunted by a lion, you know they can sense when death is near. They can't see the lion, but they can sense him, and they start moving around nervously before they run for their lives. I felt like that.

But there was no place for me to run. I was thinking for my life. I had already seen some so-called Gangster Disciples become cowards under pressure. The two Disciples I was eating with weren't going to stand up and protect me or help me fight. Even though I was in command of the Disciples on my deck, I knew that these two brothers would rather watch me die than protect me. A Vice Lord came over and said, "Walk with me to Conan's cell. He wants to talk to you before you ship off to prison."

Death was calling me, and I knew I wouldn't make it out of that cell alive if I went. "I'll come down there when I'm done eating." That way Conan would think his plan to lure me into his cell was working. He could put those great big shanks—the ones he was always sharpening on the hard, cold, concrete floor—into my chest.

An officer sat behind a caged area that had a little gate that food would come through. We would set down our trays, then the gate would be unlocked and the guard would pull the trays through the caged gates. There were two gates, one on our side and one on the officer's side. We never had contact with the officer. The little corridor between the two gates was about four feet wide. That gate was my key to saving my life. I got up from the table and whispered through the bars to the guard. "I am leaving this morning for prison, and someone is trying to do me harm before I go. Will you let me stand in the corridor behind the locked gate? Please let me wait there." He opened the gate and I stepped in. The gate locked, just as Conan entered the dayroom wearing his robe, his hair in braids. He was walking fast, flanked by his Vice Lord soldiers, and his eyes were on fire. As he entered the dayroom, he opened his robe and pulled out two ten-inch pieces of steel with taped handles. They were sharpened to a razor point. When he saw me behind the gate, he swung one knife against the steel gate. The clashing steel made a piercing sound. "Nigga, you just saved your own fucking life," he said and went back to his cell. I saw my life flash before my eyes. If you have ever been truly close to death, you know what I mean. In one brief moment, you visualize yourself as a baby, in school as a child, your mother's face, the first time you had sex, and your first love—along with a thousand other images.

That angel was there again, protecting me from certain death. I often wonder what would have happened if that officer hadn't been there. Suppose he had been in the bathroom. That was my first near-death experience. I was a lucky eighteen-year-old that day. Many Gangster Disciples never had the chance to reflect on the gravity of avoiding being killed. They simply woke up in heaven or hell. And I don't believe there are any gangsters in heaven.

The officer opened the other gate and I went to be processed. There were about 100 other guys on their way to prison. I avoided any conversation with the brothers that I knew. I wanted to reflect on the moment. I had almost been killed. But my biggest test was waiting for me at a maximum security prison. The show of my young life was about to take place in Joliet, Illinois.

CHAPTER 11

Joliet Maximum Security Prison

On the bus ride to Joliet Maximum Security Prison, some talked and joked. Many of the older guys had been there before. For most black men in the prison system, prison is a cycle that they repeat for their entire life. Many black men either die in prison, or on their way to prison in the street.

There was a saying in the 1980s that went like this: "It's hard to get into prison, with all the endless probations and slaps on the wrist. But once you finally get there, it's easy to come back." That government policy position was changed in the 1990s. I didn't know it then, but I would be a living example of that old saying.

Some were visibly scared. If you listened hard enough you could hear their hearts beating. Those brothers would be like lambs to the wolves. There were the young brothers who had never been to prison before, who hadn't fared as well as me in the county jail, who had been beaten down and/or raped.

The guards sat in the front separated from the prisoners by a steel cage and held shotguns ready to shoot any of us, or anybody who might try to stop the bus. I sat in silence, my hands and feet shackled, taking it all in: the sounds, the smell, the motion of the bus.

I looked straight ahead, my face showing nothing but strength and confidence, preparing myself for the unknown and the unexpected. I had already chosen between a shield and a sword or a scarf and a skirt, months ago, and my weapon was polished and sharpened. Ready for battle, I wondered what my family and friends were doing. What were Cliff and Earl doing at Morehouse College? I looked at the lonely highway and images of my grandmother drifted in and out of my mind.

Whenever I was having trouble at home or in school my grandmother had encouraged me, "Victor, you can make it." My being in prison was much more than my grandmother could deal with. As a family, we all agreed it would not be a good idea for her to see me here. Although I would have liked to have seen her, the thought of some prison guard touching my grandmother or searching through her things was something I couldn't stand. But I wrote to her often and she wrote me back. Those words "You can make it" now applied to a situation she could have never imagined I would be in.

I was snapped away from my thoughts as the Joliet population sign of 30,000 popped into view. My stomach jumped—the way you feel riding a roller coaster when it drops you down. On the outside, I was cold as ice, but inside, I was scared. But as in the armed robberies, I had to make fear work for me, harness that adrenaline, excitement or fear, or be consumed by it, destroyed.

Anybody who says they weren't scared when they approached a maximum security prison is lying. Joliet looked like a castle. It was a large old complex, surrounded by a huge wall, with an enormous gate. It was a nightmare come to life. You could hear a pin drop.

We didn't go directly into the prison. The bus stopped down the street at the Annex. It was like a little county jail. We would stay there for two to five days while being processed.

They unloaded the bus and took us inside. It was a routine I now knew well: doctors and nurses, the standard questions. There was a new identifier here, though. If you were known as a snitch, there was a chance that somebody might recognize and kill you. So you could be put in protective custody. You're locked up twenty-four hours a day, with no recreation, and your food is served in your cell. I had no such problems and was given a cell with a young brother. I got the top bunk after our initial introduction. Neither of us said much to the other.

If I was on my way to the major league, the Annex was the tunnel leading into the ball park. I had my game face on. I knew no one. I was truly alone. You only have one time to make a first impression. I wanted to be seen as a strong, self-assured brother. Some Latino brothers walked up and spoke Spanish to me, but, I quickly proclaimed my blackness, and told them I didn't speak Spanish.

We were locked down day and night. The only time we got out was to eat. I noticed how fast everybody ate. Instead of the long lazy way we ate at the County, everybody ate as if it were their job to eat that food. "Time's up, lockdown," the guard yelled halfway through my meal. We had only fifteen minutes to eat. I grabbed some bread and headed back to my cell. We had no radio or TV in our cell. I was left with my own thoughts. Sometimes you're fortunate to be in a cell with a brother you can talk to. My cellmate was clearly not that kind of brother. He was young, stupid and only wanted to talk about girls, sex, and getting high. There were no women to be had, and I didn't get high, so there was little to talk about with him. The sad truth is most men spend their time in prison talking about women, using or selling drugs, or lifting weights. On the fourth day, I was told I was going inside the prison. On the one hand, I was glad because I was tired of being locked up like an animal. On the other hand, I was nervous as hell. I had seen Joliet Maximum Security Prison when we initially arrived. It looked menacing. Beyond those gates lay serious drama, drama that I could only imagine, and drama that I was determined to deal with and survive.

They loaded forty of us onto a bus, handcuffed in pairs of two. As we drove, nobody spoke. You could hear a mouse piss on cotton, as they say in prison. The bus stopped at the dark and grimy medieval prison and I wanted my mother, father, grandmother, a friend—somebody—to rescue me. I sat there as the gate opened, almost outside of myself. Joliet was where Al Capone had once been locked up. I had wanted to be a gangster, and now I was doing what gangsters do—go to prison. In gun towers on each outside corner of the prison, armed guards were perched with shotguns. A huge wall and razor-sharp barbed wire surrounded everything. My heart pounded as I took it all in.

I harnessed my fear, determined to make it and aware the wolves would be watching us get off the bus. As we were led off the bus, my face showed no emotion.

Inside, the prison was massive, loud, and dirty, and brothers looked hard and mean. Several made eye contact with me, but they didn't see any sign of fear on my face or in my eyes. I converted my fear into a hard look and stared right back at those seasoned convicts.

"Billy Dee," one of my Disciple brothers from the County called out. We greeted each other, locking our hands, and making the sign of pitchforks with our fingers, the Gangster Disciple handshake. The brother helped me to my assigned tier and cell and introduced me to other Disciples. There must have been over a hundred Disciples on my tier alone.

My cellmate was a young brother named Junior, who had twenty-five years for murder. We hit it off pretty well. That is the most you can hope for when you're thrown into the cell with a stranger. The routine inside the prison was different from the Annex. We were locked up twenty-two hours of the day. We got to go to the recreation yard for two hours. We ate in a large chow hall. We were in a cell house for new prisoners. Some would be sent to another prison and some of us would stay at Joliet. A series of evaluations by prison administration and doctors determined where an inmate would serve his time.

One of my Disciple brothers asked me to "spit some literature," tell him some of the laws that govern Disciples. The six-point star represents love, wisdom, life, knowledge, loyalty and understanding. The chairman and our leader was Larry Hoover. The first of our sixteen laws is silence and secrecy. I had studied well and began reciting more Disciple literature that he knew. I was then officially greeted by the brothers. I met the Disciple who was running Joliet, Don Slick, a big, dark-skinned brother with braids, around forty years old. I was told that Mr. Hoover had made him a don. He had no less than seven bodyguards around him at all times. We marched out in lines of two like an army platoon. Everybody, including me, had a shank or a razor blade melted in a toothbrush. Any piece of metal could be transformed into a shank by sharpening the metal. After melting the end of a toothbrush with a match, you could then insert the piece of metal into the end of the brush, forming a handle.

In the chow hall the noise was deafening. There were hundreds of men. It was just that big. In each corner of the chow hall were four watchtowers. Each tower was manned by a guard with a riot pump shotgun looking down on everybody who ate. This was something new. Those guys sitting up there with shotguns left no doubt; that plenty of shit happened and that they would shoot to kill, if necessary.

Don Slick sat at a table with his bodyguards and other important Disciples. I was just a soldier and ate with the soldiers. All the brothers at the table with Don Slick got loads of extra food, because most of the cooks in the kitchen were Disciples. I watched everything and everybody in my new environment, and reveled in the thought, *Al Capone once ate here*. I had graduated to the big time.

I was finding my way into the mix, while keeping Phil Leonardi's advice at the forefront of my mind. Everybody called me Billy Dee.

Homosexuals were constantly saying "Billy Dee, hey, baby, let me suck your dick." We called them "gumps." They walked, talked, and acted like women. By themselves they were harmless. However, many have killed and been killed fighting over gumps. I always told them that I wasn't interested, laughed and walked away.

One day a gump came to see my cellmate. Junior gave the gump two packs of cigarettes. I continued reading a book my mother had sent me, Kareem Abdul-Jabbar's *Giant Steps*. As I looked up from reading, to my horror, Junior's dick was hanging out between the bars, and the gump was on his knees, sucking and smacking loudly, while my cellmate moaned. I had never seen anything remotely like that. I just kept reading and doing page four—"minding my own business." After Junior came in the gump's mouth, the gump ran down the gallery and, I imagine, spit the semen somewhere. Junior got into his bunk and went to sleep.

On some nights, I could hear my neighbor having sex. It sounded like he was having sex with a woman, with all the "ooh, babys," "fuck me daddys," and the bed squeaking. Inmates don't look down on the guy doing the fucking. Only the guys who take it up the ass are considered homosexuals.

Some guys were never going home. Prison became their whole world. A life sentence will aid one's loss of perspective. Hearing and seeing that type of thing let me know I was completely in another world. If I had stopped and looked around, I would have lost my mind.

I tried to fit into my new environment by wearing a blue bandanna on my head. Blue is the Disciple's color. I also grew as much of a beard as I could. I stood out too much, and facial hair and headgear helped me tone down and blend in. In the County jail, my speech had gradually changed and by Joliet, I was speaking broken English, and talking like hip brothers raised in the projects.

There were about ten galleries—rows of cells—each on a separate level stacked on top of one another. You weren't supposed to go up or down to another gallery, but you could hang on the bars and jump down or pull yourself up. One day while I was walking on the main floor, I heard a frightening scream. I looked up and saw a brother falling, headfirst to the ground. He had been beaten and thrown off the top gallery, about forty feet down, to his death. I looked for a split second and kept walking. Nobody stopped. Everybody did page four.

The guards rushed into the cell house and herded us all back into our cells. After a couple of hours, they let us out for dinner as if nothing had ever happened. I heard that night in chow hall that the brother who died was only eighteen years old. The word was he owed some Vice Lords money because of a gambling debt. I knew I was in the worst situation of my life.

After two weeks, they finally processed my visiting forms, and my family was allowed to visit. It was great seeing my parents and two sisters. My mother was immediately concerned because I had the look of a wild animal, especially in my eyes. She noticed that right away. I couldn't turn off that prison face when I walked into the visiting room. They could not imagine what I was going through. Most of it was too deep to tell them.

I saw a brother I knew visiting with his family. He and his family were collectively crying their eyes out. That brother was weak. I knew others saw the same thing and one of the wolves would be looking for him. The wolf would give him a shoulder to cry on before pulling his pants down and raping his ass.

I wanted to cry, too. But there was no room in my survival kit for crying. My parents looked in disbelief at the other prisoners' wild and crazy looks. I know they felt sorry for me. But there was nothing they could do. Before they left, I smiled, and told them I was OK. I went back to the hell that I couldn't escape.

As I returned from my visit, I had a chance to go by Don Slick's cell while most brothers were locked up. It was my first opportunity to talk to him alone. I had been observing the security around him and believed that I had found a flaw. I had selfish reasons for pointing that out. For one, I was a soldier and the soldiers were the first to be sacrificed. It was just a matter of time before I was sent on a "mission." A "mission" involves administering payback by sticking a shank into someone for something they had done. If you were told to stick a guy, you had to stick him a certain number of times. If you made a mistake, your reward would be to get the shank stuck into you.

Being a bodyguard was a step up from a soldier. I talked to Don Slick and told him that when we marched to the recreation yard or chow hall, we could be marching into an ambush. I suggested we send two brothers ahead as advance scouts. One brother would walk into the location. The other would be close enough to hear if everything was OK, but far enough away to get back and warn the group if an ambush awaited. The Don listened and told me that somebody would get back to me. I ended the conversation by telling him I would be honored to be one of his bodyguards.

The next day there was a big mess. Apparently, a new brother joined our gallery and said that he was a Disciple. But before he was screened and questioned about the laws and policies as was the protocol, the chief of security introduced him to the don. From my understanding, the don was furious with the brother who breached security. I only got the tail end of everything because I was a soldier. That night in the chow hall, I was called to the don's table. One of his bodyguards came over and told me to walk over to the table.

The second-in-command was an older brother whom I barely knew. He told me what I had already heard about the chief of security's mistake. What I didn't know was the don wanted me to violate that brother. That was my test to see if I was up to being a bodyguard. I remember feeling as if I had set myself up.

I asked to speak to the don, who was engaged in conversation with some other brothers. When he finally spoke to me, he asked, "Have you been told?"

"Yes," I answered and tried to speak, but he interrupted me and said, "Nigga, take care of it." That was it. They wanted me to physically violate the chief of security. I was told I could take one soldier with me to help.

The brother in charge of security was named Black. He was about six-one and 190 pounds. He outweighed me and was taller. But I knew how to fight, and he didn't know I was coming. Given those two advantages, I figured I could carry the order out. If I did, I believed that I could write my own ticket with the don.

I picked up a brother, not much bigger than myself, to help. My plan was to roll up a magazine and carry it like a stick. Once we were back on the gallery, I would wait for Black to enter his cell. When his back was turned, I would break his lightbulb that hung from the ceiling and coldcock him as he turned around. I would follow this with as many blows as I could land.

After chow, we all marched back to our cells. I told the other brother that once I got Black down, to come and join in the beating. When I got to Black's cell, my heart was racing and my adrenaline was pumping. He was turned away from me, pissing in the toilet at the back of the cell. He turned his head and said, "What's up?" As the sound of his piss splattered in the toilet, I hit the light with the rolled-up magazine. The cell went dark as the glass shattered. He turned around into my right fist, then a left uppercut, followed by another right to the head. The other brother joined me by throwing and land-ing several punches. Black was screaming, "What did I do?" I said, "You know what you did, nigga. This is from the don." I walked out of that cell with the mission accomplished and the respect of my fellow Disciples.

The next day, there were no hard feelings between Black and me. We hugged. Violations were part of being in a gang. He had gotten off easily, though he was clearly wrong. Later that day I was called to Don Slick's cell and formally put on his bodyguard team. I was given a real shank—my own personal sharpened piece of steel, fashioned like a knife. It had to be carried at all times.

My suggestion for sending advance brothers was adopted. I became close to the don in the weeks that followed. The older brothers contin-ued to see considerable potential in me to be a great criminal. Don Slick told me stories about Larry Hoover who, at that time, was at Stateville prison. I was fascinated by Larry Hoover. I knew he must be a great leader to have thousands following him and to control most, if not every, state prison in Illinois. Mr. Hoover was a mythical character to me because I had only heard about him.

Prison life was people screaming, fighting, and taking drugs. The scene was out of control. I struggled to maintain sanity in that insane place. Showers were twice a week in the shower house, where twenty-five to thirty brothers wash at once. The last time I could remember standing in a shower with a bunch of men was in high school. Even County had separate shower stalls. The gumps held their penises from view between their legs, trying to act and look like women. It was sick. Prison life—the absurd had become my home.

It was summer and I knew Earl, Cliff and Robert were enjoying it. I lay in my bunk worlds away from them, but determined to survive and get back there with them. There was nobody trying to kill the don, and things went on as normally as could be expected. Making the move to bodyguard proved to be a smart one.

After about a month, I was called to the counselor's office. She wanted to talk to me before deciding whether to keep me in a maximum security prison or send me to a medium or minimum facility. I shaved my beard, and took off my bandanna for that meeting. I knew that I could survive anywhere, but I had heard stories that some medium and minimum security prisons were equipped with a key to your own room and had spacious well-kept grounds. I wanted to go somewhere like that. I walked into the counselor's office as if I were on a job interview. I extended my hand and introduced myself to the white woman in her forties. She seemed immediately impressed with my demeanor.

I quickly dropped my cold, hard mask and told her I was scared to death, that I had never been in trouble before. I looked at her with my big brown eyes, and tried my best to look like a frightened deer. I said I was afraid of the gangs, although during our meeting I was carrying a shank. "I'm recommending you to Centralia." It was a medium security prison in the southern part of Illinois.

I shared with the don my news that I was leaving in a couple of days. He wished me well. Guys familiar with Centralia said it was nice; you could eventually work your way to a single room. When the day came for me to leave, I was shackled and handcuffed to a brother I didn't know, much like many of my ancestors on slave ships before me. We were herded out to the bus with about eighty other guys. On to my next adventure.

CHAPTER 12

Centralia Medium Security Prison

The trip to Centralia Medium Security Prison was about seven hours. If you had to use the bathroom, they passed you a bucket. It was hard to urinate in handcuffs, holding my penis, aiming into a bucket, as the bus moved, with eighty people watching. That was a humiliating experience. But I was so happy to be moving on, I didn't care where I urinated or who was watching. I sat eating bologna sandwiches and drinking milk, feeling good. I had survived the worst. Many guys were sleeping. Not me, I was alert. I never sleep around people I don't know.

Centralia was a bunch of one-story brick buildings surrounded by a fence, not a wall like Joliet. It looked like a college campus, neat and clean. We got off the bus and were taken to where they received the new inmates. Inside, it was the same old mess. Stupid questions about whether you were scared, thinking of killing yourself, if you were homosexual, or couldn't live with the general population. Again, I answered, "Hell no!" to all of those questions.

After five hours of waiting and being refingerprinted, I was allowed to go to the chow hall. It was closed, but they opened it for us. It was a Ponderosa restaurant compared to the one in Joliet. They served us hamburgers and french fries.

While I was eating, I looked up and saw a tall, pretty, light-skinned black girl working in the kitchen, but a brother laughed and said it was a gump. In Joliet, the gumps looked like men. After I ate, I walked to my assigned unit. The units looked like cottages, brown, built with metal and brick.

Inside, a brother asked if I was "Folks." I identified myself as a Disciple, and showed the brother love by spitting literature and shaking his hand in the traditional way. That had become old hat for me. I had paid my dues in the County and Joliet. I had earned the right to be a Gangster Disciple.

I was put into a cell with an older brother named Milt, a born-again Christian. The Disciples came and met me one by one, and asked if I needed anything. We were like a family. There were the usual questions about my nationality. People mistake me for Puerto Rican, Iranian, East Indian. I told them I was born in Detroit from two black parents.

Milt played basketball. I couldn't wait to get to the gym. I spent the night asking him about everything from the food to how often we could go to the gym.

I had orientation to learn the rules of the prison, before I could go out. We were given blue shirts and khaki pants. We were also allowed to wear Levi's blue jeans that could be bought at the prison commissary.

Centralia had controlled movement, which meant you could only go to the gym or library on the top of any hour. After that, doors would be locked. To be caught out past that time, except in the yard, was considered out of bounds and you were subject to disciplinary action—going to the hole (a jail within the prison) or given extra work duty.

Unlike Cook County jail or Joliet, everybody had to work or go to school. I hated school, but I hated work even more. I quickly signed up as a full-time college student. Teachers came into the prison from the local college to teach accredited classes. If you were unfortunate to be there long enough, you could earn a degree. I only positioned myself to get out of work.

In Centralia, the Disciples outnumbered any other gang. The head Disciple was known as Cold Power. I knew guys in Centralia from County and Joliet, including my old friend T Bird from the County. I relaxed a little for the first time in over a year, and enjoyed fresh air and relative freedom. Centralia was full of problems, but they were not as intense, on some levels, as the County or Joliet. I continued to stay close to the advice that Phil Leonardi gave me. I stayed away from gambling, homosexuals and drugs. Most importantly I did page four.

I met a young brother named Kevin, a good-looking kid and a good basketball player. There was only one problem, he was a Vice Lord. Vice Lords and Disciples didn't mix because why make friends with somebody you might have to kill the next day, or who might be ordered to kill you? Still, we became close. We played basketball together, and shared books, magazines, and snacks. Some of my Disciple brothers resented my friendship with Kevin, and let me know it. I let them know that I knew what side of the fence I was on.

I took psychology, business, and history classes. I spent my days playing basketball and went to school at night. I was one of the best point guards there and usually one of the first players picked to play ball.

I stayed away from Gangster Disciple politics at Centralia. There was always some power struggle about who was going to be in charge. Usually, somebody who had met Larry Hoover, or had been instructed by a brother who sat on Mr. Hoover's board, ran the prison for the Disciples.

I stayed on the sidelines because my main concern was to survive and go home. I wasn't there to run for public office or be anybody's campaign manager. To me, all the guys had black faces, white faces, or Latino faces. I never saw a Vice Lord, Disciple or Latin King. I didn't grow up running from bullets that were shot at me from a rival gang. I took everybody at face value and talked to everyone. Unfortunately, many of the brothers' loved ones were murdered by rival gang members. So most of the brothers hated each other simply because of the different organizations they belonged to.

I met a few interesting characters in Centralia. A white guy, Dino, was about forty years old and had been the drummer for Chaka Khan's band. He had pictures of them together and letters where she had kissed the paper with those big beautiful lips, and written Chaka beside it. He had a huge tape collection. We would listen to music for hours, and he would explain the different musical sounds on the tapes.

My parents sent me money for a TV and occasionally came to visit me, staying in a hotel over the weekend. I looked better in Centralia, and my mother felt better, although it was still hard for her to see her only son in prison. Tomasa also came to see me about twice a month, making that six-hour pilgrimage from Chicago. We would sit there kissing and holding hands, and making plans for the future.

Prison life at Centralia was full of oddities, like any other prison. Every time I went to the shower, a big brother named Sampson looked at me. His cell sat across from the shower. I thought he was a wolf looking for a victim. A solid 240 pounds, he bench pressed 500 pounds, and squatted over 650 pounds. He was awesome. I had seen him in the weight room. He would bark just like a dog when he worked out. He had won every prison weight-lifting competition in the state of Illinois. His room was filled with over a hundred trophies.

When I walked by his cell, he would be sitting in a chair at the foot of his bed. We would always make eye contact. I hoped that I wouldn't have to fight him, but I was prepared to, if necessary. One day as I passed he said, "Hey little brother, I see you like to keep clean." In prison, a lot of brothers skip daily showers. He was also extremely clean and neat and kept an immaculate room. I turned to look at him; we both broke into a smile. I introduced myself and we shook hands. In the days that followed, we got to know each other and became best friends. Sampson was from Chicago. He had been down for four years already, for burglary. He wore his hair in braids and was about five-ten.

He wondered how a brother from a good family, good-looking and smart, ended up in prison. At Centralia, I let go of the broken English and crazy behavior and it was apparent that I was different.

Sampson confessed to me that he could barely read or write. No one knew but me. I would read all his mail and help him write his letters. I also helped him learn how to read and study for the GED exam.

He took me to the weight room and taught me how to lift weights. He was always on me to stop playing so much basketball. He told me that basketball and lifting weights didn't mix.

Sampson knew all about fixing things. He often bragged that he could build a house from the bottom up, including wiring and plumbing. We made plans to get together in "the world." He introduced me to one of my favorite snacks: peanut butter and honey on a saltine cracker. I still eat that to this day. Sampson swore on that as a great protein snack. We spent countless hours eating and talking. A quiet man, he wasn't in a gang and rode by himself. I felt privileged to be his only friend.

One day Sampson got into an argument with a Vice Lord about the telephone. The brother refused to get off the phone during Sampson's time, talked shit about him, too, since he had his gang behind him.

Sampson went to his room, put on workout gloves and gym shoes, and prepared to fight. It wouldn't have been much of a fight because Sampson would have kicked the brother's ass and put him in the prison hospital. I walked into his room, stood in the doorway and refused to let him out. Sampson was mad. "Little Vic," he told me, "get out of my way. I'm going to kill him." "You'll have to fight me before I let you throw away all of the plans we've made over some mark," I insisted. Sampson was up for parole and scheduled to leave that summer.

"When you get through talking, Little Vic, I'm going to kill that nigger."

"You're going to have to kill me, too, before you kill that brother." We talked for more than three hours before he finally calmed down.

I didn't know exactly how Sampson would fit into my life when I got out, but I knew I would need him one day. After that, our friendship was stronger than ever. Sampson eventually got parole and went home. Before he left, we hugged, exchanged addresses and promised to see each other on the street. It was a promise I knew we would keep.

I got into only one fight at Centralia. One day Prince was on TV, and one brother said he looked good enough to fuck. He then commented in front of everyone that I looked like Prince. Everybody watched to see what I would do. I punched him, knocked him to the ground.

After about six months, I applied to a minimum security facility in East Moline, Illinois. I had to go before a committee of counselors and the warden to be transferred. My record was clean and I had not been in any trouble. With my good manners, sincere "I have learned my lesson" look, and the humble tone in my voice—they unanimously voted to send me on my way.

CHAPTER 13

East Moline
Minimum Security Prison

I made another several-hour trip to a new facility, East Moline Minimum Security Prison. I had only about six months left on my sentence when I arrived at East Moline in the summer of 1985. I couldn't help but think about Earl and Cliff graduating from Morehouse College, as I continued my bizarre journey.

East Moline wasn't originally a prison. At one time it was a hospital, overlooking the Mississippi River, and surrounded by a fence. Inmates were outside when I got there. Trees were everywhere. It looked lovely.

Unlike Centralia, there was no controlled movement. All you had to do was sign out with the officer in your unit. You were free all day until you had to report back for one head count at 4:00 P.M., and another at 9:00 P.M.; then you were locked down in your unit until the next day.

To avoid work, I took a horticulture class. They had a greenhouse and I eventually got certified in horticulture. I cheated throughout the course. But anything short of cheating at that stage of my life would have been unacceptable.

The Gangster Disciples were the biggest gang there, and again I was screened and met the brothers. I paid my two dollars a week dues to the box for buying soap or cigarettes. I also came a little closer to meeting a legend. I met Larry Hoover's codefendant, DD. Mr. Hoover and DD had been sentenced to 200 years in prison on a murder charge.

DD had done about fifteen years when I met him. He was small, dark-skinned and wore his hair greased back. He always had a small entourage with him. I still left prison politics to brothers who would be there for a while. I was just passing through on my way home. As usual,

I quickly made friends on the basketball court. Tomasa followed me to East Moline; we were in love, and looking forward to our future.

I met some interesting characters. KeKe, a master thief, counterfeiter and con man, was a polished player, a perfect gentleman, handsome, brown-skinned, with short hair. He was around thirty-five years old. When he told stories, a crowd would listen. He would tell how he ripped people off, played women and cashed checks he had stolen. He had forged some checks for over $25,000. I paid attention to everything he said, especially about credit card fraud.

KeKe ran with all the high-level players at East Moline. One friend was in prison for impersonating a lawyer. His roommate, Tops, was the biggest player in East Moline. They called him that because whatever he got involved with, he finished on top.

Tops was a Black Stone Ranger, which was affiliated with the El Rukins, who had been down for ten years for murder. He had light skin and was good-looking, with a strong build. He stayed to himself, and only associated with the other players. He was about twenty-eight years old. Rumor was he controlled the drug trade at East Moline.

KeKe had taken me under his wing, and was schooling me night and day. He introduced me to Tops, but Tops paid very little attention to me. I was sure he dismissed me as one of the many misfits at East Moline. One day I was slap-boxing with one of the brothers, and getting the best of him. Tops asked if I wanted to go a few rounds with him. I was sure he expected me to back down, but I looked at him and said, "Sure, let's go." He responded, "Let's go to the laundry room."

I started throwing body punches and combinations. The guys who watched were surprised at my aggressiveness, and so was Tops. Tops was about 225 pounds, and his punches almost knocked me down; however, for that performance, I had won his and everybody else's respect.

After that, Tops was a lot nicer to me. He even stopped to talk to me once in a while. But, he had a lot of things going on, and I was still on the outside. Another time he caught me bragging about playing basketball, and challenged me to a one-on-one. I knew he couldn't deal with me on the court.

We headed out after count one afternoon, again with a crowd watching. I was raining jump shots, and dribbling around him. I was so fast back then, he couldn't stop me. I kicked his natural black ass out on the court. Like a true player, he knew how to win and how to lose. He shook my hand after he lost.

One day while I was using the phone next to him, I noticed that he had an attorney's card whose name I recognized. He was about to call Angela Simpson, the woman who had represented Mark Dellums in the armed robbery case. I told him I knew her because she had been counsel to a friend of mine. Tops wanted more details, so I explained the whole case to him. I proudly told him that before I pled guilty, I told the judge that her client was sleeping in the car, and knew nothing about what was going on. Consequently, the case against Mark was dismissed.

Tops was using Angela Simpson to represent him at a parole hearing. I told him to ask her about me. It turned out that she was coming to see him the next day.

I don't know exactly what the attorney told him, but I do know she said I was a stand-up brother who had saved her client from a jail sentence. Furthermore, I was someone who could keep my mouth shut.

After that, Tops treated me differently. He also began asking me questions about my case. I started hanging with KeKe and Tops all the time. Tops called me his little brother.

One night, Tops, KeKe, and I were listening to some music in their room. They were sharing stories about life in the fast lane. Tops asked me if I knew about Stan Wilson. I didn't. Tops and KeKe laughed and Tops pulled out a bag of white powder.

Stan Wilson was Tops's name for cocaine. He used that alias so he could talk about it over the phone, or anywhere else without any prison authority knowing what he was talking about. I didn't know anything about cocaine, except what I saw in *Scarface*. They offered me some, but didn't pressure me. I declined. Drugs weren't and still aren't my thing.

Cocaine makes you want to talk, and they told me a lot. Tops was smuggling in marijuana, heroin, and cocaine. He even had needles for guys who wanted to shoot up. Just then, an officer walked into the room unexpectedly. I jumped up, and blocked the cocaine from the officer's view. After that, I was truly accepted by Tops.

In the days that followed, Tops explained to me that he killed some people over a drug deal gone bad. He had an eight-year-old daughter who lived in Chicago. He also introduced me to a guard at East

Moline who worked for him. Because I was generally not known at East Moline, I was perfect to carry messages back and forth to the guard and inmates for Tops.

I was on the inside. KeKe and Tops took me to school, and I loved it. Tops had prostitutes from Chicago coming out to sleep with the white guards, so he had permission to get away with anything short of murder. He had so much weed, he would pass out free joints to everybody in our unit on the weekends, to keep everybody happy, so nobody would trick on him.

I finally tried some weed for the first time and liked it. We spent days smoking weed and eating pizza from the commissary. Tops and KeKe told me that with my good looks, I never had to steal; all I had to do was ask for money, and women would give it to me. KeKe explained that by wearing a suit and a tie, I could go anywhere, especially since I knew how to talk to people. He also told me how to change my name, and use other people's credit cards.

Tops explained about the life I had chosen, calling it *the game*. He told me there was a right way to go down a wrong road. He taught me not to be a renegade, meaning don't steal from your friends, don't be a snitch and rat on people you got caught with, and do your own time. He told me to balance my scales in life—always have the good things you do outweigh your bad things, have so much good shining, that it blinds people from the bad.

I listened to the words of wisdom Tops shared, as if my life depended on it. I was getting the formal training I needed to be a player in *the game*. That was the knowledge I had needed before I set out on my life of crime in high school. Some say Tops was wrong to school me in *the game*. They say that if he was my friend, he would have told me to go to school and get a job.

But Tops was a player, and he loved *the game*. You can't blame a player for being a player, any more than you can blame a tiger for being a predator. I wanted *the game* and he gave me something he loved, much like a father gives his trade to his son. I was finally receiving the advice and the schooling I had been searching for. I will always be grateful for the things he taught me, and I'm proud to say that I never showed disrespect or dishonor to *the game*.

He also told me about brothers who would be jealous of my looks and abilities, and try to kill me and take me out of *the game*. Tops would say, "The game is cold, but it's fair," and "Everything that glitters isn't gold." The most important words of all were: "There's a price to pay for playing *the game*. Everyone who plays pays. *The game* might reward you with cars, money, women, and everything your heart desires, but sooner or later *the game* will come calling for you to pay your dues. You may pay with a prison sentence or your life, but everybody pays."

In the 1990s, you have a new wave of criminals, who try and cheat *the game* by becoming informants. Today, people want to play, but try to never pay. Eventually, they will find out that nobody cheats *the game*.

I made parole in January 1986. KeKe had already left. So the job of seeing me out on my last day of prison was left to Tops. He walked me to the gate and hugged me. I walked out of his embrace to Tomasa's. She was waiting for me on the other side of the gate. I vowed to Tops that I would come back and visit him, *and* I promised to honor *the game* that he had so beautifully given me.

I left East Moline a player. I had graduated at the top of my class, with the highest honors. I was given an education. You can't ask for *the game*. It can only be given to you by a master player, one who has chosen you, and you him. He told me to hook up with another master when I got out. He left me by telling me to resume my rightful place in the world, and in *the game*.

CHAPTER 14

The Transition from Prison

I had spent a year in state prison honing my skills as a player. I was anxious to come out into the world and show people that prison hadn't destroyed me. I had yet to find my inner self and my true spiritual purpose in life.

Tomasa was waiting for me with her best friend, Stacy. It felt great but also very strange to be out. I didn't talk much as we drove down the highway in Stacy's car. I had left prison, but my mind was still there. It took a while for my mind to catch up. I saw a lot of brothers' faces in the highway of my mind.

Stacey dropped us at the Ramada Inn by O'Hare airport. The whole time I was locked up, all I could think about was being with a woman. Whenever Tomasa came to see me, I was horny as a dog in heat. But when I finally got into that hotel room, I was nervous. "Let's go down to the restaurant for dinner," I suggested, but Tomasa pushed me down to the bed.

"I have been waiting too long. I want to make love now!" Her long, reddish brown hair fell on my head as I began sucking her breasts like a hungry newborn. Her hot Latin juices flowed. She was screaming, and moaning, and saying my name. After I exploded, I stayed erect, and we did it again. We eventually went down to the restaurant, then headed back upstairs for more. We ordered champagne and spent the night fulfilling our sexual appetites.

The next morning, I boarded a plane to New York. My family had moved to the East Coast while I was locked up. My parents had a plane ticket waiting for me at the airport. I kissed Tomasa good-bye, and promised to send for her when I got on my feet and found an apartment. I had a drink on the plane, and in less than two hours I was greeted by my mother and father. We hugged and kissed, and shared a warm embrace. My relationship with my parents had always been turbulent. However, they truly loved me and were glad to have me back home. I believe they were praying for the best.

My parents lived in a beautiful town in Connecticut. My father had gotten another promotion in the Fortune 500 company and relocated to New York. The house was beautiful. It cost over $500,000 and sat on several acres, surrounded by trees. Often, you could see deer in the backyard. My parents' new neighbors included Diana Ross, Paul Newman, and Harry Connick Jr.

My grandmother, Mary Louise Martin, was staying with my parents. We suspected that she was developing Alzheimer's but she still remembered everybody. Her love for me was still very much alive. My grandmother's eyes sparkled when she saw my face. We shared a spiritual closeness and it felt good to be able to hug her again. Just the very touch of her hand was soothing and calming.

My mother found me a job at Saks Fifth Avenue unloading trucks. The father of one of her students was the manager. I immediately started casing the store, just as I had during my armed robbery days. I quietly watched and listened to everything. The people I was working with were basically young people like myself. Upstairs, where I had to deliver clothes, young white guys in suits sold the merchandise, and managed various departments. I could tell they looked down on me because I was black, and also because I unloaded those trucks.

It was that bullshit corporate mentality, that "I'm better than you, because I have a better position" attitude. It was what Joe Citizen lives for. Often, Joe Citizen has very little power in his overall existence. But on the job, he was king over somebody, anybody. If something needed to be cleaned or mopped, they would call me up from the basement. I despised doing it. In my position as the grunt work guy, I was the one who was looked down upon. Such was the way in corporate America working in the basement.

To amuse myself, each day before the store opened, I stole something, a belt or a pair of socks. Then I graduated to expensive perfumes, watches and sunglasses.

I hid stuff in the store, and took it out piece by piece. Then I became bolder, stealing from the trucks, throwing boxes of shoes into the outside garbage, retrieving them at night, after work. I sold the loot at the park to brothers I played ball with, who lived in the bad part of town. It wasn't a good day on the job if I didn't steal something.

After a few months of freedom, I decided to explore the night life. I went to a couple of bars in town, and hung out. I started dating a good-looking girl with a nice tight body on my job, Cynthia, and I did what any brother who had just gotten out of the joint would do—had sex with her as much as I could.

One day I was home by myself and remembered KeKe's words about transforming myself into a sophisticated gentleman. I put on one of my father's sports coats, a shirt and a tie, and picked up one of his old briefcases. I immediately felt comfortable and I looked good. It was time to put my teachings in *the game* to use.

I took all of my next paycheck and used my employee discount to buy my first suit. It was blue, with pinstripes. I also bought red suspenders. The white man who sold me the suit asked, "Why do you need a suit like this?" All he saw was a "nigger" who worked in the basement. I smiled and said, "I need a suit for church."

That weekend, I dressed up, got into the old Lincoln Mark V my father had given me, and headed out on the town. Just like KeKe said, people treated me differently dressed in a suit. To get used to my new role, I went to a bar in a fancy hotel, and just sat there. Older women checked me out, but I was too nervous to approach them.

My parents were still chanting, "This is our house and you're going to follow our rules." We were back to fighting all the time about what time I was coming in, what I should or shouldn't be doing with my life. Things came to a head one night when my mother found a suitcase full of stolen goods from Saks. She was understandably hurt and upset. We had a Woods family discussion.

"What are you going to do, spend the rest of your life in prison?" one of them said. My grandmother had been listening in the next room and walked right into the kitchen, and told them, "Stop talking to him like that."

My father had resented my grandmother, because she always stuck up for me, no matter what, but he never dared to disrespect her. With my grandmother showing signs of Alzheimer's disease, my father and sisters had taken to being disrespectful of her. Their standard joke was: If you put Grandma on the stairs, she wouldn't know if she was coming or going.

It always angered me to hear those cruel remarks about my grandmother. On that night, when my grandmother, Mary Louise Martin, entered the room, my father yelled at her. "Our discussion is none of your business. Get the hell out." I jumped up and threatened, "If you ever speak to her that way again, I'll kick your ass." He jumped up like he wanted to slap the shit out of me.

It looked like slow motion to me, the same way people moved in the joint. My eyes were fixed in a hard, cold, steady glare. I was ready to hurt my own father. I moved on him for the first time in my life. I had been lifting weights. He backed down, could see the fire in my eyes; he didn't want any part of me. I had a lot of anger built up in me, and he *almost* was the recipient of it. He looked at my mother, who was shocked at my behavior, and said, "Honey, that boy has got to leave this house."

My father gave me about $1,000, and some old suitcases to carry my clothes, and I returned to Chicago. Tomasa moved out of her parents' house, and got a small one bedroom apartment for us. She even flew in to help me drive to Chicago. I spent one last night with Cynthia before Tomasa and I left for Chicago in that old Mark V that my father had given me.

CHAPTER 15

Finding *the Game*

Tomasa's family wasn't happy about her moving in with me, unmarried. They were a hardworking, old-fashioned family. The parents barely spoke English, so it was hard to communicate. Tomasa worked as a full-time waitress at a luxury hotel and for a few weeks, we got by on Tomasa's meager earnings, but I needed some real cash.

I looked up my buddy, Tony Pappas. I heard that he was in prison for selling drugs while he was out on bond for the armed robberies he did with me. Tony was sentenced to twelve years in state prison, which meant he had to serve six. I went with his family to visit him at Joliet. It was strange going back into that godforsaken place. That night after seeing Tony, I settled back at the apartment, sipped beer, and tried to figure out how to best run *the game* I had learned from Tops. I had Tomasa buy some suits for me, but I wanted real cash to go along with those new clothes. I remembered what Tops had told me about balancing my scales; I got a job at the *Chicago Tribune* selling newspapers over the phone, at night.

I looked up another old friend from junior college named Carlo. He was an Italian pretty boy. I remember even my mother saying that he was nice-looking. Women fell all over Carlo. But he was conceited about his looks and would frequently say, "How could God have made somebody so beautiful?" I invited him over to the apartment and we shared stories, filling each other in on what had been going on in our lives. After the small talk, I explained to Carlo my plans to make money in *the game*.

Carlo introduced me to Sonia, a beautiful Puerto Rican girl. She owned a restaurant, but was also into big-time drug dealing. We were immediately attracted, but I never tried to bone her. I didn't want to take the chance of blowing a business connection over a romance.

I began to hone the teachings from Tops and KeKe about making money in *the game* and became involved in numerous illegal business activities and scams. Like anything else, you get experience and, hopefully, get better.

My new lifestyle and a relationship with Tomasa weren't compatible. It saddened me to have our relationship end. She had been good to me at a time when I needed support; however, I loved *the game* more than any woman.

With each new facet of *the game* I participated in, my understanding and level of complexity and sophistication increased. Some of them netted me large sums of money, others did not. But my intellect within *the game* kept evolving.

It was a nice Chicago summer day in June 1987. The sun was shining and it was hot. I imagine most people who were not in *the game* were at work. I spent my days at home, lounging in my shorts and T-shirt, living the life of a player. I enjoyed watching movies, playing Nintendo, and washing my Corvette that sat in the driveway in its splendor. Instead of a nine-to-five job in an office, I was a middleman. I was the guy who brought two parties to the table in drug deals. When the deals went through, I stood to make a generous fee for my services.

During that summer, there was a shortage of drugs in Chicago. Everybody was scrambling for the powder, mother of pearl, or bubble gum—better known as cocaine. What that really meant was a big shipment from Florida or Texas got busted on its way to Chicago. So I was trying to hook up a deal to introduce some "haves" with some "have nots."

I got a call from Hector. He was a Mexican I had met through Sonia, who had some keys (kilos) of cocaine for sale. His asking price was $21,000 for one and $19,000 each for two. While it sounded good, I knew in *the game* that everything that glitters wasn't gold.

Nevertheless, I took a chance and didn't listen to my instinct, which can be fatal in *the game*. I, in turn, called a brother named Cool Breeze—CB for short. I met CB through a parole officer who was selling drugs.

I explained the details to CB, and he jumped all over the deal. Two hours later, he and his girlfriend came over to my place in the suburbs. He was short, with kind of a square face, wore glasses, and he was extremely intelligent. CB liked to be in the middle of everything, always looking for a way to cut you out of a deal, and cut *himself* in. He was a brother who was greedy, and loved to make fast money.

CB followed me in his car to meet with Hector at a seafood restaurant called the Rusty Pelican. Once we arrived, Hector wanted to take CB's money to his people, *alone*. However, CB did not trust Hector, and wouldn't part with any of his cold cash.

I didn't want the deal to go south, so I stepped up and offered to ride with Hector. Since I was the middleman, I told CB I would be responsible for the money. After all, CB didn't know Hector. But, wouldn't you know it, CB didn't trust me either. Hector explained that his people didn't want to meet anyone else. However, CB would hear none of that. He insisted on going. He was somebody who couldn't see the forest for the trees.

I just watched out of my window, no more than five feet away. After ten minutes, Hector got back in with me. CB went over and got into the car with $21,000 to complete the deal. About five minutes later, there were undercover police everywhere. In fact, everyone in the restaurant and parking lot was an undercover agent.

With guns drawn and video cameras rolling, they pulled us out of our cars. I was facedown on the ground as they handcuffed me. I looked at Hector and CB, and they looked crazy. They had the look on their face that only a guy who had just gotten busted can have. One ounce of cocaine carried a minimum sentence of six years and a maximum of thirty years.

On the way to the police station in the backseat of an unmarked car, I was wondering if CB or Hector was an informant. Who was under surveillance? CB, Hector, or even worse, me? I was racking my mind determined to figure out who brought down the heat. I was also wondering if the guy in the car had heat on him; or if he was an informant; or even worse, an undercover agent.

Once at the police station, the agents asked me my name. Since they didn't know my name, then I could claim I was just in the wrong place at the wrong time. At first, I refused to give my name. You see, it was time for me to play Joe Citizen.

I was demanding to talk to whoever was in charge. I was telling them that I was only a passenger in the car, and asked why I was even there. It turned out the prosecutor, who was present at the arrest, determined that they didn't have enough evidence to hold me. Fate was kind to me that day. Hector and CB were charged.

It turned out that the guy in the small car was an undercover agent. If CB had trusted Hector, or even me, he would have been able to walk away. But greed will get you every time. A few days later, CB was out on a $100,000 bond, and he and his family were screaming that I had set him up. Since I walked away from the charge, I could see why his family could come to that conclusion without knowing all the facts.

However, if they knew the facts like CB did, they would have known that wasn't true. After all, it was I who suggested we let Hector do the deal by himself. Since CB insisted on being a part of the deal, he got what his hand called for. To play *the game* is to know *the game,* and *the game* is one of chance.

Months later, I heard that CB had gone to prison. My understanding was he departed with a four-year sentence—two less than the mandatory minimum of six years for possession of one ounce of cocaine, let alone what he got caught with during our encounter. So I safely assume that he found somebody to rat on.

In the 1990s, when a guy got busted in the drug business, the issue became how much you knew, and how quickly you were willing to inform on someone else to the authorities.

CHAPTER 16

Never Judge a Book by Its Cover

It was another beautiful summer day in 1988. I was out cruising with the top down on my Corvette. I pulled up to a red light in downtown Chicago. A sister pulled up next to me in a black Fiero. She was checking me out, and she motioned for me to pull over so we could chat.

A beautiful dark-skinned sister with a crushing body walked over to my car. She gave me her business card that said she was a cosmetologist. I gave her my beeper number and told her "to hit me on the clip sometime."

About a week later, I was cold chillin' in my friend Jazz's apartment. Jazz was in the process of putting some deals together, and was counting out about $80,000 in cash stacked on his glass coffee table. I was on the couch checking out his new nine-millimeter handgun, when I got a page from who I would discover to be the sister I met in the black Fiero. I invited her to go out to the movies with Jazz and me.

Once she decided to accept my invitation, I decided to have some fun with the sister. Instead of putting away the money, I told Jazz to leave it out and put his gun on top of the pile. I then put my gun on the table, too. After about an hour, she arrived. I waited patiently for the doorman to send her up, anxious to see the look on her face when she came in.

When she entered the apartment, I expected her to freak out. She surveyed the place and saw the money and guns on the table. However, she was as cool as could be. Then, after meeting Jazz and exchanging small chitchat, the sister did something that shocked both of us. She looked at the guns on the table and said, "Oh, isn't this a nine millimeter?" After I told her it was, she picked it up, popped out the clip, checked the chamber, and popped the clip back in—all within a matter of seconds. She knew how to handle a gun. We left for the movie, but that woman's familiarity with a gun weighed heavily on my mind.

We went back to Jazz's apartment after the movie. I took her into Jazz's room to see if I could get laid. Shortly thereafter, Jazz called me out of his room. When I came out to the living room, Jazz was holding a police badge and a photo ID. On a hunch, Jazz searched her purse, and discovered that she was an Illinois state trooper. That immediately explained her knowledge of firearms.

Jazz was like "What are we going to do?" Well, I knew that to do anything crazy to the woman was out of the question. If she was an undercover cop, someone else knew she was in the apartment. I turned my attention to figuring out whether she just happened to be here because she was attracted to me, or was I the target of an undercover investigation? I decided I would just go back into the bedroom and try to have sex with her. I figured that if she had sex with me, then she was not there on police business. It would mean she was just hanging out.

After an hour of foreplay and "You won't respect me in the morning" rhetoric, we had sex. After that, I began asking her if she had anything to tell me. At first, she said she didn't. I kept after her. She asked if I went through her purse. I said, "In my business, we can never be too careful." She then admitted to being a police officer. She tried to explain that she lied because a lot of guys don't want to date her when they discover that she was a police officer.

We hung for about a month. It was interesting literally fucking the police, but she was getting too attached, and that concerned me. A jealous rage, or an argument that got out of hand, could end with my imprisonment.

I decided I had to cut the state trooper loose.

It was around the fall of 1988, when a guy I knew named Barry hit me on the clip. When I returned his call, he explained that he wanted me to set up a transaction for him to purchase some keys of cocaine. Barry wasn't really a player, he was just an investment banker in his late twenties, looking to make some extra cash.

I told him that I knew some business associates coming in from Florida, and I would meet them at the downtown Hilton hotel. I told him that I would need $100,000 up front.

I was expecting Barry at 8:00 P.M. at my apartment. He arrived around 8:15 P.M. He gave me a card that opened the door to his apartment building. I told him I would be back in two hours. The money was in a blue duffel bag. We left my apartment together, and I caught a cab as he drove away.

While heading to the hotel, I thought about how I had made $100,000 in forty-eight hours for basically doing nothing. I got out and paid the taxi driver. I headed through the front doors of the Hilton, and then walked right out of the hotel through the side doors.

I had played Barry out of $100,000—now I had to really get away with it. The task at hand was to convince Barry that he hadn't been ripped off. The next day I called Derrick. He was a police officer whom I had met in *the game.*

Derrick liked to use drugs occasionally, so I hooked him up with some players who dealt drugs. Derrick rewarded me for the hookup by providing me with privileged police information. He would tell me about undercover operations and expose informants to me.

On that occasion, he got some arrest and bond papers for me.

That night I met Barry in my loft, and showed him the bond receipt and made-up charges. He was blown away. I told him I was probably going away for ten years. He thanked me all the way out the door.

The game is a dangerous and delicate road, with many perils and pitfalls. There is a saying in *the game*—"Stick to what you do best, and never try to play another man's game." I didn't adhere to that. I jumped anywhere and everywhere I thought I could make money. In the three stories I related to you, had I made any mistakes in judgment, or in my actions, my life could have been lost, or I could have found myself back in prison.

I talked to a good friend of mine in the car business named Chuck Trumbower; everybody called him CT. While I was in prison, CT was one of the few friends who consistently supported me. When I called on him, he was there.

Eventually, I opened a dummy investment company called IFIS. For $60 a month, an answering service answered the phone in the name IFIS. I gave them a list of bogus names and titles. I instructed them to never reveal to anyone calling that they were an answering service because we wanted to appear to be a big company, so our customers would feel comfortable.

If somebody called in the morning, and asked for the personnel department, the operator might say he wasn't in, or he was in a meeting.

I always called the number myself to check. I would press them to tell me when Mr. Magoo would be in. One time the operator became frustrated and said, "I don't know when he will be out of the meeting, sir, this is only an answering service." I immediately called her supervisor and raised hell. Once I got it running smoothly, I would just call and check my messages on the hour.

If I wanted a car loan, the loan department called regarding Victor Woods, and I would ask the personnel director at IFIS to return the call and say: "What's that Victor up to now?" The agent would tell me that Mr. Woods was trying to buy a new car, and he needed to verify employment. I would put him on hold while I supposedly checked the file, then come back in three or four minutes and verify my own credit application, employment, salary, and how long I had been employed.

That's how I got my Corvette. To this day I love Corvettes. They are beautiful, powerful, fast cars. I drove that car as fast as it would go every chance I got. Having honed my skills in *the game,* in 1988 I moved downtown near the Gold Coast and the Magnificent Mile, to a penthouse apartment in a fifty-floor building named Harbor Point. I moved in there the same way that I bought my Corvette. I used IFIS for my employment. Harbor Point overlooks Lake Shore Drive and Lake Michigan, and is right off Chicago's famous Michigan Avenue. I could see Navy Pier from my window.

I rented a one-bedroom condo overlooking the lake for $1,500 a month. A full-time doorman, underground parking, indoor pool, sauna, Jacuzzi and weight room were only a few of the conveniences available to the residents. A dentist's office, grocery store and dry cleaner were in the building. You could call and have groceries delivered and your car washed by one of the parking attendants. Most residents were in their forties, fifties and sixties. I was twenty-three. My girlfriend moved in with me. Lisa was African American mixed with Japanese—long black hair, a nice body. The downside was Lisa liked to snort too much cocaine. The upside was the sex was great when she was high. When she came down, she was a real bitch.

I met only one other young couple in the building. The wife was Linda Johnson, whose father owned *Ebony* magazine and Johnson Publishing Company. In the elevator on our way to the parking garage, I introduced myself and told her how much her magazine had been a part of my family's life. With my suit on, briefcase in hand and good manners, I fit right in, like KeKe said I would at East Moline.

In light of my success, I decided to go back and see my teacher in *the game*. We had talked on the phone, but now it was time to check in with my mentor. I wrote him and I told him that I was coming to see him. An officer who was hooked up with the drug ring at East Moline worked the visiting room. The other connected officer worked the front gate. That was perfect because ex-convicts aren't allowed to return to the prison and visit. I drove down one weekend, wearing a black Armani suit, a white shirt, red tie, my gold Longines watch, and Porsche sunglasses. I carried about $4,000 cash on my money clip.

Tops's dorm was on the side where you could see the visitors coming in. We had spent many days together looking out that window as the visitors drove in. I took up two parking spaces with my Corvette.

When I walked into the visiting room, a few brothers with whom I had been locked up, immediately recognized me. We politely smiled at each other. Tops rose and greeted me with a big smile and a hug. "As you walked up, you looked like a movie star. You're one of the chosen few."

I spent the day telling him everything I could not tell him by telephone. When my visit was over, Tops asked, "Do you have a quarter?" I reached into my pocket and gave him one. He held up the quarter and said, "Heads." He flipped the coin into the air, and caught it on tails. "Avoiding tails," he warned. "Remember the rules of *the game*." I knew tails was prison. That was his way of telling me not to get caught up in the money and glitz, to stay on top of *the game,* and to be careful.

CHAPTER 17

Fools Rush In
Where Wise Men Fear to Tread

L isa went off the deep end one night when I told her she had to stop spending my money and getting high. She tried to set my face on fire with a cigarette lighter after I refused to give her money for cocaine.

I got so mad I grabbed the telephone cord and wrapped it around her neck. I got hold of my senses, released her and said she had better be gone by the time I woke up in the morning. I locked myself in the bedroom and went to sleep. The next morning, I found that she had locked herself in the bathroom. After calling her name from the hallway for half an hour and getting no response, I broke the door down. She had taken everything in the medicine cabinet. She was lying on the floor, unconscious.

The sight scared me to death. Her mouth was blue because she drank a whole bottle of Nyquil. I called an ambulance, her parents and her best friend, a white girl named Eve, whom I had met only on two occasions. She came to the hospital and we talked about Lisa as we waited.

Eve stared at me as we talked. I had noticed it when we met before. Eve's stare was a bit much. She came back to my apartment that night. We talked a bit about Lisa, and said good night.

Lisa was in drug rehab when Eve called me saying she had left her watch at my apartment. I searched the apartment, found it and told her she could come by and pick it up. Before she hung up the phone, she said, "I had a dream about us. We were in bed having sex and Lisa walked in."

"Sounds interesting," I said. "We can talk more when you come over to get your watch."

Eve stood five-ten, had beautiful blond hair, long legs, big blue eyes, and a small, sexy chest. She came over wearing tight jeans and a fitted sweater. Those jeans accented her behind perfectly. I made a couple of drinks, and we talked for about two hours at the kitchen table. She excused herself to go to the bathroom, and I moved to the couch.

When she came back, she sat next to me. I made my move and kissed her. She was waiting for it, and wanted it. We took each other's clothes off and had sex on the couch. She was real vocal. I like that.

I had intended to just have sex with her; she was nothing more than a freak. But Eve spent the night, and she never left.

I'm a very sexual person, and Eve exuded raw sexuality. We connected in that way. Other than that, we didn't have much in common. I was outgoing and came from a totally different background. She was quiet and reserved, and worked in accounting. But in bed, we found our similarities. We fell in lust or love, or both.

A month after I met Eve, my sister Valerie flew in for my birthday. Eve bought me a stereo, served me breakfast in bed, sent to me from an outside restaurant, and then she took us all out for a seafood dinner. My sister said, "Watch out for Eve. She wants something from you." Woman can read each other like that. Eve wanted me. But I was beginning to want her, too.

Eve knew nothing about my illegal business dealings, and having to hide my lifestyle from her was becoming a pain. Each morning, I had been leaving the apartment pretending to go to work. Then, when Eve went to work, I would come back home. I came back one day before she left for work and she asked me if I had forgotten something.

I sat her down and told her everything: that all the things in the apartment came from my being in *the game;* IFIS was a dummy company I created; and I had no job. I told her I had been in prison and why. I also told her I would understand if she wanted to move out. She walked over to me, told me she loved me and didn't care what I did for a living.

Shortly thereafter, Eve and I decided to have a baby. Then, just as quickly, I asked her to marry me. I was lonely, looking to make some sense in my life. My parents came into town and the four of us went to dinner. My parents' position was that I was too immature to get married, and I didn't have a job. My mother probably thought what every black woman probably thinks when her son brings a white girl home.

As usual, I didn't pay any attention to my parents. I then turned my attention to Eve's parents.

Eve had had bad relationships with black men before, and her parents frowned on interracial relationships. We went out to dinner with them, and it was evident that they didn't approve. But with my good looks, manners, and high-level investment broker job at IFIS, I was a black man they could halfway accept. Especially since Eve was pregnant, her parents bought into IFIS hook, line, and sinker. Her father even asked me to invest some money for him. We got married in St. Thomas, Virgin Islands—right on the ocean. Her parents joined us for a beautiful time. My parents were totally against my getting married and refused to come to the wedding.

A lot I didn't know about Eve became more apparent in the months that followed. She had a temper and was extremely jealous. She was pregnant and we stopped having sex frequently. Our relationship began to change as our differences surfaced. Other than the daily routine of married people, life was treating me rather well.

One Tuesday, I decided to go to 34's, Walter Payton's club in Schaumburg. It was attached to the Hyatt hotel, near where I grew up. It was a beautiful club; 34's was 90 percent white, with mostly suburban folk partying. I enjoyed partying in a different atmosphere every now and again.

Since I had been married to Eve, all the women I was fooling around with were sisters: dark brown or light, it didn't matter. Since I was married to a white woman, it didn't make sense to me to fool around with a white woman. Like I said, I love all women of all races. Nothing makes me more sick than those brothers who get on TV and "dis" black women, and say they only will date white women. Especially since a black woman probably brought him into life. It's not like that for me. I don't date any particular race at the exclusion of another race. Women of all races have it going on, and that's all I have to say, period.

I love to dress in black. I had on a beautiful black Armani suit, and I was clean. I pulled up to the front of the club, and valet-parked my Corvette. My hair was slicked back with gel and my gold watch hung off my wrist. Most of the white people were looking at me, trying to figure out who I was. When I stepped in, I walked over to the bar to get a beer.

As I walked to the bar, I immediately noticed a white woman sitting with a friend, staring in my direction. I knew who they were looking at. I flashed them a smile, and kept moving. As I walked away, I noticed that the blonde, who couldn't take her eyes off me, was gorgeous. But like I said, I already had a blond-haired, blue-eyed honey at home. I was just hanging out, and not looking to hook up with anybody.

I didn't ask anybody to dance, I just walked around checking everything out. I started to notice that everywhere I went, I saw that blonde. I wasn't sure if I was being followed, so I walked over toward the dance floor, and she followed. I got a good look at her. She had long, beautiful, blond hair and a nice figure.

I started to hang out again, mostly with black women. I'm turned on by all women—black, white, Latino, Asian, dark-skinned, light-skinned, nappy hair, long hair. I'm a connoisseur of fine women. If a female green Martian came down from Mars, I would probably be attracted to her.

My old friend, Mark Dellums, called me one night and said one of his customers had ripped him off of two keys of cocaine. He gave the guy two keys, and waited in the car for him to go into a house to get the money. The guy walked in the front door, and out the back door. I was familiar with that trick. Mark rang the bell half an hour later and the people said, "Oh, Mike left about half an hour ago." I couldn't help but laugh. Mark was pissed off and out of $50,000.

Mark brought in two other guys on the campaign to recover his loot. One of them was a big brother, about six-three, introduced to me as Flex. He was sitting down with his shirt off.

The first place we went was the dude's mother's house. Mark rang the bell, and the mother said her son wasn't there. After she shut the door, Flex threw a brick through the window, and then opened fire on the windows of her house with his gun. Mark got mad at him, but Flex said, "We're out here like this, so fuck it." I liked his attitude. We searched the projects where that punk hung out and couldn't find him. I let Flex drive my Corvette back to Mark's place. He had never driven one and immediately fell in love with it. We parted that evening as friends.

I saw him again about a month later. I was driving down Michigan Avenue, and he drove up alongside of my 'Vette in his girlfriend's car.

Flex quickly hopped in, and we chatted for a moment before exchanging numbers. Flex had a lot of heart and was interested in playing *the game*. He might fit in to some of my plans. I invited Flex over to Harbor Point. By that time, Eve and I had moved into a two-bedroom apartment. He couldn't get over it. I don't think he had ever been in a building like Harbor Point before. Flex was like a kid up in my place— looking out the window at the city, marveling over the leather furniture, and tripping over things. Flex was street-smart. He was a little wild, but a lot of fun. He had played football for the University of Indiana, had rugged good looks, and a perfect physique that women loved.

During that time, Eve was pregnant. I had been taking Lamaze classes in Lake Forest, another rich Chicago suburb. I was in the delivery room with Eve when my daughter was born. I always thought I was going to marry a beautiful black woman. So I always thought my children would be nice-looking. But, with the interracial thing, I was unsure and a little scared.

Most of the time, interracial unions bore nice-looking children. But what if I was not fortunate, and my children came out looking crazy. My fears were immediately dispelled when I saw my daughter. She was beautiful from the first moment she was born. I know most people say that their children are beautiful, but we've all seen some ugly babies. However, my child was truly beautiful, with big black eyes, a head full of curly black hair, and a light-brown complexion.

After my daughter was born, I continued to expand my lifestyle in *the game*. I was living life on the edge. I had to stay one step ahead of the police, my parole officer, and my criminal friends. I slept with one eye open.

On my monthly visit to the parole office, I met Phil Bergman, a white guy who worked at the Safer Foundation, where I reported for parole. We spent hours talking. He was a graduate of Northwestern University, and during our many conversations in the months to come, Phil encouraged me to go to college. He was relentless and used every chance he got to sell me on the idea. School was the last thing on my mind, but his persistence paid off. Phil was friends with the dean of students at Northwestern University and arranged for me to take the admissions test. If I tested well, the dean promised to admit me. I did well on the test, and was soon matriculating at Northwestern

University. I took public speaking, business, and philosophy classes. Eve and my parents were both excited and proud of me. They all thought I had a lot of potential.

At first, I was intimidated. I expected the students to be out of this world intellectually. But in my public speaking class, I was easily the best speaker and I held my own in the other classes. One day I was driving along in my wife's Mercedes with another player. We were in the middle of a business deal at the time I was supposed to go to class. I closed that deal opting not to go to class and never went back. The education I was getting in life was more intoxicating.

Every day above ground and out of prison was a good day for a player. Many lives are lost daily in *the game* to prison, and for some unfortunate players, the graveyard. So when the season changed to winter and brought on the Christmas holiday, I was happy to be able to enjoy it.

The game had many advantages. One of those was to be able to play Santa Claus in a big way. I bought my friends and my whole family gifts. My little baby had more toys to play with than she could handle. At a young age children are funny; you can buy them an expensive toy, and all they want to play with is the box the toy came in. I bought Eve everything she wanted—jewelry and thousands of dollars' worth of clothes. I even surprised her with a beautiful cocker spaniel.

But Eve and my parents were pressing me to get a job, since I was now a father. Again, I relented to the pressure. I got a job at running a nail technician school. The woman who interviewed me was the vice president's wife. The job entailed recruiting women to sign up for the school. The students got a federal grant and the company got paid from the government, off the top.

She took one look at me and hired me on the spot. My office was on 79th and Cicero. The building was full of young women—black, white, and Latina. You could hear a pin drop when I walked into the office. I was clean, and wearing one of my Armani suits.

I expected a small office, and was surprised I got one upstairs above the school, with hardwood floors, a beautiful modern desk and chair, track lighting, a couch, mirrored walls, a refrigerator, and my own bathroom. I played it cool like I expected it. The job was perfect. I could do it while continuing my illegal business. It dawned on me that having that job was what Tops meant when he said, "A player has to balance his scales."

I became the top recruiter. If a mother brought her daughter in to inquire about the school, I would sign them both up.

My office became a freak show. I was boning more women than I could count. But all good things come to an end if you don't handle your business correctly.

The trouble began when a wealthy Greek woman, a doctor's wife named Sofia Papagus, started taking me out to lunch. Sofia and her daughter were there to learn the business and then open their own shop. Sofia and I slept together a couple of times. She knew right away my job was a front and told me so. But she was no threat. She just wanted the "black experience" and I was doing my best to accommodate her.

I got a call from the vice president explaining that Sofia's husband was a personal friend of the owner and warning me to stay away from Sofia. After that, he singled me out for every little thing he could. I decided to quit after only four months. I had enough drama in my life.

Once you have made fast money, it's almost impossible to settle down in the real world. Time is our most precious commodity, and trying to hold down a job and pay into a bank was too time consuming. So I spent my time in *the game*, where I could make the most money.

Living downtown with a wife and a child was costing too much money. I decided I would get more for my money in the suburbs. Eve and I moved into a brand-new three-bedroom town house in a Chicago suburb called Streamwood. The house had a fireplace, a nice yard, and two bathrooms. I used the extra bedroom for my workout room. Two months later, Eve was pregnant again. When she gave birth I was again in the delivery room, and again we had a beautiful baby girl.

CHAPTER 18

Hell Breaks Loose

In Streamwood I got lazy. I spent my days playing Nintendo, cooking steaks and lobster, and drinking imported beer. Eve and I weren't getting along. But we were still having sex, our common thread. Plus I had a couple of fine black girlfriends in the city. I saw them every time I had to go into the city on business.

During my experience in *the game,* I was often treated like a celebrity. Women love gangsters and players. With all kinds of money, fancy clothes and cars, you attract all kinds of attention. Plus, you have no job to worry about, so you had free time to profile, just like a celebrity does. At restaurants and clubs, you might not be recognized like a Michael Jordan, but trust me, after you give the doorman $100 for opening a door, or tip a waiter or waitress a couple of hundred for a Coke and some fries, they are going to remember you and treat you like a celebrity.

I didn't have to wait in line at restaurants or nightclubs. All things considered, I felt like life had been good to me.

Around that time, John Cappas, a young white guy, was busted for selling drugs. Highlights from his trial were on the six o'clock news every night. Eve and I would watch the news report on the trial every evening. I was fascinated with his case. He came from a good family, and his father owned several businesses. He drove a Corvette and had been accused of having a big network of drug dealers and customers. He lived in a $300,000 house, with a swimming pool.

The DEA (Drug Enforcement Agency) was investigating the Chevy dealership where he bought his Corvette with cash. He was good-looking and cocky. During his trial, he swore at witnesses on the stand. Like me, he chose *the game,* when he could have easily made it in the legitimate world.

At sentencing, the federal judge gave John forty-five years. He would have to serve 85 percent of that sentence.

Many states would adopt what is known as the "Truth in Sentencing" law in the 1990s, where prisoners must serve at least 85 percent of their sentence, similar to the federal law. In Illinois, prior to the Truth in Sentencing law, prisoners served around 50 percent of a sentence.

For the first time I started thinking about a way to get out of *the game*. I knew that sooner or later I would have to deal with the other side of the coin that Tops had tossed.

Meanwhile, my relationship with Eve become a disaster. There were times I would stay away from home for two or three days at a time. When I came home, she often greeted me with a loaded gun, asking me where I had been. We weren't having sex much anymore. Our marriage had become a big mess. Being in *the game* and being married doesn't work.

The game gives you a license to do anything you want. Women don't ask players questions. You do not tell your wife where you're going, and with whom. In *the game* a man might have to go out at any time. A woman has to accept that if she wants to be with a player. Eve forgot whom she had married.

One day, I was pleasantly surprised to receive a page from Flex, especially since we hadn't talked in six months and I thought no news was good news. I went out to his parents' house in Markham. He met me outside and got into my car. He told me he was broke, his parents had moved out of the house, there was no running water or heat, and there were maggots in the toilet. He broke down and cried. I took him home with me to help him get back on his feet.

Eve didn't like Flex at all. She figured it would be a good time to visit my parents in Connecticut, if he was going to be staying at our house. That was great. With Eve out of my hair for six weeks, I could hang out with Flex and run wild. I told Eve she could go, but under one condition: she wouldn't tell my parents any of my personal business. My mother was always fishing for information.

With Eve out of town, I would just go from club to club and hang out. At closing time when people were beginning to leave, a white girl walked right up to me and whispered in my ear, "You are gorgeous."

She pushed her business card into my jacket pocket and said, "Call me." I've known some bold white women, but that move got my attention. She didn't look or act like the typical white woman who goes for brothers—who wears tacky tight clothes, tries to talk black, and hang out at black clubs. That kind of white woman disgusts me. It's a freak thing for them; they literally just want some black dick, no matter who it's attached to.

But that woman was different. She didn't send off those kinds of vibes. I didn't pay any attention to that business card until the next day. I discovered that she was a manager of a Ramada Inn. She also had written her home number on the back. I decided to give her a call at home. She seemed surprised that I called. I let her know that her boldness got my attention. We made plans to go out the next weekend.

I really didn't get a good look at her before, because I had been drinking, and the club was dark. But that girl was clearly fine. Even her name was beautiful—Delilah. Actually, she looked like Cheryl Ladd from *Charlie's Angels*—pretty and sexy-looking.

We hung out that night until about 3:00 A.M. She invited me up for a nightcap. While on the couch, we kissed, but she stopped me when I tried to go under her sweater. But it was clear she wanted to go further.

With Eve gone, I started having Delilah over to the house. I took down every picture of Eve and anything else that would indicate a woman lived there and transformed the house into the ultimate bachelor's pad. Everything about Delilah was different from Eve. I loved to drive fast. It wasn't unusual for me to go 150 miles per hour with a date in the car. I loved to see them scream, scared to death, hollering at me to slow down. But Delilah loved it. She said, "Hey, pull over and let me drive it." Then she would go 150 herself. She liked to live on the edge.

During our time together, we became so close that I confessed to her that I was married. I said if she didn't want to see me anymore, I would understand and I left her apartment. Ten minutes later, she called me on my car phone and told me my being married didn't matter. She then invited me out for dinner.

Two weeks later, we were saying we loved each other. In less than two weeks, Eve was coming home. I called my mother's house to check on Eve and the kids and my mother began yelling at me. "I know you are into all kinds of illegal activities." "Stop tripping," I said curtly. But then she went on to tell me some of the specific things I was doing and I knew Eve had told them everything. I had told my parents that I was selling cars.

When Eve got on the phone, I cursed her out. She was talking crazy. She and my parents had been watching *America's Most Wanted*. A man got busted on TV. The police broke the door down, the children were crying, and they told the mother they were going to put her children in a foster home.

My mother had said, "Oh, my God, that's what's going to happen to you, Eve! They're going to take away my grandbabies." Eve had broken down, started crying, and began telling my parents everything I was doing. She said how terrible it was living with me, that there were guns in the house, and that she was scared.

My parents fed her a lot of "We know how bad it must be for you, honey," and "We're here for you." She said she wasn't coming home unless I stopped doing illegal things. I stopped calling Eve at my parents' house. A few days later, I didn't even call to wish her a happy birthday.

Eve called a week later to tell me she was coming home that Sunday and that if I wasn't going to get out of *the game,* she would move in with her parents. I said, "Fine, move in with them." When she arrived at O'Hare airport, I was at home barbecuing on the grill. I got a call from my mother telling me, "My grandchildren are at the airport, and you better pick them up."

"Eve is waiting for her parents," I said nonchalantly to my mother.

"Get your butt down there and pick them up!"

When I arrived, Eve was looking at me as crazy as I was looking at her. It was good to see my two little girls. I had gone to a toy store and bought them all kinds of stuff.

Eve started crying as we pulled up to a toll booth. As I slowed down, she jumped out of the car and ran toward a field. I sat in broad daylight with my black ass in traffic, with two kids in a car seat, and a white woman running from my car, crying.

I pulled over to the side of the road. Eyes were bugging as I chased and yelled that I was sorry. Eventually, she got back into the car. We drove home in silence. She slept upstairs that night with my youngest daughter. My oldest daughter and I slept on the couch.

The next morning Eve told me she was leaving me, and going to pawn all of her jewelry. That was the first time she had threatened to pawn the jewelry. Ordinarily, when she threatened to leave, I would say, "There will be none of that, honey," and calm her down. This time I told her to go ahead. "It'll be a long walk because your car belongs to me and I won't let you drive it to the pawn shop."

She grabbed a butcher knife and demanded the car keys. I gave her the keys. Fifteen minutes later, she was back banging on the front door. I refused to let her in the house. She had taken our youngest child and now started screaming for our oldest and waving a butcher knife outside the window. The neighbors were enjoying the entertainment. She poked holes in my new red Corvette, scratching through the paint. She yelled that she was going to turn me in to the police, and sped off.

I called Delilah and explained what happened and asked her to come by. She drove right over. I put my gun and bullets into a duffel bag, and put it into her trunk. I had on a pair of shorts and a T-shirt. My oldest daughter was in diapers.

We drove by the Streamwood Police Department, about ten minutes from the house. As the police station came into view, Eve's car was visible in the parking lot. That was one of the worst feelings of my life. We returned to the house immediately, to get my money and clothes out before the police came.

The police were in the process of surrounding my house when we turned into my street. I ducked down while Delilah pulled into a driveway and turned around. It was unreal. I was sick. I was still wanted on an outstanding warrant for a car chase I was involved in from the previous year. I had a gun in the house. I was an ex-con. Eve had just set me all the way out.

Delilah took me to the hotel where she worked and got me a room. I told her to drive back to my house and tell me what was happening. What she reported was astonishing. "There were police everywhere! Detectives in suits were all over your house. Every door was open. All the neighbors were outside watching, and Eve was in the house with the police, acting as their personal tour guide."

I was beyond disgusted. The police missed me by only a few minutes and they were pissed. Looking back, I guess it was a cry for help on Eve's part. I guess if I had just handled the situation differently with her on Sunday night, all of that probably could have been avoided.

Never one to miss a Kodak moment, I went to a pay phone and called my house. A detective answered my phone with the standard line by which they hope to acquire information. For example, if you're selling drugs they'll ask the caller what and how much is needed. Then the buyer will be invited over to be arrested. If the caller is really a fool, he could be persuaded to bring some drugs of his own to sell.

The officer who answered asked me my name. I said my name was Victor Woods. He said it real loud, "Oh, Victor, what's up, where are you?" I just laughed and asked him to put my car in the garage, because it was about to rain.

I called my parents and thanked them for sending my wife back home with her head all screwed up, after all that talk about the police breaking down our door and our losing the children. Eve and I separated after that episode. She moved back home with her parents, and I got another apartment in Mt. Prospect, Illinois. I bought another black Corvette from a white guy named Saul Regan, a con man who had his hands into a little bit of everything.

My new apartment was OK for Joe Citizen, but it lacked the luxury I was accustomed to. I saw my children every now and then. I was still furious with Eve for what she had done. Even though I slept with her at times, it was only sex. I vowed that I would never live under the same roof with her again.

The game generally had been good to me. I had been out of prison for three years, and I started to feel like nothing could happen to me. I was living my life the way I wanted to. But detectives from many suburbs were searching for me.

A cashier at the local White Hen Pantry near my new residence told me as I was buying some juice that detectives had been in the store looking for me. "How do you know it was me they were looking for?" She said, "They were looking for a good-looking black guy, who dressed nicely, and drove a Corvette." I said, "Yep, that would be me, except for the good-looking part." After a pause, we both laughed.

A player has got to be like a shark. A shark sleeps while it's moving and is always in perpetual motion. I was like a shark when I first got out of prison. But I had become like a lion. I was still deadly and dangerous, but I was also lazy.

But that happens to guys in *the game*. Too many women, too much alcohol, too much steak and lobster, and you get soft, and forget about the cold prison cell. A player has always got to be looking for a way to keep his edge. I was starting to slowly lose mine.

Delilah was hosting a convention at the hotel where she worked. I planned to cook steaks and lobsters on the grill. I had bought some wine for the occasion, and I planned to pick her up at 10:00 P.M. for a late dinner. My Corvette was in the shop, so I was driving her Beretta. I went inside, and she was at the bar with a bunch of white business-men. I walked up to her, put my hands over her eyes, and then kissed her. I loved the expression on the white guys' faces when I kissed her.

We headed back to my apartment. When Delilah drove into the parking lot, we noticed two white men sitting in a car. "Drive right past them, then circle back around so I can check them out," I said. I sensed danger. The car pulled out of its parking space and blocked us in, when they saw that we weren't going to park. "Remain calm. Relax." Both of the officers got out with their hands clearly on their weapons. I asked them why they had stopped us and the officer on Delilah's side said, "There was a hit and run accident in the area, and this car fits the description." I said, "As you can see, this car hasn't been in an accident." The other officer, who was closest to me on the passenger's side, watched my movements.

I sensed it was much more than a routine traffic stop. When the detective on my side of the car asked me for some identification, I sur-mised they were looking for me, but I didn't recognize either detective and concluded they wouldn't be able to identify me from an old mug shot. I was wearing a suit and tie and we were in the darkness of night.

I had been using a driver's license of a friend who looked like me. When I handed the detective my identification, they both pulled their guns. "Victor Woods, get out of the car." They cuffed me and put me into the backseat of their car. One of the detectives, a big guy, 250 pounds, blond hair and glasses, started beating me, and hitting me on the head while I was handcuffed in the backseat. He yelled accusations that I committed some armed robberies in his town. His partner had to pull him off me.

They asked Delilah to get out of the car and got her permission to search the vehicle. They found a loaded .38 automatic pistol. That cop acted like he had hit the jackpot. Some backup patrol cars came, and they took me down to the police station. I was put into a little room and locked in. I was clean that night, wearing a tan Armani suit and a red silk tie. I had already been arrested for an outstanding warrant for the car chase I was involved in. More seriously, however, I had been arrested for being a felon in possession of a firearm.

I immediately told the sergeant who walked in to interrogate me that I had been hit in the head by one of the officers. He looked at me blankly, and said he didn't know what I was talking about. Police officers are excellent liars, and I marveled at the sincere matter-of-fact way he ignored my accusations. The detective (the one who didn't beat me) said that he didn't care about the car chase or the gun. He wanted to talk about the armed robberies he said I had committed in another suburb called Glenview.

The detective then said that he had my phone records from when I lived in Harbor Point and it showed that I called Glenview. I just laughed and said, "Let me get this straight, because I called Glenview and a crime took place around the day I called that town, that makes me a suspect? You must have a lot of suspects, gentlemen. Surely, you can do better than that." They left the room red-faced and disgusted by my arrogance.

Ten minutes after they left, I got up and looked at the glass window, which I discovered served as a two-way mirror. In the adjoining room, I could see the detectives had surrounded Delilah and were yelling at her. She was crying hard. I felt sorry for her. I figured she had broken down, and was telling them all she knew.

Another officer stepped into the room and saw I was watching through the window. I was then moved into a cell. About two hours later, the lead detectives who wanted me for armed robbery shouted out loud for my benefit that they wanted my fingerprints to check against the prints at the robbery scene.

The next day I was transported to court for being a felon in possession of a firearm. When they brought me out from lockup to stand before the judge, Delilah was standing there too. I was shocked. I naturally thought that she had told them everything. She had been charged with having an unregistered firearm. It turned out that she told the detectives absolutely nothing. I couldn't believe it.

She told the cops that she had just met me a few days prior. I was proud of her for keeping her mouth shut. It made my feelings for her even deeper and stronger. Bond was set at $30,000. I couldn't make bond, because I had an outstanding warrant for the car chase. It was

still haunting me, as well as a bunch of other outstanding warrants
for speeding. Delilah was released on a signature bond.

Cook County jail was all I remembered and worse. It had twice as
many inmates. I was a veteran but it was still hell. I was placed in
Division 6. Immediately, I was approached by Disciple brothers who
knew me. Division 6 was more filthy than when I left, the food was
worse than I remembered, and the inmates seemed harder. People
were sleeping on mattresses on the floor, or wherever they could find
space. However, in those four years, they had added an extra phone
that helped ease at least some of the tension. I spent my time on that
phone with my lawyer trying to get the hell out of Cook County jail. I
had retained a good lawyer for that case. He was an old Harvard-
educated Jewish lawyer named Seymour Vishney. He handled a lot of
murder cases. Mr. Vishney was bald, had false teeth, and was a chain
smoker. He was a no-nonsense, thorough lawyer who understood the
ins and outs of the courtroom. Judges and lawyers knew him and
respected him.

I had to resign myself to hell in the county jail for a little more than
a week. Since there were no available cells, I laid my mattress on the
floor near a corner and settled back into the madness that I thought I
would never see again. I stayed away from all of the usual mess, while
my Mr. Vishney was resolving the issues so I could bond out.

In court for a gun charge, the car chase was now small. The prosecutor agreed to give me nineteen days in County. With the ten days in,
I had already served my sentence. I posted bond for the gun case and I
was out. I felt sorry for some of the guys as I left. Many would never
see the streets again.

CHAPTER 19

Back to *the Game*

Delilah picked me up, with a chilled bottle of champagne and two glasses waiting. All appeared well, and I was happy to be out. But I knew that those detectives were investigating me closely. I had to tighten up my whole program.

After that ten-day stint in the joint, the first thing I did was make plans to move back into the city because I was under surveillance. Living in the suburbs is great until your cover is blown, but it is too easy in the suburbs for the police to lock in and investigate you. In Chicago, so much goes on, you can just blend in. There were too many other people in *the game* in Chicago that the police didn't have time to pay attention to me, as long as I wasn't obvious or stupid. I wasn't big enough to attract attention from top-level law enforcement, nor was I the street criminal who attracts the common police.

Marco Calabrase, a young Italian who was in *the game,* stopped by my apartment while I was preparing to move. He showed me a blank Visa Gold credit card. Marco said he had many more and asked me to check around to see if anybody wanted to buy them. "Leave the card and I'll check," I said and returned my attention to moving.

I moved into a beautiful downtown Chicago apartment, in Huron Street Lofts, a block away from the Hard Rock Cafe, four blocks from Michigan Avenue, and across the street from Walter Payton's America's Bar. The loft was new and it was sharp. It had wide-open spaces, with no doors other than to enter and to the bathroom. A Euro-style kitchen and exquisitely exposed brick walls set it off. There was a twenty-four-hour doorman. Rent was a cool $1,300.

Once settled, I started thinking about that Visa Gold credit card. Saul Regan was into a little bit of everything. When I called, he expressed interest and wanted to know how many I had. I learned Marco had 4,000 blank Visa Gold cards. He said a friend had stolen them from a security transport at O'Hare airport. I relayed that information to Saul.

Saul called back a few days later, and offered $60,000 for all the cards. I hadn't figured they were worth that much. Then I did some simple math. Each card had a $10,000 limit, and there were 4,000 of them—$40 million! That number was staggering to me. Of course, I had absolutely no idea how to make a blank card be worth $10,000. However, if Saul was willing to buy the cards for $60,000, knowing how greedy he was, they had to be worth at least $150,000 to him. So I decided to up my asking price.

Saul and I met at Carson's Ribs in downtown Chicago and I told him that my people wouldn't settle for anything less than $150,000. Saul hemmed and hawed saying his people were firm at $60,000. I didn't budge, and he got up to make a telephone call.

He came back and said his people wouldn't pay any more than $100,000. I was sure Saul would be making money on the deal, and guessed he was running the whole operation. I acted perturbed at his $100,000 offer, although, inside I was delighted with that figure. After some more posturing, we agreed on the $100,000 for 4,000 blank Visa Gold credit cards.

I told Marco I found a guy who *might* pay $25,000 for all the credit cards. Marco and his friend were sitting on a bunch of plastic cards with no value, and they didn't know what to do with them; $25,000 quick and free sounded good. I suggested I receive a $5,000 finder's fee. He readily agreed.

I would get $75,000 from Saul, and $5,000 from Marco; $80,000, all in a day's work.

Saul was paging me frequently, eager to get the cards. I set up a meeting at Kevin Reilly's house, because he knew Saul and me. I wanted to stay as far in the background as I could, so I got another friend, Frank, to act as the middleman in the deal. Marco was to give the blank Visa Gold credit cards to Frank. Frank would take the cards to Kevin's house, where he would meet Saul, and make the exchange. I would give Frank $10,000 and Kevin $5,000. It was worth $15,000 for me to be safe, and not find myself back in prison. Prison was an unacceptable risk.

The transaction was to take place on a Friday night at 10:00 P.M. At 10:30 P.M. Saul called Kevin's house, and said he didn't like something he saw around the area. He was afraid that the whole thing was a setup. We rescheduled the meeting. I was disappointed, but I was used to that kind of stuff. People in *the game* were always nervous and scared. Plans were often changed for protection, because one false move and you were back in jail, or worse.

I then had trouble contacting Marco and Saul, and suspected they were planning to cross me out.

One day I tried to call Saul, Marco, and Kevin. When I couldn't reach any of them, I paged them. When none of them returned my page, I figured they had all hooked up somehow, and were in the process of crossing me out of the deal. My guess was if that were the case, it was all at Saul's behest. That was exactly the kind of stuff that goes on in the so-called legitimate world every day, although it would be something like an account, client, or commission taken. The only difference was that, in *the game,* when you get crossed out it might be with your life.

I finally caught up with Kevin. My plan was to tell Kevin that I had talked to Marco, and he told me that he and Saul were out drinking the night before. I was hoping that Kevin would confirm what I already suspected. When I called, and ran it down on him, he admitted that the group had been out drinking at a local bar.

I hadn't told Marco or Saul about each other's involvement, nor the cool $80,000 I was going to make on the deal. It stood to reason that if Marco, Saul, and Kevin were together having drinks, they had figured out what part they all played in my game.

As I continued to talk with Kevin, I just played it cool. I didn't let on that I was upset or concerned. *The game* was on, and you never let your left hand know what the right hand is doing. I said good-bye and started to figure out how I was going to deal with that development. Knowledge is everything, and I knew something they all didn't, and that was that they had crossed me out of the deal. I was still in *the game,* only I was on the sidelines for a moment. It was time to wait for an opportunity to get back in.

About a week later, I got a call from Saul's wife, who said that he had been arrested for some bogus business dealings. She was frantic, and said Saul was scared to death. Five minutes later, Saul called my apartment.

He sounded happy to hear my voice, even though I could sense his fear and tension. "How are all the brothers in jail doing?" I asked him sarcastically. He was not a white person who ever hung out with black people, unless he could make money. Saul was a middle-aged white guy who had never been in jail. He was in Division 6.

After I stopped laughing, I said, "Saul, ask one of the brothers if there are any Disciples around."

He said, "What?"

"Just ask anybody if there are any *Folks* around."

In an instant, one of the brothers told Saul that he was Folks. "Put him on the phone." I told that brother my nickname was Billy Dee and I was Folks. It turned out that the brother knew me and I asked him to look out for Saul, and let him ride as a guest in our house. The Disciples would protect Saul while he was in jail, as a favor to me. Saul would be able to use the telephones, and not be worried about being raped, or stolen from. I told the brother that Saul had cash, and he would look out for the brothers during his stay. Saul got back on the phone and I said, "It will be smooth sailing until you leave. Now, hey, why are you trying to cut me out of the deal with Marco?"

Stuttering, he said, "The kid approached me. When I get out, I'll make it right."

"Saul, tell Marco that his people have to do the deal this weekend. Say they don't want to meet anybody new. Tell him that since you're in jail, the cards are to be delivered to Kevin, who will do the deal with your people. Marco trusts Kevin. Kevin will then give me the cards, and I'll hold the cards myself for you until you get out of jail."

Saul agreed. He had no choice.

"Tell Marco that Kevin will call him with the details."

When Saul called Marco to explain the new plan, he immediately called me back to say Marco wanted to ride with Kevin to make sure that he wouldn't be ripped off and to make sure I was nowhere to be found. Marco had found out that I was going to make $80,000 on the deal, and he only $20,000, when the cards belonged to him. Marco was pissed.

Marco's insistence on being there made things more difficult. I decided to have Kevin meet Saul's people with the money at the Marriott hotel across from O'Hare. It had a Polynesian bar where I would be waiting for Kevin to make the exchange, while Marco sat in the car.

Before the exchange took place, I went to Delilah's Christmas party at the Ramada Inn and hung out for a few hours. Then I parked at the Marriott side entrance, went in and had a drink before Kevin arrived at 10:35 P.M. He had a black duffel bag with him, and sat beside me at the bar. I bought him a drink. He told me Marco was outside in the car, waiting. Kevin said Marco had asked him over and over if I was involved, and he had told him I wasn't. I told him to have Marco call me once Marco discovered that I was behind the whole thing. With that, I picked up the heavy duffel bag, it must have weighed about fifty pounds, and left the bar via a side door. I returned to my car, put the cards into the trunk and returned to the Christmas party, just as calmly as I left.

I opened the duffel bag for the first time the next morning. The credit cards were inside eight long white boxes, 500 per box. They were beautiful. Colonial National Bank Visa Gold Card was printed across the top in black letters and an eagle was pictured on a metallic background on the left. Each credit card had a dark strip across the back, and a blank space for an authorized signature. They needed only names and account numbers to bring out their true beauty.

It was then that I started thinking about keeping the credit cards for myself. Why sell them for $100,000? Or even $250,000? They were worth $40,000,000. Somebody was going to activate them and make a killing. Why shouldn't it be me? I didn't know how to print them, but I could figure it out. How hard could it be?

I had taken the phone off the hook the night before, expecting Marco's call. The moment I put it back, Marco called, screaming and cursing me incessantly. Making fun of him, I said, "If you continue to use that tone of voice with me, then I will have to hang up." He continued and I hung up. He called back, threatening me. "My partner is going to kill you!" Again, I hung up. He called back and began talking sense.

"Victor, the cards aren't mine, and the people who own them are serious. They won't take it lightly that you took them." The kid didn't know anybody, and I didn't care if he did. With Sampson and my crew, I could dance with anybody. "Tell your people that the deal is still on, but I'll hold the cards until Saul gets out of jail. If they don't like it, they can try to take them back."

He didn't like it, but there was nothing that he could do. Ten minutes later, Kevin called, saying Marco broke his nose in the Marriott parking lot when he found out I had the cards. He had to go to the hospital. When Marco called I told him, "I'm sorry about your nose. For that you get an additional five thousand. That's fifteen bills for the job." The bonus definitely made him feel better.

The more I looked at those cards, the more I thought about keeping them and figuring out how to use them for myself. I remembered going to a Y.M.C.A. once in high school to play basketball. A man at the front desk had just bought a membership, and they were making him a membership card. It was plastic and resembled a credit card. They put it on a funny-looking metal machine that resembled a strange typewriter, that imprinted his name in raised letters just like on a credit card.

I called the Y.M.C.A. and asked for the front desk. A nice lady answered the phone. I asked for her name and asked how she was doing. I introduced myself as Robert Smith and said I was a past member. I was planning on opening a video store, and wanted to make ID cards for my customers. I remembered the Y.M.C.A. had a machine that printed names on plastic ID cards. Such a machine might be useful for my video business. She told me the machine was called an Addressograph and explained its function, but had no idea of its cost.

Now that I knew the machine I needed to print the credit cards, I had one half of the puzzle figured out. The next task was to secure names and expiration dates to print on the actual credit cards.

I abandoned the idea of selling the cards to Saul Regan. I couldn't milk it for $40,000,000, but I could get 25 percent, say $10,000,000. That was a realistic number. From that moment, I became obsessed. I called everybody I knew in *the game* for leads regarding credit card names and numbers. I even contacted people who weren't in *the game*. Some so-called good citizens have more larceny in them than many criminals. In my zeal to obtain credit card account numbers, I even crossed state lines. Sylvia, a good friend from Washington, D.C., had friends who worked at major hotels as managers or at the front desk. She could get me Visa Gold credit card account names, numbers, and expiration dates from those contacts.

The credit card project was clearly too big for me. I needed a partner. I trusted Flex, and I felt he could help. I ran the whole game down to Flex, and he listened to me, but like most guys in *the game*, he was afraid to venture out from what he knew. Flex didn't understand how I was going to make it work, but he knew me well enough to know I would find a way, so he accepted my invitation to get involved.

The first step was to steal the Addressograph from the Y.M.C.A. I called my friend Jazz, who had graduated from college and was a stockbroker. Despite his credentials, Jazz dipped and dabbled in *the game*. Intrigued by the amount of money involved, he agreed to steal the machine.

Steve, a white mechanic, who at times worked on my Corvette and occasionally participated in some of my illegal business activities, was the getaway driver for Jazz. I drove in another car with Flex to watch the show.

We arrived at the Y at about 11:00 P.M. The Y had been closed since 7:00 P.M. that evening; it was completely dead. I sat in the car sipping my favorite beer, watching Jazz, who is six-eight, was wearing black, and looked hilarious as he crept up to the glass window. Imagine someone the height of Magic Johnson, trying to walk and move discreetly in a crouched position. I was laughing so hard at the sight, I almost couldn't sip my beer. After Jazz disappeared from our view behind the bushes, I heard a loud crash. Minutes later, Jazz reappeared, running fast, with the Addressograph under his arm.

We all drove to Flex's apartment complex in the Presidential Towers. Once inside, we all looked at the machine and then at each other. The Addressograph was gray metal, and had a mess of buttons all over the top. None of us had the slightest idea how to work the thing.

I left the machine at Flex's, and went home. I could feel the wolves at my heels, detectives who wanted me badly. I might go to prison on that gun case. I was into another adventure, but life felt more serious.

One night while Delilah and I were having dinner at my favorite restaurant, Nick's Fish Market, she started crying. "What's wrong?" I asked her.

"You've been distant. I feel left out."

"I am only trying to protect you by leaving you out of my business," I said. "It's because I love you."

She just cried and said, "I want to be a part of whatever you're doing."

Any player knows to keep women out of their business, but I was intrigued that she wanted to get involved in criminal activity. Lots of women like being around players and spending money, but few want to get into *the game*. And of those women who want to get in, even fewer have the potential to play.

Delilah was beautiful, smart, and could lie with a straight face. She had kept her mouth shut while in the police station under pressure. I was fascinated by her interest and I decided to let her in. I quickly brought her up-to-date with what was going on. I took her over to Flex's apartment the next day and showed her the Addressograph machine.

Flex shared an apartment with Rhonda, a beautiful, dark-skinned, sexy young sister, even though he had his own place on another floor in the building. Flex always had a lot of women around him, and I liked that in him. Unlike me, he had his women in check.

Rhonda and Delilah were assigned to figure out how to use the Addressograph. We left them with some blank cards to practice on and a picture of a Visa Gold credit card that I tore out of a magazine. Flex and I played basketball in the health club in his building, while the girls worked on the machine.

When Flex and I came back from playing ball, the girls each had their hands behind their backs, with a surprise for us. When they brought their hands out, I saw a beautiful sight. They were each holding a Visa Gold credit card with the names and numbers perfectly printed. Delilah put my name on it. I hugged and kissed her. I knew we were all going to be rich. We all went out and celebrated.

I called Sylvia, who told me that she had gotten a credit card number from a friend who worked in a hotel in D.C. I asked Sylvia to call me back on a pay phone. I never talked about business over the telephone. To do so might have led to imprisonment. I got the credit card name and number.

Jimmy, one of my Greek friends from high school, stopped by. He was always looking to make fast money. He had a beer belly, big nose and kinky hair. His hair was as kinky as any black man's. Many Italians and Greeks have "black" in them, but often try to deny it. But with Jimmy, there was no way to deny it. He was looking for some credit card names and numbers for me. One night he had stopped by to show me his new white Cadillac. I told him I had received a credit card number. Together, we headed over to Flex's apartment.

At Flex's, I gave Rhonda the name, number, and expiration date and within about fifteen minutes, she printed the card perfectly. Now we had to figure out how to program the metallic strip, but I could figure that out later. Having the information on the front of the credit card was enough to get me started. The same information printed on the front of the card is on the metallic strip to allow for faster and easier use of the card.

Since a metallic strip can be easily demagnetized and the information canceled out by touching another credit card in your wallet or purse, the machine in stores is equipped with a manual terminal. A salesclerk can punch in the information.

I decided to test the card at a gas station minimart. We drove to the gas station to fill the tank up. I went inside to pay. There was a short line and I stood nervously waiting for my turn.

When I gave the clerk the credit card, she ran the metallic strip through the back of the machine. Of course, it didn't work. She unsuccessfully ran the card through a couple more times, before she turned the card over and began manually inputting the account number into the machine. She waited a few moments, and the screen remained blank. She repeated the manual procedure and received another blank screen.

The clerk was puzzled, and so was I. I paid her cash, retrieved my card, and walked back to the car trying to figure out what went wrong. The answer had to lie in the numbers Sylvia provided. I called and said something was wrong with the numbers she gave me. A few hours later, she told me what I already suspected: Sylvia's contact mistakenly thought any Gold credit card number would suffice, so she provided an American Express Gold credit card number, instead of a Visa Gold credit card number. Two days later, Sylvia called back with two Visa Gold numbers. Rhonda and Delilah printed up two cards.

We drove to another gas station and I was holding my breath as I gave the credit card to the clerk, who ran the metallic strip through the machine, unsuccessfully. Then she turned the credit card over, and punched in the account number. I stood there; my heart was beating hard and my adrenaline was flowing. About ten people stood behind me.

The cash register beeped and buzzed, processing the card. I gently let my breath ease out. I had finally cracked it. I walked out to the car, got in, and screamed, "We are going to be rich!" Even Flex could see we were on to something huge.

We drove to Anabelle's, a seafood restaurant in downtown Chicago, and spent $500 on dinner. We had wine, steak, and lobster tails, as we planned what we could do with the rest of the credit cards. I gave the waitress a $300 tip.

The next day, we went to Water Tower and started buying any and everything, running the credit cards close to the $10,000 limit. I was reveling in excitement.

But *the game* was still unfolding. I likened the credit cards to the armed robbery ring years before. I was learning as I went along, without the benefit of a guide. That experience ended in disaster. I would have to be very careful with the credit cards.

I was constantly on the hunt for account numbers. A friend's girl-friend was a waitress at a restaurant, and she fed us more credit card numbers. Sylvia continued to feed us numbers and I was quick to reward Sylvia with a few cards of her own. After I got a feel for using the credit cards, Delilah and I went shopping. She took to using the cards like a fish takes to water. She wasn't the least bit nervous. Delilah shopped with such authority that I was almost convinced the cards were hers.

As soon as I received new numbers from my resources, I gave credit cards to everyone in my crew. I began to see how greedy everybody could be. I would give someone a Visa Gold credit card on Tuesday, and on Wednesday, they would be back for another one. Many were like children at Christmastime. I needed to get a steady source of Visa Gold credit card numbers; then I could sell the cards. After two weeks of asking everyone I thought could help, I caught a break. One of my old friends from high school, to whom I had sold one of the video recorders, had a girlfriend, Paula, whose cousin worked at Visa head-quarters in Elgin, Illinois.

I met Paula and, after some small talk, I asked her to find out how many credit card numbers her cousin could get. She got back to me with news that sounded too good to be true. Her cousin worked at the Visa office that had access to as many names, account numbers, and expiration dates as I needed. I never let on to my high school friend, or Paula, what I was planning to do with the information. I told them I was trying to buy things through the mail and would pay $25 per account name and number. Paula's cousin wasn't making much money at Visa, and making some easy cash was interesting. Paula's cousin went for the deal. If Paula and her cousin knew I would be activating those credit cards to the tune of $10,000, there was no telling how much they would have charged me.

I didn't feel bad about it either, not one single bit. Making big profits is the American way. The whole premise of the Fortune 500 is to make their products as inexpensively as possible, and sell them for the most the market will allow. Or perhaps a better example is the whole savings and loan scandal. It is my understanding that George W. Bush, the current president, walked away from that scandal with millions of dollars, and wasn't even indicted. I was greedy, and I was in good company. I kept what I was paying for the credit card numbers a secret from everybody, except Delilah. Now *the game* was truly on.

CHAPTER 20

Losing Mary Louise Martin

My grandmother's memory loss continued to decline. I missed our long loving conversations. Although I called her regularly, it became increasingly difficult for us to hold normal conversations.

My grandmother's condition had worsened. The official diagnosis from the doctor was that she had Alzheimer's disease. My mother and aunt were unable to provide the necessary attention for her everyday living, because she needed full-time care. It was a hurtful and stressful time for our family.

My aunt made arrangements to place my grandmother in a retirement home in Detroit. It had a special floor devoted to the special needs of residents who were afflicted with Alzheimer's. Visiting my grandmother became a very painful ordeal.

My grandmother, once so full of life, with her special sense of humor and wit, at that point had almost completely forgotten who her family was. Although Alzheimer's had wreaked havoc on her mind, the insidiousness of it couldn't make my beloved grandmother forget about God.

Despite forgetting family names and faces, at any given moment, she would praise God. She would also break out and sing gospel songs. Her favorite was "His Eyes Is on the Sparrow." She sang it perfectly and never missed a word.

My grandmother often told me, when I misbehaved, that one day I would have a little boy who would also misbehave and worry *me*. She would always finish that statement by saying that she wouldn't be alive to see that, but I could count on it happening. I could never imagine my grandmother dying; I would always tell her that she would be alive to see her great-grandchildren.

Shortly after my first daughter was born, I brought her to see my grandmother, even though she could no longer recognize me. I felt it was important for my daughter to meet her great-grandmother. I believed that my daughter, just being in the arms of my grandmother, would be a great blessing for all of us. Furthermore, I received my own personal satisfaction in making my grandmother's prediction (of not living long enough to see any of my children) wrong.

It's hard to describe the feelings you have when somebody you love so deeply and means so much to you, no longer recognizes you. There are no words that could adequately explain the immense pain, emptiness, and deep sorrow I felt in the midst of my grandmother's suffering.

During 1990, my grandmother passed away. Although I mourned her passing, I felt a strange sense of joy that her suffering had ended. I knew that she was in heaven with the one who meant the most in her life: God.

The funeral was held in Detroit. My parents, sisters, and I stayed at my aunt's house. The funeral service was at Newlight Baptist Church—the same church where my grandmother had been a faithful member for decades, and the very same church that her husband, my grandfather, died preaching in the pulpit.

I stood in line waiting for my turn to look into my grandmother's sweet face one last time. When I was a boy, she would often talk about her passing on from this world. My grandmother was a true child of God, and death was something that she never feared. I drew strength from that thought, as I approached the casket.

I thought I would kiss her on the cheek. At first, I reached out to touch her hand. I immediately felt the ice-cold feeling of death. I realized that the spirit that had dwelled in that body, that I called my grandmother, had long since gone. Kissing her at that point would only have been in vain, so I did not. In my heart and mind, I knew that I had spared her no kisses while she was alive.

As I stood over my grandmother's casket, with tears in my eyes, I painfully realized that no earthly person had held higher hopes for me or believed in my potential more than my grandmother. I felt ashamed that I had failed to live up to her many expectations. The honest-to-God truth was I hadn't lived up to any of them.

I had secretly hoped that one day I would straighten up my mixed-up life and make her proud of me. There is nothing on earth that can compare to a grandmother's love.

I sat in my grandfather's church and embraced the shame of what I had and hadn't become in my life. My thoughts of failure were broken by the powerful words of the great Reverend Charles Adams. Reverend Adams studied under my grandfather at one time. He is now the pastor at Hartford Memorial Baptist Church. *Ebony* magazine once acknowledged him as one of the 100 most influential black Americans in the United States. My grandmother adored him and always had kind words for him while I was growing up.

Reverend Adams was preaching on behalf of my grandmother, and in the middle of his sermon, singled me out from all of the grandchildren. He said that he wanted me to know that I had a special place in my grandmother's heart. I knew that Reverend Adams's words were meant to soothe me. However, they actually stung. Again, I was forced to reexperience the shame of never living up to what my grandmother had expected me to be.

Later that day, we said our silent good-byes, among our tears, as they laid my sweet grandmother down to her final resting place. I left the cemetery that day with a heavy burden on my heart—the burden that I had disappointed the one person in my life who adored and loved me the most. That feeling would continue to plague me in the days, weeks, and months that followed.

Whatever motivation I might have had to make a positive improvement in my life, was gone. My life returned to the perpetual state of madness that had become familiar. I lacked the spiritual wisdom and understanding to recognize that my grandmother's spirit and prayers never left me, and never would.

CHAPTER 21

Shop Till You Drop

I bought $500 worth of numbers. I didn't want to buy too many at first, in case the numbers weren't correct. I met Paula's boyfriend at a bar. He had the computer printout of the names, numbers and expiration dates. I paid him and went right over to Flex's apartment. After the cards were printed up, I gave Flex ten cards and kept ten for myself. I mailed two to Sylvia.

Then Delilah and I went absolutely shopping crazy. First we spent $500 on dinner. Then we bought clothes, shoes, accessories, and jewelry at all the finest stores—the kind of stores where you don't have to show ID when buying something with a credit card. It is considered an insult to be asked for identification at stores like Gucci, Cartier, Ralph Lauren Polo Shop, Saks Fifth Avenue and Marshall Field's.

In order to avoid suspicion, we got dressed up to go shopping. In America, a white guy can go into nice stores in gym shoes, dirty jeans and a T-shirt and spend $10,000 without being given a second look. A black man dressed that same way is immediately a suspect.

I once went into a gas station wearing a pair of Levi's with holes in the knees, a baseball cap, and a blue jean jacket and I tried to pay with one of the Visa Gold cards. The white woman in the booth, Gold card in hand, looked me up and down, as if to say, "No way a black man dressed like you has a Gold card." She asked me for my driver's license.

"How dare you!" I went off and said, and demanded my card back. The bulletproof glass prevented me from just snatching the card from her. "I'm going to call the police," she said. "You'd better call, before I do," I replied calling her bluff. She picked up the phone and I dashed to cover the back of my license plate with paper, so the woman couldn't copy it down.

After that incident, I made it a point to be extra sharp every time I used one of those credit cards—Armani suit, perfectly starched white shirt, polished shoes, gold Longines watch. Delilah would always have on an expensive dress or suit. The salespeople never blinked an eye at her when she spent $7,000 at a time for clothes. When I was dressed well, they didn't pay much attention to me either. But, a young black man buying like it was going out of style often raised a few eyebrows.

White people aren't accustomed to seeing black people spend the kind of cash I was spending. After dropping $9,000 at a store, some white salespeople couldn't help themselves. They asked me what I did for a living, cleverly or matter-of-factly. Sometimes, I was a model or actor. Other times I was an investment banker from New York. My suburban upbringing allowed me to put white salespeople at ease.

In *the game* we call that "rocking somebody to sleep." Ordinarily, if a white person asked a black person, shopping in their store, what they did for a living, it would be considered an insult, cause for outrage. I played right along, because the goal for me was to get out of the store with $9,000–$10,000 worth of their merchandise.

Delilah became obsessed with shopping. She was in seventh heaven. We usually shopped together as a team, with his and her Visa Gold cards. One day at Saks Fifth Avenue, Delilah left me in the men's department, as she shopped in the women's department. I was furious. If something went wrong, I wanted to be there. After that incident, I told Delilah that I wanted her to stay in my sight at all times when she shopped. I knew I could handle just about any store security guard.

One day we walked into Mark Shale on Michigan Avenue, after leaving Gucci's across the street. When we walked in, loaded down with bags, the salespeople ran toward us, and hustled our bags from us. A saleswoman wanted to take Delilah upstairs to show her some clothes. And a salesman wanted to show me some suits.

I gave Delilah a look like, "You better not go upstairs where I can't see you." But she just gave me a big smile, and whisked off. She laughed and smiled at me all the way up the escalator.

I spent about $3,000 on suits, and went to the cashier to pay for my clothes. The salesman shook my hand, and left me with the cashier. I gave her my Visa Gold card and waited, as I had done so many times before. Instead of an orderly sale, the woman got on the phone. I kept my eyes on her. Finally, I asked if there was something wrong. She then turned her back to me. I walked around the counter, and asked loudly, "What's the problem?" She started yelling for the manager.

I snatched my card out of her hand, grabbed my bags, and was on my way out, when the young guy who sold me the clothes came over to see what was wrong. He saw that I was leaving without the merchandise. His commission was about to walk out the door and he wanted to know why.

He grabbed my arm and said, "Hold on." I put my bags down and looked him in the eye and said, "This is beyond you, get the hell out of my way before I break your neck." He quickly stepped aside.

I wanted to run upstairs for Delilah, but I had to leave her there. There was no sense in both of us getting arrested and going to jail. At least I would be able to bond her out when she called.

I took a cab home and waited for Delilah to call from the police station. I was certain they would check her ID when they remembered she was with me. They'd learn she had a counterfeit credit card, too. I sat on the window ledge, wondering what happened to Delilah and I glanced down to the street, hearing a car horn. Delilah smiled and waved at me from her car. Security at Mark Shale never even stopped to question her. She just walked out after she shopped. I was glad to see her, but I didn't allow that joy to stop me from admonishing her about going off alone.

Meanwhile, Flex, Jazz and Sylvia were shopping wherever their hearts desired. Flex even took his shopping to other cities. He would use the credit cards to purchase first class round-trip airline tickets to California. He would then check into one of the best hotels and spend a few days shopping. On those excursions, he would take three or four credit cards with him.

My favorite designer has always been Ralph Lauren. I love Polo. There was a Ralph Lauren Polo store on Michigan Avenue on the Magnificent Mile. While I had shopped at that store before, I had never shopped with the vengeance that I did with my homemade Visa Gold cards.

I walked into that Polo store, and got stupid. When I bought cologne, the salesclerk asked if I wanted spray or splash. I took both. I bought Polo in every color: shirts, sweaters, and shorts, with matching belts and shoes, as well as a few suits. I also bought clothes for Delilah and some of my friends. In all, I spent over $9,000 in that store. Then, I marched across the street to the I. Magnin store (where Borders bookstore is now), with another card.

When I. Magnin salespeople saw me walk in with all those bags, they went crazy trying to help Delilah and me with our bags. They knew we were going to spend money. They treated me like a movie star, so I acted like one. I bought a few Armani suits, a matching crocodile belt, sunglasses, and a purse for Delilah for a total of $5,000.

From my source at Visa, I learned that sporadic purchases may alarm security. Instead of going to a mall and buying shoes, baby clothes, and tires, I purchased complementary items at the same time. For instance, if I purchased a television, I might get a video recorder in the same department, as well as some video cassettes. That was how Joe Citizen shopped. I made it my business to know how the system worked, so I could take advantage of it.

The only problem with all that lavish spending was the increased difficulty in finding stores to shop at. A good salesperson will remember your name, making it difficult to go back to that same store with another card. On one occasion, Delilah and I were at Saks and a woman approached her as Ms. Johnson. At that point, Delilah couldn't use a credit card with a new name on it. Delilah said we were just browsing. After the saleswoman departed, we did too. At that point, we had pretty much burned out downtown Chicago as a shopping resource. We started shopping in the suburban stores.

I had bought so many clothes with the credit cards, that one day I gave all my old ones to some black children who were always trying to shine my shoes or wash my car windows. Things they couldn't wear, I told them to give to an older family member. I didn't have enough room in my closet for my new wardrobe. My dresser held more cologne than the display case at Marshall Field's.

Delilah was missing so much work by constantly shopping that she lost her job, but that didn't matter. With all the money we were making, she bought a brand-new Alfa Romeo Spider from Loeber Motors. We took the car to the stereo store, and picked out a $6,500 Blaupunkt stereo system with a compact disc player. They wanted to keep the car overnight to install the system, but I couldn't allow that because we were charging it on one of the credit cards. If Joe Citizen happened to use the card during the night and was denied because he had reached his credit limit, he would contact Visa and we would hear police sirens.

To avoid that kind of drama, I gave them an extra $500 to put it in, while we waited. After it was installed, we went to the Sound Warehouse and bought $500 worth of CDs.

We became accustomed to luxury and extravagance. We shopped during the day; and we ate out every night at the finest restaurants Chicago had to offer.

I knew most people wouldn't find out that we used their credit card information until the end of the month, when their bill came. Depending on when I got the number, I had a few weeks to use the card, but it only took Delilah and me a couple of hours to spend $10,000. I was having the time of my life, but I continued to stress to everyone the importance of being careful.

Almost everybody wanted a Visa Gold credit card. People who wouldn't normally rob, steal, or run scams, jumped at the chance to use one of my cards. It wasn't like a found wallet or a purse. With one of those cards, you had to use the cards before they were canceled. You could easily get busted. With my program, Joe Citizen had his credit card in his pocket. I simply had Joe Citizen's account numbers printed on another card. You could take your time and shop at your leisure. It had a universal appeal. How many people do you know who wouldn't jump at the chance to go on a $10,000 shopping spree without repaying on the charges? Everybody felt safe with my program.

One day Delilah, Jazz, and Flex were over at my loft. Everybody was drinking, laughing, and exchanging stories about which stores they had ripped off and what they had bought. Delilah was putting on a fashion show of her new designer clothes.

I interrupted the festivities to let everybody know that we had to tighten up. I told them that we had to be careful because if we got caught, we would all go to jail. They all laughed, especially Delilah, as she put her hands together pretending to be handcuffed. "Take me now," she said. Everyone laughed even harder.

We were on heads. It was sweet. But I knew that could change to tails in an instant.

CHAPTER 22

Mastering the Possibilities

I soon tired of shopping. The bottom line with me had always been money; it was time to organize the program and get paid. I had to come up with a way to start making some real money.

Delilah and I would sometimes buy a $100 gift certificate, then turn around and buy a shirt, and get the change in cash. My thought was to buy $500 worth of gift certificates in $100 increments from department stores, buy a pair of socks for two dollars and get the change. It was too risky for me to do myself; however, if I had a team of women who spent the entire day doing that, I could make a killing.

Alisa, a girl I knew from Detroit, was perfect for the scam, along with her two sisters Allison and Audrey. After she and her sisters agreed to the plan, I sent them credit cards to go shopping with, as an advance token of my appreciation. She and her sisters had a ball shopping with the cards, and introduced me to Mrs. Washington, an older black woman who owned a travel agency, who wanted to buy five cards a week for $1,000 each. I gave her a few cards to try. If she was satisfied, I would have more cards delivered to a location of her choice.

My cousin was home in Detroit from Florida A & M University for the summer and could be my delivery person. Earlier in the year he had called me when he found a woman's purse in a restaurant. It had a wallet full of credit cards. He asked me how to use the stolen credit cards and not get caught.

I had advised my cousin to get rid of the credit cards because he didn't know how long the purse had been missing. There was no way to determine whether the woman had already reported the credit cards as lost or stolen, and had them canceled.

I called him in Detroit and ran *the game* down to him. He was all too eager to deliver the credit cards to Mrs. Washington. I began FedEx-ing Visa Gold credit cards to his house, and my cousin would deliver them to Mrs. Washington. I always sent an extra card or two for his personal use.

Alisa and her sisters flew in for one week to learn the gift certificate scam. I told them that it was a job, and it should be taken seriously. I got them up at 8:00 A.M., and we were out shopping from 9:00 A.M. until 5:00 P.M. I took them to the high-end stores on Michigan Avenue: Saks Fifth Avenue, Gucci, I. Magnin, Marshall Field's and Mark Shale.

They entered the stores together, and went their separate ways inside. One by one, they would make their way to the cashier's office and buy $500 of gift certificates. After some minor shopping, they each came out with at least $400. I paid the ladies $50 for every $500 they made. I was pulling in about $5,000 a day from the ladies' shopping. Plus, I had money coming in from selling cards to Mrs. Washington.

Flex was also selling a lot of credit cards at $1,000 each. I got half of his proceeds. A friend of a friend, Razor, owned a jewelry store on the south side of Chicago and was interested in some cards. Razor was a dark-skinned brother with a jheri curl. He had a hooked nose and was city slick. I knew that he couldn't be trusted, but as long as I had his money up front, we could do business. I started selling credit cards to Razor for $1,000 apiece. He was running the cards through his store, charging all kinds of stuff, and pocketing the money.

One evening I went by Flex's apartment to talk business with him. When I got off the elevator, I heard music blasting from his apartment. Flex had about a dozen guests, none of whom I knew. Women were walking around half naked; people were getting high. He had boxes and packages everywhere; his apartment looked like he was moving in, or moving out.

"Flex, you need to chill and tighten up your game. Having all these people up in your business is not only ridiculous, but dangerous," I admonished him. He acted like he was listening, but I knew he wasn't. As I left his apartment, I had an uneasy feeling—like something was chasing me. I knew that something was the law.

We had been running the cards for about ninety days, and I felt sure there had to be a big investigation going. The next day, Delilah left to go shopping and discovered that her car window had been busted. She came back to the loft crying because her portable tape deck and her CDs had been stolen. She was upset about being robbed, while stealing every day herself. What was going around was starting to come around. She didn't understand that, but I did. That afternoon, an old friend called me with alarming news. His girlfriend, who worked at Carson Pirie Scott, told him that there had been a storewide meeting. Store security told all the cashiers and salespeople that if they saw any Colonial National Bank Visa Gold credit cards, to call them immediately.

I gave 3,000 blank cards to my mechanic friend, Steve, to store in a junked car at the auto body shop where he worked. It was time to stop shopping. I called everybody and told them the party was over. I sent the girls back to Detroit. I ended the relationship with Mrs. Washington.

The only safe thing to do with those cards was to learn how to program their metallic strips, to get cash advances from automatic teller machines (ATMs). I could milk the remaining 3,000 cards I had, for millions of dollars. ATM machines have security cameras, but we could disguise ourselves and run the cards through the ATMs.

There was a limit on how much could be withdrawn on a given day, but I could use a card repeatedly over a few days. Just $1,000 from each card would yield millions. I called Jimmy, my Greek friend, to see what he knew about programming the credit cards. I really didn't have the slightest idea on how to program those magnetic strips. However, I knew I could find someone who did. Jimmy said he knew a computer programmer. Everything in life, criminal and legitimate, is who you know.

I started thinking about how to handle the new development. If I could program all the remaining cards, Flex, Jazz, and Jimmy could each go to a major city and run the cards through ATMs simultaneously. Visa wouldn't know what hit them. We would rendezvous and split the money. I would leave the country and put my share of it in a foreign account and chill. It was within reach.

Jimmy had a contact who knew how to program the computer to access the magnetic strips. Jimmy and I bought the modem that we needed for his contact to scan the magnetic strip. I asked Paula's cousin at Visa to get the personal identification numbers (PINs) for the credit card numbers I was given. For the PIN numbers Paula's cousin wanted $75 per account. I hemmed and hawed about the $50 increase, but I was still getting over. Instead of making $9,975 on each card, I would only make $9,925. I could live with that.

Despite a full-scale government investigation, I still felt that I could salvage the project. I should have never started shopping with the cards, but rather figured out a way to program the magnetic strips from the get-go. But, just like the armed robberies, I was learning as I went along. That continued to worry me.

I woke up the next morning feeling good. It was a beautiful day. I could see the sky and the clouds. It was one of those days when you just feel good, and I was getting ready to pull down a couple of million tax-free dollars, and go lie on the beach on a warm island.

Flex called and said, "Victor, I want to sell some cards to Tom, one of my business partners. He's a white guy who knows the manager of a jewelry store who is gonna let him buy whatever he wants." I immediately said, "No." There was no reason to take a risk.

We had decided the previous month not to do any more shopping or selling cards. We knew the heat was coming. But Flex was even more greedy than me, and insisted on selling some credit cards to Tom. Against my better judgment, I relented. "Okay, but Flex, go with Tom to the jewelry store, and take the card back after he's done using it."

Flex did not go with him, as I asked him to. Tom was a lowlife, a dirty, blue-jean and T-shirt-wearing piece of white trash. He went shopping at a store in a mall where he knew the salesperson, and then went shopping at another store in the mall that had been put on alert to watch for Colonial National Visa Gold credit cards. The police busted him on the spot.

The Coin Is Tossed

The store held Tom, not for the local police, but for the United States Secret Service. The Secret Service not only protects the president, they're in charge of investigating counterfeiting cases involving credit cards and money. Printing the cards ourselves constituted counterfeiting. The Secret Service had been investigating the case for months, and arresting Tom was the first real lead they had. They took one look at Tom's dumb ass and knew he must have just stumbled onto the credit card. There was no way he was running the credit card operation.

They interrogated him, and he told them everything he knew—Flex. They assigned a female Secret Service agent to pose as Tom's girlfriend and infiltrate our operation. Flex opened the door to his apartment the next day, and in walked Tom and the Secret Service agent. She must have gotten an eyeful—TVs, stereo equipment, all kinds of other new stuff, still in the unopened boxes.

The agent told Flex she wanted to buy six cards for $1,000 each. Flex came to my apartment to get some more numbers. All Flex kept talking about was how good-looking the woman was, and he couldn't see her being with Tom. It was obvious to me that Flex was thinking with the wrong head. That situation didn't seem right to me. I told Flex that I wanted to talk to Tom on a pay phone.

We went to a pay phone and called Tom at his place. He said his girlfriend had the money and wanted to buy some cards. After my conversation with Tom, Flex said the woman might have some connections that we could use, and that he wanted to do business with her, because he might be able to have sex with her. Against my better judgment, I gave him the credit card numbers to print six cards.

The next day, Tom and the Secret Service agent returned to his apartment. After some small talk, Flex handed the agent six credit cards, and she gave him the money. As Tom and the woman opened the door to leave, several armed Secret Service agents rushed inside with guns drawn. Flex was thrown to the ground and arrested.

He was taken to the famous Everett Dirksen Federal Building in downtown Chicago. I had seen this six-foot, 240-pound, fearless man beat the hell out of people who owed us money. We had done crimes together. I thought he was my partner. But what did Flex do when the heat was on at the Dirksen Federal Building? He started cooperating—ON . . . THE . . . SPOT! He told them everything, and everything started with me.

Sipping on a beer while getting dressed in an Armani suit, preparing to go to Walter Payton's club and have a few drinks, I heard a knock on the door. I had a doorman who was supposed to announce all guests. I didn't talk to my neighbors; it wasn't one of them. I hadn't talked to Flex all day, so I presumed it must be him. The doorman would sometimes let him up without calling me. I looked through the peephole, saw that it was Flex, and let him in.

"Dog, I got busted by the Secret Service today." I looked at him and laughed. I thought it was a joke. He said, "Dog, I'm not kidding, I'm supposed to be setting you up right now. They're downstairs." I took a second look at his expression, and knew he was serious.

I ran to the TV and turned on the security camera channel that was positioned on the front lobby. On the screen were four white guys just standing around in my lobby. I yelled at Flex, "Why did you bring them to my apartment!" He explained what had happened, said they wanted to come up, do a credit card sale, and arrest me.

I started grabbing receipts, and Visa account numbers. I didn't have a lot of cards in my apartment, maybe ten. I tried to burn the cards, but the burning plastic smelled horrible. I ran to the garbage chute and threw them out. The machine was not in my house. I was clean.

I was way beyond pissed at Flex, but there was no time for that. I changed into some jeans, a shirt and penny loafers. I told Flex we were going to walk out of the building, and let the agents follow us to his mother's house. Twenty minutes had already passed. They would suspect Flex was telling me what was happening.

We took the elevator down to the front lobby. I fought to remain calm. My adrenaline was flowing. If all those years of armed robbery taught me anything, it was how to remain calm when I was nervous and rein in my fear. We got off the elevator and walked right by the Secret Service agents. I even spoke to them and said good evening. One of the agents spoke back. We got into Flex's car, and drove south to his parents' house, which was about thirty-five minutes from the city. I watched the rearview mirrors. If Flex hadn't told me we were under surveillance, I probably wouldn't have noticed the older four-door Mercedes and a van following us.

As we drove, I was trying to figure a way out, asking Flex questions about the agents who had arrested him. Flex hadn't bothered to call our lawyer, Mr. Vishney. I knew that was our first order of business. Cooperating with the Secret Service without a lawyer was the height of stupidity. Flex said he tried not to reveal too much, but I didn't believe that, because he brought the heat right to my front door.

He was supposed to call them on their car phone, once I agreed to meet them. When we pulled into his mother's driveway, the Secret Service agents parked down the street. I had to make it look like I was going along with the setup, in order to buy some time.

Once inside, I said, "Flex, go out and tell the agents I am going for the plan. Explain that I am on the phone trying to reach Steve, my guy who hid the cards for me. And take the garbage out when you go to talk with the agents, so it looks like you have an excuse to go out."

When Flex returned, he said, "They're falling for it." I needed to use a pay phone to continue the illusion, so we drove to a busy shopping center. I could see the Secret Service agents parked about thirty or forty yards away. I pretended to use the pay phone. After five minutes I threw my hands up in the air, as if I were mad about something, and then slammed the phone down.

Flex had a "what now?" look on his face, as I got back into the car. I told him, "Look, man, you're already out on bond. A judge gave it to you, and only a judge can take it away. Drive back to your apartment." I was furious with Flex, but I focused on damage control.

They didn't have anything on me so far. Since Flex didn't tell the Secret Service that Rhonda, his pregnant girlfriend, lived in the building, my plan was for us to spend the night at Rhonda's apartment in Presidential Towers and in the morning, Flex and I would catch a cab to Mr. Vishney's office.

I looked from Rhonda's thirty-fifth floor window with binoculars and saw the Secret Service agents waiting downstairs. In addition to the gold Mercedes and van that had followed us earlier, there were about ten other cars. All of the agents were out of their cars, on the street talking to each other, looking somewhat confused. They were waiting for the cell phone call from Flex, one they never received.

I spent the night thinking about how stupid Flex was, and how much trouble we were in. First thing in the morning, I called Mr. Vishney's office. I told him a little bit about what had happened. He told me to come to his office, immediately. We jumped into a cab, and headed straight to his office, five minutes away.

I believed we were still under surveillance, but in broad daylight, with thousands of people on Chicago's busy streets, it was impossible to be absolutely sure. Once we were inside Vishney's office, I felt better. Flex detailed the sorry events while I sat with a disgusted look on my face. Flex, Mr. Macho, looked and acted like a child. He produced a business card from the United States prosecutor, Joshua T. Buchman.

Mr. Vishney picked up the phone, and said "Hello, Josh, this is Seymour Vishney." Mr. Vishney sat in a cloud from nonstop smoking, and began doing what he did best—working out a deal for us. He talked for about fifteen minutes and closed the call by saying, "Thank you, Josh." Flex and I were sitting at attention, because our lives depended on what Mr. Vishney had to tell us. Our lives were literally hanging in the balance.

Mr. Vishney took the cigarette out of his mouth, and put it out. He said, "Look, I can get five years' probation for each of you." Flex let out a gasp of air, clearly relieved. I sat there poised, because I knew the man wasn't through. Then Mr. Vishney continued, "To get the probation, you have to give up the remaining blank Visa Gold cards and the machine you used to print them on." So far, so good. I could live with that. We had lost that match, it was time to cut my losses and move on to something else. At least I wasn't going back to prison. Mr. Vishney went on to say, "The prosecutors will also need your inside source at Visa headquarters and everybody's name who was involved, which included anybody who used one of your credit cards."

That was something I could not, and would not, do. Flex sighed and said, "Dog, I would never tell on you, but we have to take this deal." I looked at Flex as if he were crazy. "There is no way I am going to turn in my cousin, friends I have known for years. Your parents, your almost baby-mama in Presidential Towers, and some of our friends are on the list! How can you even entertain the thought of telling on everybody? I can't believe it. Flex, you're turning out to be a rat," I exploded. "You wanted to be a player. You wanted to wear Armani suits, drive a Corvette and be the man," I explained. "Going to prison is part of being a player. Dealing with heat from law enforcement is part of being a player. Now is the time to be a player, and players keep their mouths shut and don't become government informants. It is clear to me that it is time to go to prison."

"Dog, you've been watching too much of those Godfather movies." Mr. Vishney interrupted us, and told me that the United States Secret Service was going to catch everyone, anyway. He recommended that I cooperate. In his many years as a lawyer, he had watched the Secret Service work on numerous cases. They were thorough, meticulous, and the most elite governmental law enforcement agency around. That's why they are responsible for guarding the president.

I looked Mr. Vishney in his eyes and said, "That may all be true. They may indeed catch everybody. But there is absolutely no way I am going to turn in my family, friends, and girlfriend. There is just no way. If the United States Secret Service catches everybody, it will be without the assistance of Victor Woods!"

Flex looked at me like I was crazy.

If I wanted to be a stool pigeon, I could cut myself a great deal. I was sitting in the driver's seat. I alone knew where the Visa Gold cards were hidden. I was also the only one who knew how to reach Paula's cousin at Visa headquarters.

The Feds offer a deal to the first person they catch. If that person informs on everyone, he receives a lighter sentence. After that, the feds indict all the remaining people involved in the criminal activity. There is no deal for the others they arrest. Usually, the people who have been informed on get the heavier sentences.

Mr. Vishney reiterated that Flex and I would get five years' probation, and stay out of prison, if we told on everybody else involved. I couldn't imagine, let alone genuinely consider that. Mr. Vishney warned me that the United States prosecutor wanted those cards, that I needed to come up with an answer quickly. I told him I would get back to him in a couple of days.

I walked out of Mr. Vishney's office totally disgusted. I went to a pay phone, called everybody and told them what had happened. I warned all of my partners, including my cousin in Detroit, about the heat. I anticipated that the Secret Service would be making more arrests. I had no way of knowing exactly what Flex told them or didn't tell them. I had to assume he told everything. Delilah and everybody else were shocked and upset but none understood the magnitude of the trouble.

I went back to my apartment, sat in the window and stared out. A car was parked in front of my building with two white men sitting in it. I was under twenty-four-hour surveillance. Mr. Vishney said Visa was putting a lot of pressure on the Secret Service to solve the case.

I needed some space. I planned to check into a hotel for a few days and clear my head. I packed a small suitcase and headed out at 5:00 P.M.—into some of the worst rush-hour traffic in this country, so it would be easy to lose the Secret Service. I caught a cab in front of my building and instructed the driver to take me to Water Tower Place on Michigan Avenue. Traveling on the Magnificent Mile in rush-hour traffic is treacherous.

As we plodded through traffic, I could see the car that was earlier parked in front of my building, boldly following me. On Michigan Avenue, still several blocks away from my destination, I paid the cab-driver for the ride, so I could exit at any moment.

A few minutes later, in bumper-to-bumper traffic, I hopped out of that taxi, and caught another taxi going in the opposite direction. It was impossible for the Secret Service agents to follow me.

I knew that sometimes the police let you see one set of detectives, while there are others hidden elsewhere, to give you a false impression that you've lost them. You'll feel comfortable and lead them directly to your illegal activities.

I had the second taxi take me to Water Tower Place. Again I paid the driver up front and again made a quick exit in front of Water Tower on Michigan Avenue.

Not knowing if I was still being followed, I ran into the crowded mall, up about forty steps to the second level, then about fifty yards to the escalators and went down. I then exited the back doors and jumped into another taxi.

I instructed that driver to take me to the Holiday Inn on Ontario Street. I arrived satisfied that I hadn't been followed. I ordered a drink from room service and called Delilah. I told her to meet me, but make sure that she wasn't being followed. Delilah arrived and after some drinks said she wanted to go visit her parents in Iowa. In light of what was going on, it was a good idea. The next morning, she went home.

I remained in the hotel contemplating my next move. I thought about leaving town. I hadn't been arrested. The Secret Service didn't have enough evidence against me. I called my parents to let them know I was planning a trip to see them and was greeted with awful news. The Secret Service had arrested my cousin in Detroit. My parents were livid and told me my aunt was even more upset. They all blamed me for my cousin's arrest.

My aunt, uncle and their two children are the epitome of the black bourgeoisie in America. Their reaction to their son's arrest was like my parents' when I first got into trouble, but unlike my parents, my aunt and uncle found a scapegoat for their son's behavior: me. They chose to ignore the fact that their son *chose* to participate in the credit card conspiracy.

My cousin had the same option that I did: turn in his family and friends to save his ass; or stand up and accept the fact that he had been caught participating in an illegal activity, that he willingly chose to participate in.

My cousin chose to cooperate with the Secret Service. He was in college and had aspirations of becoming an attorney. My aunt, who is a sitting judge on the Michigan judiciary court in the 36th District, denies having instructed, or participated, in my cousin's decision to become an informant. She says she retained a lawyer for her son and was not involved in any decisions regarding his criminal case. In her child's deepest hour of need, in a field in which she has expertise, does a mother allow her son to make a decision without her?

My cousin sold me out. And neither my mother nor father blinked an eye. There was no righteous indignation from my parents about what happened to me, in part due to their nephew. Even my own parents felt that my life had become expendable.

I truly believe that my cousin's taking that position was the lowest point in our family's history that I know of. I will be the first to admit that my life, back then, was doing very little to hold up the good family name. However, informing on a member of my own family is something that was and still is incomprehensible.

In the final analysis, I guess the end justifies the means. I say that because my cousin went on to graduate from Wayne State School of Law and is now working for American Express in New York.

In the midst of all the investigating going on, I decided to do some investigation of my own. My first order of business was to find out who implicated my cousin. I proposed the question to Flex. Of course, he denied giving my cousin's name to the Secret Service. But I knew it was him, because no one else knew about my cousin's involvement except him.

In the middle of all of my family's righteous indignation, the reality was that I never put any pressure on my cousin, or anyone else who participated in the credit card case. I simply offered them an opportunity. Back then I was dishonest, and I made the conscious decision to be so. I felt like I was doing people a favor for the chance of making some easy money, by involving them in my illegal activities.

I didn't ask people if they wanted to get into trouble. I asked if they wanted a Visa Gold credit card so they could get something for nothing. What I was doing would never have appealed to an honest person. The truth of the matter is, everybody who participated in the credit card case, whether helping me directly or buying things on the card, was dishonest, too.

So it seems to me that I shouldn't be blamed because someone got caught for their dishonesty. However, America is about passing the buck, and passing responsibility to someone or something else. My mother, father, and aunt were no different.

I called Sylvia, to make sure everything was all right on her end. The Secret Service had called her job several times, and because she never returned any of the phone calls, the Secret Service came to her apartment when she wasn't home. Her ignorant boyfriend let them walk right in without a search warrant. I listened to Sylvia, sick. I had Mr. Vishney call the Secret Service in Washington, D.C., to let them know that he was representing her, too. After that call, Sylvia never heard from them again.

On top of this drama, I was still facing the gun case in state court. Delilah returned from her parents' house in Iowa, and we went to the Rolling Meadows courthouse for the gun charge. Delilah testified that the gun in the car was hers. She was charged with a misdemeanor. With no prior record she would get supervision as opposed to the prison sentence that was hanging over my head.

After receiving another continuance, we walked to Delilah's car in the parking lot. "Victor Woods." I turned around to see who called my name. "United States Secret Service agent." In an instant, I was surrounded by four other agents pointing their guns in my face. Delilah looked shocked and frightened. I gave her a half-smile as they handcuffed me. They put me in their car and sped away. The driver was a white Secret Service agent. The agent riding shotgun was black. We drove for about fifteen minutes in silence. Polite conversation came next. The driver asked me my birth date and Social Security number. I knew they had that information; they were trying to warm me up and then progress to more incriminating questions.

"You already have that information and I won't speak without my attorney present."

The agent driving said with great pride, "We're not like the Arlington Heights police, we're the United States Secret Service."

I said nothing, and that was the end of that conversation.

We arrived at the Dirksen Federal Building by way of the underground parking garage and entered through the back entrance. We took an elevator to a huge room with cubicles and people everywhere. The agents were all in plainclothes and laid-back. Many were friendly, saying "hello" as I walked by. They put me into a room, removed my handcuffs, and locked me in.

An agent came in and started asking me questions about my clothes. "I really like your suit and watch. Where'd you get them?" I looked at him like he had to be kidding. Another agent came in and took my fingerprints.

About thirty minutes later, five agents walked in. One stood out. He had a head of white hair, wore glasses, and stood about six feet tall. Lee Seville was in charge. He said, "I know you're in charge of the credit card conspiracy. I've been following the case for months." He held a huge stack of receipts, accumulated from all the shopping, and laughed.

I was accustomed to arrogant caveman police tactics. Secret Service agents were polished and smooth, especially Lee Seville. I sat there and laughed with him, not saying a word.

I then smiled and said, "I know nothing about what you're referring to." The only agent who talked to me was Lee Seville. The other four sat at the table and stared at me while the bright lights shined in my eyes. They were trying to intimidate me, and it worked, but I had learned to deal with law enforcement interrogation tactics and harness my fear. I sat there showing no emotion, listening to Lee Seville's every word.

One agent handed Lee Seville a letter sealed in plastic. I immediately recognized the handwriting as mine. It was a letter I had sent to Flex before we stole the Addressograph machine.

Lee Seville read the short, one-page letter out loud. "Flex, let's get the machine and get rich and I'll race you to Rio de Janeiro." It was signed, "Victor."

"The machine I referred to was a video recorder. I hoped we would get rich by watching real estate videos on how to buy and sell property."

All the agents laughed. Lee Seville looked at one of the other agents and said, "I told you this guy was smart."

"That's all the talking I am going to do before I speak to my lawyer," I said.

Mr. Vishney arrived and had a conversation with Lee Seville, then came into the room. Mr. Vishney explained that the Secret Service had arrested me on an outstanding warrant for failure to appear in court on a speeding ticket.

Lee Seville made it appear that I had been arrested for the credit cards, in hopes of getting me to tell on myself, as I did ten years earlier, but I had been well-schooled in *the game*. The only evidence the Secret Service had against me was from Flex's big mouth. That wasn't enough to arrest me. They had to drop me off at Cook County jail. I had won that round with the United States Secret Service.

As I left the Dirksen, Lee Seville said, "You better help yourself. If you don't cooperate with the government, we'll bring your gun case into federal court." He was telling me something I didn't know: that three violent felony convictions and possession of a firearm could mean anywhere from fifteen years to life in prison in federal court.

Delilah bonded me out of Cook County jail, and we drove to her apartment. I was shaken up. I called everybody who was involved with the credit cards, told them what had happened, and again, warned them all to be careful, prepare themselves to be arrested, and seek legal counsel.

CHAPTER 24

The Sting

I had to get rid of those credit cards. I could have thrown them into Lake Michigan, but I still wanted to make money. I focused on selling the remaining 3,000 blank credit cards in bulk.

The first person I thought of was Razor. He was greedy, and I knew he would jump at the chance to buy in quantity. I called Razor and offered to sell him 700 blank Visa Gold cards for $30,000—a great deal for him, $700,000 worth of credit for $30,000. He said he would get back to me.

When Razor called me back, I told him I would call him back from a pay phone. I called and Razor said, "I want to buy the cards, but the Addressograph has to be included."

"The deal was for the cards only."

He kept asking, "What can I do with the cards, and no machine?"

"I'm giving you a great deal. You have to buy your own machine." We decided to meet that night at Red Lobster in River Oaks to sort out the details. I went through a lot of trouble to make sure I wasn't followed and that evening we etched out the details of our deal.

We decided to meet on a Friday afternoon at his jewelry store. Razor would have the $30,000 in cash, and I would deliver the credit cards.

All week I sat back with Delilah and carefully examined every detail of the deal. I kept everything I was doing secret from Flex. He insisted he wasn't cooperating with the Secret Service anymore, but I knew he would do anything to stay out of prison. I wanted to hire Patrick Tuite, a high-profile attorney, for Flex at a cost of $70,000, a high price for damage control, but I planned to put the $30,000 toward Flex's lawyer and go on a long vacation.

I didn't know or trust Razor, so Jimmy would wait nearby with the credit cards, and I would call him when I saw the money. Steve, my mechanic holding the cards, packaged 700 blank cards. I had them delivered to Jimmy Thursday evening.

The night before the deal was supposed to go down, Delilah and I went to a bar in another suburb where her friend was having a party. We were being followed by several cars, but since we weren't doing anything, I didn't bother to try and lose them. I had gotten used to being followed.

The next day around 2:00 P.M., I paged Razor from a pay phone. When he returned the call, I asked him if he had the $30,000. He said that he did. He said that his buddy, who was lending him the money, wanted the credit cards delivered to him at the Holiday Inn in Harvey, Illinois. We agreed to meet at 4:00 P.M.

The fact that Razor was involving another person in our business at the last minute was definitely a bad sign, but I ignored it. I would have Jimmy deliver the credit cards to the Holiday Inn, and then I would get my money. I told Razor to make sure the money was at the store when I arrived. I called Jimmy and told him to find a spot near the Holiday Inn in Harvey, and wait for me to call for the OK to deliver the cards.

It was a lovely summer day in July 1990. The sun was shining, and there wasn't a cloud in the sky. Delilah and I were in my Corvette cruising down Lake Shore Drive. I was delighted to be on my way to pick up a cool $30,000 in cash. I wasn't concerned about the Secret Service following me, because it's not illegal to pick up money from someone. I didn't have the credit cards on me, even if they did stop me.

When we arrived at Razor's jewelry store, Delilah sat in the car. Razor's wife greeted me and took my watch, and began cleaning it as she usually did. No one else was in the store. Razor and I shook hands, went to the back of the store and got down to business.

"Where's the money?" I asked Razor.

Razor, in turn, asked me, "Did you drop off the credit cards?"

I said, "I have a friend waiting to deliver the credit cards upon receiving my orders."

Razor said, "The money is close by."

I was furious. "I told you over and over and over to have the money in the store when I got here." That was the second sign that something was awry.

"OK, OK, man. I need to make a phone call to have the money delivered here to the store."

I gazed out of the front window, and saw a brother leaning inside the passenger's side window, talking to Delilah. I left the store and walked out to the car and said, "The lady is with me. Give her some air."

The scene didn't seem right. It was all a little strange. About half an hour later, a brother in an older model Datsun 280Z arrived at the store. Razor said, "There's my man," and went out to greet him.

As we approached the car, the brother rolled down his window, and Razor introduced us. I asked to see the money, and the brother showed me a ten-inch stack of hundreds in a leather bag. I wanted to get into the car, talk to him, feel him out, but the brother refused. "I don't know you well enough to let you into my car," he said.

"Once the credit cards are dropped off at the hotel, my partner will meet us, and give you your money," Razor said and I walked back inside.

I said to him exactly what I had been thinking all day: "The guy in the car looks like the police. Something isn't right. How long have you known the guy in the car?"

"I practically *raised* the guy! I've known him for years!"

I wasn't sure if I was just being paranoid. I couldn't imagine Razor being an informant, and against my better judgment, I called Jimmy and told him to drop off the credit cards at the hotel. Once the credit cards were dropped off, Razor was to receive a call to release the money. Jimmy was to call me as soon as he dropped off the credit cards, so I could pick up the money.

I waited outside for half an hour for the phone call from Jimmy. That was also strange. I paged him. It took him a long time to get back with me—yet another sign that things weren't right. All the madness of the past three weeks had dulled my senses.

Jimmy finally called. "Everything all right?" I asked.

"Yeah."

"Is the person in the hotel room cool?"

He said he was. I told him cool, and I would call him later. I gave Delilah the thumbs-up sign and she smiled.

I went back inside the store and told Razor that my guy had delivered the credit cards. He made a phone call and then after a few minutes said, "Let's pick up the money." Razor got into a new Thunderbird, while Delilah and I followed him to Rainbow Beach—a ten-minute ride on the South Side of Chicago.

As we were driving to Rainbow Beach, Delilah asked, "Do you think they might try and shoot us?"

I just laughed and said, "They already have the cards, why would they do that?"

When we arrived at the beach parking lot, Razor's friend was already there. No other cars were around, and the few people there were into their own activities. We parked about forty yards away from Razor, and his friend's car. That way, if something did go wrong, Delilah could get away. I then got out of the car and walked toward Razor and his friend who, by now, had gotten out of their cars.

We walked toward one another until we met. Razor's friend smiled at me and said, "What's up?" and tried to hand me the money in the leather bag that I had seen before.

I told him, "No thanks. Hey, no offense intended, but I don't know you." I told him to give it to Razor, and let him give the money to me.

As Razor took the money and reached out to give it to me, the whole parking lot lit up like a Christmas tree. Secret Service agents were everywhere. Cars raced to surround me, and men ran toward me with guns drawn. It was the most police I had seen since I was arrested by the task force for the armed robberies in 1984. Josh Buchman, the United States prosecutor, was even there, taking in the scene in an unmarked car.

I looked at the spectacle and froze. I slowly raised my hands. I knew one false move could get me killed. As the agents handcuffed me, Razor and his friend, I knew the former was an informant, and the latter an agent. I looked at Delilah, and guess what she did? She smiled at me, and rolled her eyes like it was a big joke. That woman never ceased to amaze me.

Handcuffed in the back of that unmarked car, I understood. Razor had been setting me up the whole time. They didn't have to follow me to Red Lobster because they already knew where I was going. We probably had been served by Secret Service agents.

I never would have gone down if Jimmy had given me any kind of clue. He walked into the hotel room, was immediately arrested by the Secret Service, and without further ado, became an instant rat. The brother who tried to talk to Delilah was also an agent, there probably to keep my mind off the task at hand.

I rode in the back of an unmarked car, as I had three weeks earlier. But I knew *the game* was over. I was headed back to prison. That felt terrible. "Tails" had arrived.

CHAPTER 25

The Informant

I found myself once again back inside the Dirksen Federal Building. Only this time there was a twist—I was sitting handcuffed to the wall. Lee Seville, the same gray-haired Secret Service agent who told me to help myself three weeks ago, came confidently strolling in. He told me that Jimmy was telling them so much that I'd better start talking before there was nothing left to tell. He knew they had me by the balls.

He said that if I didn't want to talk, then I was going to the Metropolitan Correctional Center (MCC). The MCC is the federal government version of Cook County jail, located in downtown Chicago. He then added he would see to it that I not get out on bond. At that moment, I knew what I had to do.

The game was cold, but it was fair. All the signs had been there that day. I had a chance to read them, I just didn't. It was time to go back to prison. I didn't like it, but it was simply that time. I told Lee Seville to go home.

The biggest difference between it and County was that MCC was clean. The officers sat inside on the deck with you, instead of being kept behind bars or protective glass, like in the county jail. There were vending machines, a microwave oven, and an ice machine. The cells were really rooms with carpeting on the floor. My floor was filled with white, black and Spanish people. There were four color-TV sets and four telephones. With all the white people talking on the phone, it was easy to see the MCC wasn't controlled by the gangs. In fact, it was clear that Uncle Sam controlled the facility.

Delilah had already been questioned and released and was at home. I called her to get bond money ready. Since I had been arrested on a Friday, I had to wait until Monday morning to go before the judge for a bond hearing. The MCC looked like the Taj Mahal as far as prisons go, but the rules of being in prison still applied. That meant doing page four: mind your own business. I spent the weekend in my room and Monday went to court for my bond hearing. I asked Eve to bring my children for the hearing. I wanted to play the "family man" game for the judge and the prosecution.

While waiting in the bullpen to be called into court, they told me that my lawyer was there. I was really surprised to hear that, since I hadn't been given a chance to talk to Mr. Vishney. I was taken to a wire-mesh booth. From behind that, I saw a small, good-looking white man. He told me the court had appointed him to be my lawyer for the bond hearing. His name was Thomas K. McQueen.

I was impressed with his professional manner and straightforward approach. Inside the courtroom Josh Buchman, Lee Seville, and other Secret Service agents were huddled like a basketball team during a time-out. The judge presiding over my bond hearing was a woman. Eve and Delilah were both present.

During the bond hearing, Josh Buchman argued that my bond should be high. Mr. Buchman said that I was about to receive $30,000 at the time of my arrest. Mr. McQueen countered that I never actually received that money, therefore, using that as a gauge to set bond was ridiculous. Then he mentioned that my wife and children were in court. Mr. Buchman went crazy and started yelling that I was separated from Eve, and I hadn't lived with her in months. Of course, that was information that Lee Seville had fed him while trying to keep his promise of denying me bond.

The judge gave me a bond of $10,000, of which I had to pay $1,000 to get out. The prosecution team was visibly upset. I looked at Lee Seville and smiled. Delilah posted my bond and I was out about four hours later.

Delilah had a six-pack of beer on ice waiting for me when I walked out of the MCC. We rode back to her apartment in silence, listening to the radio as I collected my thoughts. The question in my mind wasn't *if* I was going to prison, but for *how long*.

I called my family and told them what had happened. They were unsympathetic and full of "I told you sos." Once I came to grips with the fact that my family wasn't going to support me, I turned my attention to fighting my case. I didn't like Mr. Vishney's recommendation that I cooperate with the Feds, even though he was looking out for my best interest. Tom McQueen worked for Jenner and Block, a large and prestigious law firm in Chicago. He handled my bond hearing well. I was comfortable with Mr. McQueen handling my case. I liked him, and he appreciated that I wouldn't tell on anybody to save my own skin.

After my meeting with Mr. McQueen, Delilah called and told me she had been arrested again. Agents had surrounded her apartment and served her with an arrest warrant. I headed straight downtown and sat in court waiting for her to come out, just as she had done for me a few days earlier. She received a signature bond, meaning she signed her name verifying she would return for court dates and didn't have to pay any money.

I wondered what evidence the Secret Service had acquired to arrest Delilah. We had stopped shopping with the credit cards. I thought she was safe. Agents must have taken her picture at stores where we had previously shopped. One confirmation from a manager or salesperson would have been enough evidence to place Delilah under arrest.

As we drove home, Delilah cried. The amount of trouble we were in was finally sinking in. She now understood how serious it was. It wasn't fun in the sun anymore.

Delilah hired an attorney specializing in federal cases.

We were both scheduled to be arraigned in federal court and the arraignment looked like a convention. Jimmy, his whole family and lawyer; Jazz, his family, and lawyer; Flex, his family and lawyer; and everybody else involved in the case in Chicago was in the courtroom. There were even a few faces I didn't recognize. Twelve people had been indicted that day. I was shocked.

Nobody made eye contact with me. Everyone looked in the opposite direction except Jazz, who came over. We hugged. He sat with Delilah and me. Together we marveled at the spectacle that we were, unfortunately, part of. The lawyers guarded their clients like pit bulls. Everybody glanced at me, but if I looked at them, they quickly turned their heads away. All cooperated with the government, except Jazz.

We all pleaded not guilty. The Secret Service agents were sitting everywhere. Of course, this was Lee Seville's day to smile.

The judge was a straitlaced man with glasses. On his desk was a plaque that read: The Honorable Judge James F. Holderman. I would later learn his nickname among the prison population is Hang 'Em High Holderman. Wearing his black robe, he looked down at us from the bench and spoke softly and courteously. But I knew he would be trying to screw me before the case was over.

To make the circus in the courtroom complete, Flex had somehow managed to con his way into Mike Tyson's training camp as a sparring partner. His lawyer requested permission to allow Flex to fly to Atlantic City and spar with Mike Tyson. The judge granted that request. Then Flex and his lawyer went into the judge's chambers. I knew Flex was singing like the Temptations. I was surprised to see him in court, but obviously he was working with the judge and prosecutor. Mr. McQueen handed me a copy of the official indictment and advised me to stay far away from Flex. I left court disgusted and physically ill. All the people I had tried to protect were turning on me like hungry dogs.

As I rode the elevator down to the first floor, I read the indictment:

United States of America v. Victor Woods

COUNT I

The November, 1990 GRAND JURY charges:

> From in or about January, 1990, and continuing to on or about July 6, 1990, at Chicago and elsewhere, in the Northern District of Illinois, Eastern Division, Victor Woods did knowingly combine, conspire, confederate and agree together and with others known and unknown to the grand jury, to commit certain offenses against the United States.

The paragraphs following the indictment gave a detailed account of everything we did in relation to the credit card case. The government had broken down our actions into a fourteen-count indictment.

With all the drama in my life, I decided that I needed a change in environment, so I moved again. I moved into the Pavilion Apartments near O'Hare airport. It was a decent complex that had a bar and restaurant, a store, and a pool. I spent my days trying to relax in the midst of all the continuing madness.

Delilah and I went back and forth to court. She got another job as a cleaning service dispatcher and secretary to bring in some extra money. It was hard for me to make any moves because I was still under surveillance. Lee Seville was really trying to nail me for anything else he could find on top of the credit cards. I had some money saved up, so I wasn't pressed enough to break down and try to get a job for extra cash.

Everybody on the case was cooperating with the government except Jazz, Delilah, and me. Everybody signed statements against me and told everything they knew. The agents got all the remaining credit cards from Steve. Everybody was trying to get probation.

Often, across the country in the state system, a judge will give a guy a light sentence for whatever reason. Then, after being released, the guy goes out and does the same thing or something even worse, which makes the judge look like a fool.

In part to combat that, the federal government came up with "Sentencing Guidelines." In it lies a point system for any federal crime. A federal judge has to sentence you by that book. He doesn't have the same freedom as a state judge has, although many states have now adopted sentencing guidelines. After months of negotiation, we entered into a plea agreement with the United States government. I was to serve between 41 to 51 months in prison, although Mr. McQueen made it clear that I could expect to serve between 28 and 40 months. Since I had refused to cooperate with the government, they wanted to count my six prior convictions as separate offenses. Even though I had already served time for those armed robberies, I still received more time when I was sentenced for my credit card conspiracy.

Mr. McQueen assured me we could argue my sentence down to maybe thirty months. The most they could give Delilah or Jazz was about twelve months. But the mere thought of going to prison scared them to death.

I spent my days trying to understand why all my other friends were cooperating, where I went wrong. They were cooperating with the federal government by telling on me.

One day Delilah asked, "Why can't we cooperate with the prosecutor? Everybody has told on you already, so why not cooperate? Why are you trying to protect people who were already telling on you? I just don't understand why you're unwilling to cooperate with the federal government."

I went all the way off on her. "Do you expect me to be like Flex and the others? I live by the principles of *the game*. I have self-respect, character, and pride. Nowhere in my codebook of rules for *the game* is there a chapter on cooperating with the government and becoming a stool pigeon!"

She stared at me with a blank expression. "Being a criminal is a profession to me. I've been trained to be a player in *the game* by master players. I understand that going to prison is a hazard associated with my profession—no different than a professional athlete being injured, or a race car driver being killed in a crash. Delilah, you and everyone else wanted a joyride. While it was fun, and the prizes were plentiful, everyone wanted to play *the game*. Everybody was fine and dandy while they were shopping themselves to sleep. But the moment trouble became a part of the equation, everybody wanted to get off the ride. So you want to get off?"

"If you really love me, you wouldn't stand by and watch me go to prison," she said.

"Delilah, you have no code except to have fun. The ride was great and you enjoyed it. But the fun is over now, and you're ready to jump off."

"Let's both cooperate with the government. This is scary, Victor."

"I would rather die than inform on my friends and family. It doesn't matter what everybody else is doing to me. The rules of *the game* are not about telling on somebody else. The fact that everyone else is telling on me is no excuse for me to violate my code of ethics."

We argued and argued, and it was clear that Delilah had no intention of going to prison. She left the apartment in tears.

I called Big Duke to talk. I needed some advice on how to handle the situation. Big Duke had been in *the game* for twenty years. He was from the old school and had picked up being my mentor where Tops and KeKe had left off. I respected and trusted his opinion. He was a gun-toting, dark-skinned brother who always had a new Cadillac.

There I was, several months later, calling him to talk about the mess that I was in. Big Duke came over to my apartment and we talked. I began to explain the sorry state of my affairs. I was going off on everybody involved in the case. I also painfully explained that Delilah had suggested that she and I cooperate with the government.

After quietly listening to me rant and rave, Big Duke spoke. He weighed about 280 pounds, and when he spoke, you listened. He told me that first of all, and above everything else, I should have never allowed Delilah to know all of my business. He had warned me in the past about her, and he said that I was a fool to let her participate in my business in the first place.

Big Duke said that Delilah was going to go down and talk to the prosecutor, and she was telling me in so many words. He said that I had to at least make it look like I supported her cooperating with the prosecutor, so I could try and control what she said. Delilah knew a lot about my personal business, and she had met Big Duke.

The next day, I went to Delilah's apartment with a dozen roses, and told her she was right and that I was sorry. I took her out to dinner that night for seafood, where I pretended to support her decision to become a rat.

The following day, we went to Mr. McQueen's office. While Delilah sat in the reception area, I told him that Delilah, with my support, was going to cooperate with the prosecution. Mr. McQueen wasn't surprised at all. He said he had wondered what had taken her so long to start cooperating. He was a seasoned criminal attorney. He had seen parents, wives, girlfriends, and brothers turn on their loved ones when their freedom was in jeopardy.

Delilah was then called into the office. Mr. McQueen explained that if she informed on me, it would be tantamount to hammering the nails into my coffin. Delilah seemed upset to hear that her testimony could destroy me, but not upset enough to change her mind.

After we returned to my apartment, I told Delilah that I loved her, and didn't want her to go to prison. She spent the night, and we discussed what she might say. I asked only one thing of her: keep Big Duke, Sylvia and my past illegal activities out of any conversations she had with the government. She agreed.

Delilah was getting ready to do what, to me, was the unthinkable. I found it difficult to act supportive of her decision. I felt a sickening dread as we approached the time she would ultimately betray me.

The morning she had a "chitchat" with Josh Buchman, the Secret Service agents, and her lawyer to cut a deal, I tried to sustain an upbeat and supportive attitude. But as I ate breakfast with her, I felt disheartened and disgusted. I remembered our conversations where I asked Delilah to stay out of my business, the night at Nick's Fish Market that she was crying because she felt left out and wanted to get involved. As she left that morning, I gave her the Johnny Gill CD and told her to listen to the song "Fair-weather Friend." One of the lines said, "I won't be a fair-weather friend, I'll be your friend to the end."

I impatiently waited for her to return. It seemed like days had passed. All I could think about was her informing on me, helping the people who were trying to destroy me. Finally, the door opened and she was back, five hours later.

As I sat on the couch, she smiled and said, "It wasn't as bad as I thought it would be. They asked me all about the case and my personal relationship with you. They asked if you had a gun, or if you were currently involved in any illegal activity. It was actually pretty routine."

I didn't believe her. "Did you keep what we agreed out of it?"

"Mm-hm."

After that, things between us were never quite the same.

I didn't know that Josh Buchman and the Secret Service didn't give a damn about the credit card case anymore; that was basically closed. We had been on bond for several months, and Delilah couldn't reveal any information that the other codefendants hadn't already told them. If Delilah didn't help set me up in a new crime, or give them some information about future crimes, they would prosecute her to the fullest extent of the law. The options the United States prosecutor and the United States Secret Service gave Delilah, after she had already spilled her guts, was simply: Set me up or go to prison.

They knew the credit card conspiracy was a drop in the bucket, and nothing in comparison to what I had been doing since I was released from state prison in 1986. There are people doing twenty years in federal prison that haven't done a quarter of what I've done. But, then again, there are people who have done 100 percent more than I have, and have never, that's right, *never,* been to prison.

With the majority of my partners telling everything, the government knew about my various and sundry other illegal activities. Josh Buchman told Mr. McQueen that if I set up some of my friends from the South Side of Chicago who were selling drugs, then I could get off with doing a year in the MCC. They wanted me to wear a wire and work with the Drug Enforcement Agency. I told Mr. McQueen the prosecutor must be out of his mind. He laughed and said, as my lawyer, he had to tell me the offer had been made.

After court, as we walked the city streets back to his office, I expressed my bewilderment that people I had loved and tried to protect could turn on me. Mr. McQueen said he had represented thousands of clients and could count on one hand the clients who stood up to the government, who turned down probation and were willing to go to prison, rather than rat on family and/or friends. He said I was a breed apart.

A few days later, Jazz called and told me to meet him at Carson's Ribs. Once I arrived, Jazz told me over lunch that Josh Buchman offered him a deal. Jazz would receive probation and keep his broker's license if he agreed to set me up committing a felony. I hugged Jazz and told him I appreciated him telling me that.

Delilah was acting funny. She told me she was scared, and wanted a gun in the apartment. I suspected she was trying to set me up. I was beginning to see her for what she was—a rat. She knew how much trouble I could get into for possessing a firearm.

She also told me that she had keys to a currency exchange, jewelry stores, and other businesses that her cleaning company serviced. She said she wanted to give me the keys, so I could rob one of the stores. There was no doubt who was behind her sudden acquisition of the keys, nor who I would meet at those locations.

Delilah was meeting with the Secret Service agents daily at her job and updating them on my activities. She was given specific instructions to get me to buy another gun, or encourage me to commit another armed robbery. If a person has three violent felony convictions and is caught with a gun (just simple possession), the minimum sentence is fifteen years. It also carries a maximum of life in prison. The worst part of it was that I was trying to protect her, while she was attempting to destroy me.

One day I came home and realized that I had forgotten my keys. It was Delilah's night to come over, so I just waited for her to arrive at 5:00 P.M. By 6:30 P.M., I was concerned. I headed out with a friend and we drove the route exactly as she would have driven it. Since there were no accidents, we drove to her job. No sign of her at work. I had already called her apartment, and there was no answer. But as a last resort, we drove to her apartment to check it out.

I rang the doorbell. No answer. I went around to the back to look into the apartment, to make sure there were no signs of foul play. As I looked through the sliding glass doors, everything appeared to be normal. I pulled on the sliding door and gently opened it.

After surveying the apartment, I checked Delilah's answering machine. Delilah's voice sounded very nervous in a message to her roommate, saying she was at the Holiday Inn in Crystal Lake. She left the telephone number and extension.

My friend and I headed to Crystal Lake in silence as I tried to figure out what the hell was going on. I saw Delilah's car in the Holiday Inn parking lot.

In the hotel, I explained to a maid that I was in town to surprise my wife for her birthday, but I only had the telephone extension. I asked if she would give me the room number to help with my surprise gift. The maid provided the room number and told me how sweet I was for the surprise.

I told my friend to knock on the door and say that he was hotel security, that her car had been hit, and she needed to come downstairs to fill out a police report. He knocked on the door, and I hid at the side of the door. Delilah didn't go for it; she asked to see some form of identification. Then, she said she was calling the front desk. I came from the side, and yelled for her to open the door.

When Delilah heard my voice, there was first a deafening silence in the room, then Delilah's voice talking to someone on the phone. Hotel security in plainclothes approached and told us to leave. They said the Crystal Lake police department had been called and were on their way.

"I'm not going anywhere until I get my keys from her." I then hollered, "Delilah, what is the problem? Why are you locked in the room?" The hotel security held their IDs up to the peephole and tried to get her to open the door, but she still refused. Then suddenly, she slid my apartment keys under the door. I was pissed off, but I couldn't hang around. I didn't want a run-in with the Crystal Lake police.

The police had blocked off the parking lot exits and were searching all vehicles. They searched us, and then they escorted us back inside the hotel.

I explained to the police that I had locked myself out of my apartment, and I came to get my keys from my girlfriend. Several officers went upstairs to confirm the story with Delilah, while others stayed with us. I sat on the couch in the hotel, watching people stare at me as they walked by. After about twenty minutes, they arrested us for disturbing the peace.

After an hour my friend and I were released. The police had detained us to allow Delilah time to get away, for by the time the officers drove us back to the Holiday Inn for our car, Delilah was long gone. She was probably trying to get back home to Iowa. The pressure from the government to set me up, while sleeping with me, was taking its toll and she was just bailing out.

The next day I called Delilah in Iowa. Her mother answered the phone and I asked to speak to Delilah. She told me that her daughter didn't want to talk to me.

CHAPTER 26

My Guardian Angel

I was going back to prison, but I was going to go out in style. Even though I was under constant surveillance, the Secret Service didn't care where I lived. They only wanted to know where I was and what I was doing. I changed my name to Randy Klein and I was on my way again. I moved into a beautiful one-bedroom apartment in Chicago's Gold Coast, 111 East Chestnut Street on the thirty-fifth floor. I now lived across the street from Water Tower Place and the John Hancock Center, had a lovely view of Lake Michigan and was a hop, skip, and a jump from the Magnificent Mile. Jane Byrne, the former mayor of Chicago, lived in the building. In fact, I introduced myself to her one day as we rode the elevator to our apartments.

I spent my days and evenings ordering takeout food, drinking beer, and renting movies. When I did go out, I ate at the finest restaurants, going to clubs, and picking up beautiful women. I was going to thoroughly enjoy my last days of freedom.

One night I got a phone call from one of my old girlfriends who told me she had seen Earl, my high school friend, at a party. He was a lawyer, working with a law firm in Chicago. Earl and I had lost contact; I hadn't seen him in four years. I had often wondered how he was doing. I debated whether or not I should give him a call. The last time I saw Earl was in the summer of 1986. He had graduated from Morehouse and was a commercial banker in Cincinnati, Ohio, on a short visit to Chicago. I had recently moved back to the area from Connecticut and had just broken up with Tomasa. We had time to spend only one day together, getting caught up. During that last meeting, I had just gotten out of state prison. We spent a few hours hanging out before he went back to Cincinnati. Now that Earl was a lawyer, I wasn't sure if he would want to be associated with me. Since I went to prison, some people I had known before I went in treated me differently—standoffish. I had seen that reaction far too many times.

In high school, Earl was like the big brother I never had. I decided to give him a call.

When I called the law firm a woman answered the phone and transferred me to Earl. He answered with a happy, but businesslike, "Hello, this is Earl Caldwell."

I said, "Hey Earl, what's up, do you know who this is?"

He said, "No."

I said, "Come on man, you don't recognize this voice?" Then I said, "Earl, this is Victor."

"What's up, man, how're you doing?" He sounded glad to hear from me, and invited me to his office. The place smelled of success and money. My friend had come a long way since we wrestled as teenagers in the room that we shared when I lived with his family. Earl still had that same arresting smile he's been sporting since I met him in high school. His eyes were bright with excitement. We embraced.

He introduced me to the receptionist before we proceeded to his office. As we walked down the carpeted corridor, we stopped at the offices of other attorneys and Earl introduced me, explaining that we were high school friends. Earl's way with people had remained the same.

Earl's office had a big window, and a clear view of Lake Michigan. But Earl didn't act like a big shot. He was the same old Earl I knew back in the old days. He asked me none of the stupid nosy questions about prison that most of my old friends asked me.

We talked for a while, then the conversation drifted to his passion—Africa. He had African art in his office. He had traveled to the motherland a few times and said he looked forward to taking me.

Earl caught me up on our mutual friends from high school. Sitting in his office talking reminded me of talking with him in high school. It felt like we talked for days, but I had been in his office only about two hours. Earl had work to do, so I bid him farewell, and invited him to my place for dinner. He gladly accepted and I left Earl's office feeling great. It was therapeutic to see and talk to an dear old friend.

After work, Earl came by and we ordered pizza. Earl seemed impressed by my Gold Coast apartment. I shared with him the mess I was in and addressed rumors he had heard about me when he was in college and I was in prison. I tested him, to see if he was afraid of me deep down inside, like I knew many people were.

When we were in high school, we used to play-fight. Earl could always whip me, and he was never afraid to mix it up with me. After I had a few drinks, I pushed him in a playful manner and reminded him of our fights at his parents' house. Earl jumped up and started slapping my head just like in high school. His reach was little longer, but I was stronger than him. We fought until we were wrestling over the couch and onto the floor.

He wasn't scared. He didn't even hesitate. It was like we picked up fighting from the last time in his room in Highland Park. He even called me some of the same old names he did in high school. He was the same old Earl, and my big brother was back in my life.

In the days that followed, we were inseparable. In high school, we would talk for hours, and even to this day, we both still love to talk on the phone. We picked up right where we left off before Earl went to college. A few days later, I went over to Earl's apartment that he shared with his roommate, Gerald. They had met in their freshman year at Morehouse College. Gerald is a doctor at Cook County Hospital. We both love jazz, so we immediately connected on that level, and we became friends.

I started hanging out with Earl and his crowd. All of his friends were square (meaning not hip to *the game*). But I liked that. They were all good people, and it was a nice switch from how I had been living. Earl started taking me to the professional party set.

There was one party I will never forget. A group of women who called themselves "Panache" were hosting a party at the South Shore Cultural Center. There must have been a thousand or so brothers and sisters at that party, like an old Jack & Jill regional convention. There were fine, sophisticated, beautiful black women everywhere. It was the kind of crowd I had been raised to be in. I looked out on the dance floor; Earl was leading a line dance and acting a fool, just like in high school. Earl had always been the life of the party, and he hadn't changed. As the night progressed, I was dancing and having a ball. I met some ladies and told them I was there with my lawyer friend. I was so proud of Earl I always bragged about him. The ladies wanted to meet Earl. I brought him over and said, "This is my friend, Attorney at Law Earl Caldwell."

Later, Earl told me he was upset that I introduced him as a lawyer. He didn't want to be known as a lawyer. He wanted to be known and liked as Earl.

My sister, Valerie, flew in for my twenty-seventh birthday in March 1991 and threw me a party. She invited all of her friends from Chicago. Since most of my friends had become informants, I invited Earl and Lanette, a stripper I'd met at a party. They were the only friends I had left. I had my daughters for their twice-a-month visit. My daughter, who was three at the time, walked over and gave me the cake. It was a wonderful day, one I will always remember. I had no way of knowing then, but that would be my last birthday as a free man until 1997.

CHAPTER 27

Tails

The situation with Delilah quickly escalated. A few days after my birthday, I got a call from an old friend who said Secret Service agents had been at his job and were questioning him about his relationship with me. Only Delilah knew of my dealings with him. I called her parents, and was told she had had a nervous breakdown. Her mother said she didn't know where Delilah had moved to, and instructed me not to call their house anymore.

A few months before Delilah moved out, I had suspected her of trying to set me up, so I decided to take some defensive measures. I picked the lock to her strongbox and got her Social Security number for a later date. I also took her old telephone bills and saved them. Now, armed with that information, I decided to start tracking her down, so I could see exactly what she was up to.

Most of the calls were to two numbers: one in downstate Illinois and the other to a local telephone number. I called the operator, and she said that the local number belonged to a restaurant in Arlington Heights. I called the restaurant and a woman picked up and said, "Hello." On a hunch I said, "May I speak to Delilah?" The woman said, "Oh, let me page her." Bingo! I had her. As I waited, I asked the woman what Delilah's job was at the restaurant. She replied, "She's the manager."

A minute later, she answered the phone and said, "Hello, this is Delilah." I listened to her voice and hung up the phone.

Finally, it was my decision with regard to how I wanted to handle Delilah. Without question, her betrayal was evident. She had tried to destroy me, and by doing that, she was also trying to destroy my children. The more I thought about what she had done, especially since I tried to help her get out of trouble, the madder I got.

In light of those new developments, it was time to get back in contact with Sampson. One day we met at my apartment, and I filled him in on the latest details about Delilah. After tossing around a few unworkable notions, Sampson had his own idea on how to deal with her.

Sampson suggested we drive to the suburban restaurant where Delilah worked. Once there, he surveyed the outside of the building and the back alley where Delilah's car was parked. Across the street, there was another building that provided a perfect view of the alley and anyone leaving the restaurant through the back door. Sampson commented that he could wait on top of the building across the street, with a high powered rifle, and then shoot Delilah in the head as she opened her car door.

Sampson's plan was to kill Delilah. His thought was to take her out and alleviate the problem. I was furious enough with her to enjoy the thought. Death is what sometimes happens to informants. It goes with the territory.

I looked up at the roof of the building across from the restaurant, and then looked back at Delilah's car parked not more than fifty feet away. I pictured Delilah falling to the ground, the blood flowing from her head, as the bullet pierced her skull. After savoring the thought, I realized that I wasn't willing to be a part of a murder. I was angry, and sometimes when I'm angry I can't see straight. But it just wasn't serious enough to me to take a life.

It was like the unloaded guns I used when I committed the armed robberies years ago. Delilah probably will never know just how close she came to losing her life in that alley.

I could rationalize a lot of things I had done in my life. But killing Delilah was not one of them. Even though I had strayed from the path of my grandparents, mother and father, deep down inside, I was still my grandmother's little boy. I knew right from wrong, and I knew to pass on committing murder.

I called Barbie, her roommate, gave her my telephone number and asked her to have Delilah call me. Barbie said she hadn't heard from her and didn't know when Delilah would call. Delilah called me sounding nervous and asked me what I wanted. She accused me of stealing her car and said she was going to call the police. I said we needed to talk. Delilah got nasty and said she wanted her car back. Then she hung up the phone.

About an hour or so passed and she called me back. She kept saying I had stolen her car. I kept denying it. I said I didn't even know how to drive a car with a stick shift. It was obvious to me that she had a three-way call going with the Secret Service, in hopes of recording me. If I admitted that I stole her car, I would have been arrested for tampering with a witness. She hung up the phone when it appeared that I wasn't going to fall into her little trap.

Later that night, I called her roommate, Barbie, who told me that Delilah flew back home to Iowa, because I found her, and she was scared. The next morning I called Delilah in Iowa. After several rings, she picked up the phone. I quickly asked her why she was trying to destroy me.

Delilah was real nasty on the phone. She said that she hadn't done anything to me, and that I shouldn't call her anymore. I kept calling just to mess with her. Delilah was a cooperating witness in a federal case against me, but I was angry, hurt by a woman I loved and not thinking straight. The last time I called her back, she told me she was on the phone with Suzie Simpleton. Then she said in a soft voice, "I'll be seeing you real soon." She said it in an evil way. I had no idea at the time who Suzie Simpleton was.

The next day Mr. McQueen called me and instructed me to meet with a probation officer, Suzie Simpleton, who would develop a Pre-Sentence Investigation (PSI) report for the judge. In federal court, the PSI carries a lot of weight. Mr. McQueen told me that I had to go to the federal building and meet Suzie Simpleton.

Ms. Simpleton was an average-looking white woman. She was a probation officer who learned and performed her job by the book, verbatim. Ms. Simpleton was the type of person whose self-image was, in part, derived from her perception that she was better than the people whose PSI reports she was writing.

It was apparent that Ms. Simpleton already had her mind made up about me before I walked into her office. She had already interviewed most of the other people on the case, including Delilah. She was looking at me like I was a slick, smooth-talking "nigger." She asked me all about the credit card case, and especially how I felt about Delilah. She was definitely fishing for information. I knew Delilah had probably told her that she suspected me of stealing her car. Ms. Simpleton was searching for any morsel of information she could feed to the prosecutor. She wanted to know why I wasn't cooperating with the Secret Service and federal government. The fact that I wasn't cooperating with the government agitated her significantly.

I guess she was disturbed that the government couldn't turn me into a rat, begging and pleading for my freedom like everyone else.

When I said I was sorry for what happened, she would say, "If you're so sorry, why aren't you cooperating with the Secret Service and the prosecutor?" I told Suzie Simpleton that I respected myself, my family and my friends too much to implicate them in a crime. I also said that if you do something as a group and one person gets caught, you need to take responsibility for your own actions. Ms. Simpleton looked at me like I was completely out of my mind.

Ms. Simpleton had to inspect my apartment and see how I was living, as a part of the PSI report. For Ms. Simpleton to see me living like a prince downtown—across the street from the Drake hotel and the John Hancock Center, right in the middle of the Magnificent Mile—would drive her crazy.

When she arrived, there was another woman with her, probably another probation officer. After they came in, I offered them some juice or coffee. I had on a black silk robe, and Count Basie provided the background ambience. Their mouths hung open, because the apartment was so nice. They were looking out of the big windows like children who had never seen a beautiful view before.

When she left, I could see that the whole scene had deeply disturbed her. She would later write in her PSI report that my apartment provided a view of the lake and the city through one entire glass wall. She questioned how I was able to live and maintain rent in one of the highest rent districts in Chicago. Her cause became personal. Ms. Simpleton cast me in the worst possible light she could for the judge.

The next morning, Mr. McQueen called and asked me point-blank if I had stolen Delilah's car.

"No."

He said, "Are you sure?"

"As sure as you are, that you didn't steal it."

"Delilah told the prosecutor that you stole her car and are threatening her. Tomorrow there will be a special hearing to revoke your bond. Meet me in my office at two P.M. to go over everything before the hearing."

The next day in his office, I again explained that I hadn't threatened her, and that I didn't steal her car. I was telling the truth, even though I had some knowledge about who had stolen her car: my old prison buddy, Sampson.

After our meeting, Mr. McQueen and I went into court confident that the prosecutor couldn't present a successful case to have my bond revoked and return me to the MCC. When we walked into the courtroom, I saw Delilah in action for the first time. The woman who had told me that she loved me, who had held my children in her arms, was sitting with Secret Service agents, the prosecutor, Suzie Simpleton, her parents, and her roommate, Barbie.

Delilah took the stand, crying, sobbing, "He has stolen my car, and said I don't deserve to live." She went on to say I said, "You haven't seen evil until you see what I'm going to do to you."

Mr. McQueen gave me a reassuring look. We leaned our heads together, and he told me that I had to buy drinks when we walked out of court that afternoon.

Mr. McQueen asked Delilah under cross-examination if I had ever driven her car, and she said "No." McQueen then established that I didn't even know how to drive a stick. He finally asked if she knew who took her car, and she said "No." Barbie took the stand and said I was an all-around bad guy.

In the closing argument, Mr. McQueen said that I hadn't violated any of the conditions of my bond, and that Delilah and I were former boyfriend and girlfriend. He further argued that the judge should order us not to speak. Mr. McQueen concluded by saying that the court should get back to the business of sentencing the defendants, and close the case.

The judge looked down at me after he listened to both sides. With his customary polite demeanor, he said that I posed a risk to the safety and well-being of that crying white girl. Most people who get out of prison stay out less than a year before they return. I had lasted almost five. "I remand you to the custody of the United States Marshals."

Delilah looked me in the eyes and had a big smile on her face.

On April 26, 1991, my bond was revoked, and I was transported to the MCC. It was a real mess. I had no time to get ready to go to prison. I had expected to surrender myself at sentencing, which would have been in three months. But just like that, I was hauled into prison. I had left my TV on and a steak out to thaw. I went to the MCC a very angry man—angry at Flex, Delilah, the judge, the prosecutor, everyone but myself.

CHAPTER 28

Muslims and Mafia

While still in shock at being back in the MCC, I was greeted by Wilson, an older brother about forty-two years old, who used to deliver drugs for Sonia. She was one of the few women I knew in *the game*. I had often wondered what had happened to her. Wilson said he and Sonia were busted on a 600-kilo conspiracy.

He explained to me that Sonia had gone to trial and lost. They hit her hard; she received twenty-five years. She was on the women's floor below us. He led me to his cell, took his lock off his locker, and banged it on the floor a couple of times. Somebody knocked twice from the floor below. He stood on his desk, and said to a woman through the vent, "Go get Sonia."

That was how guys talked to girls down on the women's floor. The vents were the next best thing to phones. I stood on the desk waiting and five minutes later, I heard Sonia's voice clear as a bell. "What's up?"

"Hey Sonia, do you know who this is?"

"No."

"This is Victor."

"Oh my God, oh my God, what are you doing here?" I told her about my case and that I was proud of her for standing strong, and not cooperating and becoming an informant. Sonia and I had always talked about how much we hated informants.

As I walked away from the vent, I realized that when you're in *the game*, if you don't get killed, sooner or later you go to prison. Sonia had just given birth to a baby girl. Her baby wouldn't get to see her mother outside of a cage until she was a grown woman herself.

The next morning an officer came to my room and woke me up. All the inmates had jobs and I was assigned to cleaning detail. She told me I had to clean the officers' bathroom. After dressing in my uniform—a blue jumpsuit—I walked down to the officer's desk. I

approached the officer, with the other inmates watching and listening. "Look, I just got locked up and dragged here, I am fighting the
government, and paying my lawyer to do the same. There is no way
that I'm going to clean the officers' toilet."

The officer said, "You have to. Everybody has to work. If you don't
you're going to go to the hole, and I'll have to give the lieutenant a call."

"As a matter of fact, you can call the president of the United States.
But be clear, because after you get through talking, I'm still not cleaning a damn thing."

The officer got somebody else to do the work. I guess she didn't
feel like completing the paperwork to send me to the hole. The guys
were laughing as I walked away. Whatever the reason, I got respect.

The MCC wasn't the best jail in the world, but it was a hell of a lot
better than Cook County jail. You could eat the food. It was fairly
clean. There were enough TVs and telephones that using them was
not a privilege. The unit was divided into four decks, each with about
seventy men. It had an upstairs and a downstairs, with Ping-Pong and
pool tables.

The MCC separated the inmates by race. The white guys were in
one section, the brothers in another, and the Spanish in another.
Blacks were the most represented; we took up two sections. I made
friends quickly. The Spanish thought I was Spanish. They would
come up to me speaking their language and soon I met every Spanish
brother on the deck. We developed a mutual respect. I also met a lot
of white guys. Some had big drug or embezzlement cases. Most of the
brothers were El Rukins and Disciples, there from the last time I had
been locked up. Rocky Infelice, the head of the Chicago mob was
there, along with Harry Aleman, a reputed Mafia hit man.

I met many of the El Rukins, too. I was familiar with Jeff Fort, their
leader. He had been tried and convicted for conspiring to commit ter-
rorist acts while he was in prison. Many of the El Rukins were of the
Muslim faith, and were serious brothers. You didn't want to mess
with them. I had a reputation as a player. I had little to fear in prison;
I was welcomed and well-received. Prisons, for all their horrors, can
also be safe havens for those who have been true to *the game*.

One brother, whose nickname was Big, was especially nice to me.
He was about five-five, but had a deep Barry White-like voice. We
spent many hours picking each other's brain about almost anything.

He was a top general for the El Rukins and reported directly to Jeff Fort. He invited me to join them for Juma prayer. Big also gave me a Koran. I received his gift as an honor, and I began learning about the Muslim faith.

Many brothers in prison are searching for something spiritual and often turn to Islam. I was no different. The truth of the matter is that there isn't much difference between Islam and Christianity. The basic fundamental difference is that Muslims believe that Muhammad is the last prophet. I was attracted to the discipline of Islam in terms of praying five times a day and fasting for thirty days for the holy month of Juma. I never abandoned the teachings of my grandmother. Strange as it may seem, I prayed as a Muslim and as a Christian. The main thing was that I continued to pray.

The only people I couldn't get close to were the Mafia members. They all had cells next to each other in the back of the housing unit. There were about ten of them in my unit. I wanted to get to know them, and I considered that my personal challenge. In the early days of my criminal activities, most of what I had learned about crime came from gangster movies and reading about the Mafia. It was a great opportunity to meet and rub elbows with real live Mafia members, people who were born and bred in a life of crime.

The Mafia case was the biggest thing in Chicago at the time. They were on the six o'clock news every night. They would sit in the unit together, watching themselves on TV. They were always cooking. They often had something smuggled up from the kitchen to make pasta dishes, just like you see in the movies. We would be eating hamburgers, and the mafiosi had steak.

Even though I patterned my criminal activity like the Mafia, I knew they had little use for black people. Historically, the Mafia only used black people to further their business interests. It's interesting that they don't like black people, since many have a portion of black in them. The African influence in Italy is well documented. Many white women like Italians because of their dark skin and wavy hair, which is, in part, a result of their African genes. Sicily is the sacred birthplace of many Mafia members, which is separated from Africa only by the Mediterranean Sea. Some Italians are even darker than me. What's even more interesting is that many Italians, as well as past popes, have worshiped at the shrine of the Black Madonna and her black child.

The prisoner management team in our unit found out that the Italians were smuggling food into their cells and decided they were living too well. The team decided to split up the Italians and put them in cells with blacks. I didn't have a cellmate and was watching TV when Harry Aleman, the alleged Mafia hit man I had seen on TV every day for three months, walked into my cell. Until then, he had walked by me without as much as a hello.

A small man, about five-six and very thin, he was clean-shaven and a perfect gentleman. He told me he was my new cellmate, shook my hand, and proceeded to move all of his stuff into the cell. He had a lot of stuff, especially food. He opened his locker and said, "If there's anything you need or want, don't ask, just take it." It was a classy move, and I extended the same courtesy. I immediately noticed how neat and organized he was.

We quickly became comfortable living together as cellmates. He had a habit of getting up around 3:00 A.M. to eat chocolate chip cookies. I joked that he looked like a giant mouse, sneaking a meal. Eventually we became friends. I would keep Harry up late at night asking questions about his life, and his thoughts on different lawyers and prisons. He was impressed with my knowledge of the Mafia, of Lucky Luciano and Al Capone. I did my almost perfect imitation of Don Corleone from *The Godfather* for him one night and he laughed hard. He liked it so much, he asked me to do it for Rocky Infelice, the head of the entire Chicago Mafia.

Infelice was an older man in his sixties, who stood six-two and weighed 230. To me, he was huge, not only in size, but in stature as well. I wasn't sure how he was going to react. Harry assured me that Rocky would get a kick out of my Godfather impression.

The next night, there were about six or seven Italian men in Rocky's cell, eating pasta and chicken. Harry left our cell to join them. Before he departed, he told me to come down when I got a chance. After an hour or so, I ventured to Rocky's cell. I could smell the food and hear the laughter as I approached. When I opened the cell door, everyone but Harry had a surprised look on their face. I walked right into the cell and said, "Excuse me," using Marlon Brando's voice in *The Godfather*. But, my "Excuse me," sounded more like, " 'Scuse me."

I walked over to Rocky Infelice and shook his hand and said, "One day I will call upon you to do me a favor, but until that day, consider this a token of my good will." I continued to talk like the Godfather, and I told them about Harry getting up in the middle of the night to eat cookies, and ended by saying, "What am I going to do with this guy?"

Everyone in the cell was cracking up with laughter. They loved it, especially Rocky. He almost choked on his food, laughing. Rocky told one of the guys, "Fix him a plate." As we ate, Harry introduced me to everyone. After that night, I was on speaking terms with the Chicago mafiosi.

In the MCC, we could only have two visitors a week, but because Earl is an attorney, he could visit me as often as he liked, which was almost daily. He began coming to see me after work and even on some days during work, if he had to be out of the office or in court. He also came to all my court dates. He would be there every time I came into the courtroom, sitting there quietly, supporting me, giving me his energy. The last time I was in prison, my parents said they would never sit through court with me again. They made good on their promise. It really meant a lot to see Earl out there. Court can be a lonely place; I appreciated his constant support.

Earl and I spent hours talking in the attorneys' visiting room. He is a really good listener. He suggested that I begin to change some of my habits. My nerves were bad and to calm them I began smoking a lot and eating junk food. I had gained weight. He recommended that I give up eating red meat, pork, and junk food. He also suggested that I drink eight glasses of water a day to keep my body cleansed during my incarceration. I listened intently, but I wasn't ready to make that kind of positive change in my life.

Sonia had begun sending me love letters saying she had always loved me. Because I was married at the time, she had kept it a secret. She also told me she had breast enhancement surgery. Her letters were a welcomed distraction from day-to-day life in the MCC.

I found out from another inmate that a lawyer could call two inmates down to the visiting room at the same time. I asked Earl to call Sonia down to the visiting room the next time he came to see me. I contacted her through the vent and told her that I was going to hug her in twenty-four hours. She just laughed and said, "I wish." I told her to be ready at noon.

The next day, Earl arrived slightly before noon and went through the process for getting two inmates together in the attorneys' visiting room. I arrived at the visiting room first. Five minutes later, Sonia arrived, a confused look on her face. That look quickly turned into a smile. Sonia was shocked. She also looked fantastic: long brown black hair, a perfect behind, and now she had big breasts. She had full lips, big brown eyes, and pretty white teeth. I gave her a big hug and kiss. I introduced her to Earl and they shook hands. We talked and got caught up in that visiting room for what seemed like days, but was only about an hour. That was the last time I would see her. She was shipped off to a women's prison a week later.

I began to adjust to life in jail. In late-night conversations, Harry told me he respected the stand I took on my case. He believed the people who told on me were rats, and respected my character and integrity for not becoming an informant.

The criminal in the 1990s, he warned me, was a new breed—one who would tell on his mother, or mothers who would tell on their children. Harry told me that the gangsters I read about lived before I was born. "If you don't change the direction your life is going in, you'll die in prison," he explained, "like many of my partners will," he finished somberly.

Hearing those words from Harry Aleman, alleged Mafia hit man, planted the first seeds in my mind to give up my life of crime. I couldn't accept what he said from anyone else, but here was a real live gangster saying it. It hit home. Harry said, "There's only one mob in this country, and that's the United States government!"

CHAPTER 29

The Car Chase

I finally received my PSI report in the mail. I was expecting to get around forty-one months. When Suzie Simpleton finished calculating how much time she thought I should serve, I was looking at a sentence of almost eight years. She tried to suggest that I serve extra time for the car chase case I was involved in a few years before.

Now, let me give you some perspective on the car chase that Ms. Simpleton wanted to enhance my sentence with. My sister flew into town to see me. That evening, I needed to meet with one of my friends, Jack Marshall, regarding his drug business. He was a young white guy in his twenties who was a low-level drug dealer. I drove out to Buffalo Grove, a predominately white northwest suburb of Chicago. Over dinner, we discussed expanding his business. After that, I headed back to the city. I was going to hang out with my sister that evening and show her a night out on the town. It was about 9:00 P.M. when I left to return to the city. I was driving on the main road, about to get on the expressway. While stopped at a traffic light, out of nowhere, a police car pulled up beside me.

As I looked at the officer, he just stared back at me. It wasn't hard to figure out what that white officer was thinking. He was suspicious of seeing a young black man, wearing a baseball cap, driving a Mercedes, in a mostly white neighborhood. I knew the officer would be looking for any reason to stop me and search my car. Being stopped and questioned by the police was (and still is) an unfortunate reality for black people driving a nice car in this country.

To avoid all that drama, when the light turned green, I pulled right over into a Mobil gas station. I was hoping the police officer would keep on going. Well, as you can imagine, that cop pulled in right behind me and cut on his flashing lights.

Buffalo Grove was the same town where I had been busted for the armed robbery ring. I knew all the officers remembered me out there, and all I needed was for some nosy detective to see me down at the police station, then learn I was living at Harbor Point and driving a Mercedes.

As the officer approached, I was thinking about all my possible options. The officer tapped on my window; I looked to see if traffic was clear. I had never cut off my engine, so I just put my car in drive and drove off. The officer's eyes got big, like he was shocked that I was pulling away.

I drove out into the busy street and began speeding toward the expressway. It was a two-way street, with two lanes going in one direction, and two lanes going in the opposite direction. There were cars in front of me, and I had the officer behind me in hot pursuit. I drove between two cars to stay ahead of him, almost causing an accident.

The expressway was in my sight, as I hit the entering ramp. I kept wishing that I was driving my Corvette. In my 'Vette, that cop wouldn't have stood a chance chasing me down the street speeding and switching from lane to lane. However, in the Mercedes, the officer was able to stay fairly close. Once I got on the expressway, I thought the Buffalo Grove police officer would stop pursuing me, because I was out of his jurisdiction. Wrong!

An officer in hot pursuit could follow you anywhere. I could see his flashing lights behind me. As I weaved in and out of expressway traffic, reaching speeds over 100 miles per hour, I cut off my headlights. I was making every effort to fade out of his view.

I assumed that he had already called ahead to the Illinois State Police. I thought there might be a roadblock somewhere down the line. So I decided it would be best to get off at the next exit, and try to lose him in the suburb of Palatine. Since I had a nice lead on him, I felt I could make some quick turns and lose him. But as I got off the ramp and onto Palatine Road, I saw what looked like a huge Christmas tree all lit up, coming toward me. There had to be at least ten police cars approaching.

Initially, I was only trying to get away from one cop. Now, I had three different police departments chasing me. I was driving through red lights and stop signs, and doing everything I could to get away.

The police had called my license plate number into the police sta-

tion. The car was registered in Eve's name. They used that information to track down our apartment telephone number, and called her
at Harbor Point. The police asked Eve if her car had been stolen, and if
her husband was black. Eve hung up the phone on them. She knew
better than to just divulge information to law enforcement.

She then called me on the car phone. I pushed the hand's-free button and talked while I was driving. Eve was frantic. She asked me why
the police had called her. I told her that they were chasing me right now,
and I hung up. Naturally, I thought the worst: that once they caught
me, they might try to kill my black ass. From then on, I was really determined to get away, because I believed my life depended on it.

I drove down what appeared to be a side street, but was actually an
apartment complex with only one way out.

When I realized that I had no way out, I jumped out of my car and
tried to escape on foot. To my horror, all those town houses were connected. There was no way for me to run between them and get away. The
police cars were filing into the apartment complex. There were over forty
cars from all the police departments. They were cursing and hunting
intensely for me. I was hiding in front of a house, behind a Christmas
tree. It was cold as hell, about fifteen degrees above zero. After the police
searched for about an hour, they abandoned the scene, one by one . . . all
except the officer who started the chase in the first place.

He was out front writing his police report, and waiting for a tow
truck to take my Mercedes to the police pound. I was freezing and had
been outside for over two hours in nothing but a leather jacket. I figured that I would make a move when the officer left. I would go to a
pay phone and call somebody to pick me up.

I guess the man who owned the house was out in front of his
house talking to the officer. When he walked back into his house, as
luck would have it, the man walked up the sidewalk leading to his
front door, instead of going through his garage. He immediately
noticed me hiding behind the Christmas tree on his front porch. I
looked that man in the face as if to say, "Please be cool." But that
white man was gone in a flash; and that cop was there in a blink of an
eye, with that ugly gun pointing at my head.

The police officer yelled for me to get facedown on the cold concrete.
I knew the police officer was alone and probably scared, in spite of his

brave-looking face. If I made one false move, I would be shot full of holes that night. So I calmly lay facedown on the cold sidewalk, and put my right hand behind my back so the officer could handcuff me.

I had really underestimated the extent and the degree to which Ms. Simpleton was out to get me. I felt sick inside after I read the PSI report. I called Mr. McQueen at his law office and he tried to calm me down. He told me that we would fight the PSI report in court.

CHAPTER 30

Sentencing

Jail was taking its toll on me. I used to smoke cigarettes occasionally if I was out drinking with friends. Now I was smoking over a carton a week. I was twenty pounds overweight, and had fallen into a deep funk. Eve rarely brought the children to see me and filed for divorce.

A bright spot came when my mother and sister flew in to see me and brought my daughters with them. But after their visit I received awful news: Mr. McQueen had contacted the State of Illinois to get a record of my armed robbery convictions and discovered an inquiry from the Bureau of Alcohol, Tobacco, and Firearms (ATF). He said that there was a rumor of another indictment coming down from the federal government. The sky was falling down on me; my world was coming apart. Because I had over three violent criminal offenses, I was a prime candidate to receive a fifteen-year minimum sentence. Every day I had a sick feeling in my stomach.

To maintain a sense of balance, I continued to read the Koran and the Bible. God sent me an angel on earth; Earl watched over me. He came to see me almost every day. He always talked positively about life and my future. I couldn't see anything good in my future. My life seemed to have ended. The further I fell into depression, the harder Earl would impress upon me that there was a light at the end of the tunnel.

Earl took advantage of my being in prison. With patience and persistence, he began talking to me about becoming a spiritual person. He never forced any of his beliefs on me, but he patiently waited until I was receptive to hear him. Earl believed in a higher spirit and an energy force that binds us all together. He wasn't much for conventional religious practices, such as going to church every Sunday. Then he would explain his philosophies in life, and teach me African and world history. I listened intently, but I was still much too angry and bitter to think seriously, let alone embrace, any of Earl's views on life.

I was lonely and scared to death that I might get a life sentence. I continued to abuse my body by eating everything I was served in the chow hall. At night, I would sit up and think about killing people involved with the credit card case, especially Delilah. One night, as I lay sleeping in the cage that I was calling my home, I heard my grandmother talking to me through a dream. Looking down at me with her beautiful face, my grandmother's soft voice said, "Tinky, you can make it. You can make it. Victor, I love you and believe in you." I also saw my grandfather's face beside my grandmother's, as if for reinforcement. When I woke up, I knew I couldn't give up, and I had to get hold of myself.

Slowly, I began to change my habits. I stopped smoking, and cut back on eating so much food. I started thinking about what Earl said and began seriously considering my future. My thoughts turned to surviving the prison experience.

If I had to be locked up for six years, or worse, fifteen, I would have to do it and be strong. Many were happy to see me in prison and expected me to die, or at least come out with a broken spirit and a destroyed soul. I became determined to survive whatever came my way, so I could one day face my enemies.

Once Earl saw that I was trying to move in a positive direction with my health and mental state, he was quick to help me along. I wasn't ready to give up meat yet, but I did give up pork and began drinking eight glasses of water a day. I became even more drawn into Islam. It is a beautiful religion, and I drew strength from Allah, which became an extension of the Christian faith my grandmother passed on to me.

Eight hard and emotionally charged months had passed in the MCC. The big day arrived. It was time for me to be sentenced. On the day that I was sentenced, only Big Duke and Earl were present. No one from my family was there. I was hurt. Much of my demise was due to the fact that I had refused to cooperate with the prosecution in an effort to shield a member of my own family from a fate similar to mine. Now, on the day of my sentencing, I hadn't received so much as a thank you from my aunt or cousin.

The fact of the matter was that I was perceived as the villain, especially in my own family. I was the sacrificial lamb. My life was deemed expendable. My parents never took a stand on my behalf. They addressed that situation by saying it was entirely my fault. The fact that all of my friends, and even a family member, informed on me, just came with the territory as far as they were concerned. I understood my family's disposition: My cousin was earmarked for law school; and I, the family outcast, was headed back to prison. In their eyes, his life was still worth saving. However, I was left alone to hang in the balance.

To this day, my parents have never confronted my aunt, uncle, or cousin about their cooperation with the federal government against their own son. I assure you that if the circumstances had been reversed, my aunt and uncle, the good judge and doctor respectively, would have confronted my parents if I had told on their son, and he was on *his* way to prison. As it was, my aunt had the nerve to tell my mother how disgusted she was with me for involving her child in my criminal life.

The reality, of course, was that her son was a thief long before I approached him with free credit cards. I would later learn that my cousin was conspicuously purchasing all kinds of things from department stores in Detroit with the credit cards I gave him. He was also actively recruiting other people to join in on the free shopping spree that was afforded him.

My guess was that my aunt and uncle were unable to deal with the truth about their son. That, in spite of their social and economic status, as well as their professional degrees, they had failed to raise an honest, law-abiding son with good morals and values. Theirs was the real-life Cosby family. But now, however, their blanket of righteous indignation had been pulled off and exposed the skeletons in their closet. That's why it was easier to blame me for what had happened to their son, as opposed to dealing with their own personal family issues.

What my parents never really understood, was that to not stand up for their son was in essence standing up for their nephew. My aunt and uncle rallied behind their son when he needed them most. I may not have been a perfect son, but I still needed the kind of support my cousin received from his family. Close to a decade in prison was ahead of me, and my cousin helped the prosecution seal my fate. How my parents could just sit by, and still associate with my aunt and uncle, is still beyond me. If the situation had been reversed, I assure you, my aunt would not have hesitated to sever their sisterly relationship.

My parents and I have been engaged in an ongoing war for most of my life. I understand that, for whatever reason, this is how we deal with one another. Through the battles, the ugly words, and periods of not talking, I have never stopped loving them. I don't think I will ever quite comprehend the stand they have taken with regard to my aunt, uncle and cousin. But I will always love them. They are the only parents I have.

I believe the stance I took was a righteous one. I was faced with cashing in the lives of people that I loved and cared for in exchange for my freedom. I chose to sacrifice my freedom, not to mention leaving my two daughters in the world without a father to care for and protect them. I wonder if my cousin ever considered that fact in his zeal to liberate himself. People have been informing on each other dating as far back as the days when Jesus Christ walked the earth. I'm sure that each person, then and now, romanticized and philosophized why they became informants. Nevertheless, I was crystal clear that informing on people in an effort to escape the ramifications of my own behavior and actions was unacceptable.

I walked out into the courtroom escorted by two bailiffs. I saw Earl sitting right up front, and I drew strength from my brother and my friend. On that day, Earl took the place of my mother, father, sisters, ex-wife, and children, all balled up into one. I am a very proud man, and I am reluctant to admit I need anybody for anything, but on the day of my sentencing, I needed my best friend, and Earl was there. He was there as he was when I needed him in the past. I will always be grateful for his love and friendship, displayed during all those prison days, and especially that day, when I needed him most.

During sentencing, the defendant is allowed to make a statement. Mr. McQueen wanted me to make a brief statement to the judge, basically, "I'm sorry, I'll never do it again." I told Mr. McQueen I would do as he asked.

However, after I watched the judicial process turn from justice to "just me," I was determined to give the judge, the Secret Service, and the probation department a piece of my mind. The judge asked me if I had anything to say. I was so anxious to finally speak, I just said, "Yes, I certainly do."

Mr. McQueen stepped to the side, and I took the podium as though

I were a lawyer myself. Mr. McQueen gave me a stern look like, "Don't you start talking." But, at that point, I didn't give a damn.

"The credit card case was never about justice," I began. "It was about who could tell the most on people the quickest. Since I decided to exercise my constitutional right to remain silent, I was facing prison while everybody else on the case who informed would receive probation and stay out of jail. I am the only one who accepted responsibility for their actions on the case." I walked around the front of the courtroom. I even motioned with my hand toward Suzie Simpleton, and reiterated what I told her: I had no ill will toward Delilah. I spoke to the Secret Service agents, and said I knew that they and Delilah had tried to further involve me in criminal activity. Moreover, I informed them I knew it was their intention to lock me up for the rest of my life and had conspired to see that it happened.

I praised God in the courtroom. I also thanked Mr. McQueen for his excellent representation, even though the cards were stacked against him. There was a deafening silence in the courtroom.

I carried on for about fifteen minutes without a prepared statement. When I finished speaking, the judge said, "As I sit here, and I listen to the articulate way you can speak, the sincere tone in your voice . . . your ability to be persuasive is somewhat frightening, when it's turned toward criminal ends. I sentence you to the custody of the Federal Bureau of Prisons to serve seventy-eight months." The Secret Service agents had happy faces. Suzie Simpleton looked proud. Josh Buchman also joined them, like they were a football team celebrating after scoring a touchdown.

Earl's face was the picture of strength and friendship. Prison time wasn't the gift that I had planned to give him on his twenty-eighth birthday. As the bailiff led me out of the courtroom, I looked back at the man in charge of my case for the Secret Service, Lee Seville. He and his soldiers wore weary but smug looks on their war-torn faces. For them the war was over, at least where I was concerned. The fight had just begun for me.

Aboard the van that transported inmates, I rode in silence, trying to come to grips with the fact that I wouldn't be free again until 1996. Silently, I wondered what my future held. The most painful thought was that I wouldn't see my daughters grow up during their early years. It was almost too much to bear.

Back at the MCC, I could not complain about my six and a half years. Harry Aleman had moved back to his cell with his Mafia friends, who were all probably going to receive life sentences. My new cellmate was accused of killing a federal informant. He had a life sentence and was playing cards as if nothing had happened. He was a player.

I played *the game*. I had to deal with the good and the bad. That was what *the game* taught me. I had enjoyed everything good that *the game* had to offer: women, clothes, cars and money, in abundance. I now had to pay for all of that splendor. I understood *the game,* and accepted its consequences.

CHAPTER 31

Oxford Maximum Security Prison

It was about a four-hour ride to the Maximum Security Federal Prison in Oxford, Wisconsin. On the bus, shackled and chained, I tried to prepare myself for prison life. Although I had been in before, I was mindful of the unexpected things that could go wrong. The prison sat in the middle of nowhere. It was built in dense woods, surrounded by two parallel twenty-foot fences of barbed wire, and another razor-wire fence sandwiched between the two. There were four watchtowers strategically situated in each corner of the prison grounds. Each tower was manned by a guard toting a shotgun.

My cellmate, Scottie, was doing fifteen years for drug conspiracy. A blue bandanna hung on his shelf. Blue is the color of the Gangster Disciples. "Are you a Disciple?" I asked him and when he said yes, I reached out and shook his hand as only another member could.

The next morning, during orientation, what I saw amazed me. The prison grounds looked more like a college campus than a prison. There were four tennis courts, a gym and track, soccer and softball fields, and plenty of basketball courts inside the gym and outside, a hobby shop and a pool room. Oxford had a good library and a school that offered college courses.

Scottie introduced me to other Disciples. The organization was changing. Mr. Hoover had moved to growth and development, stressing education, and sociopolitical awareness. I still had never met him, but had come to admire him and respect his words of peace.

Mr. Hoover's agenda was to push members to graduate from high school, as well as college—to use education as a tool for legitimate business activity, political involvement and empowerment. Unfortunately, the majority of the Disciples I had met in state and federal prison were more interested in selling drugs and fighting Vice Lords, Bloods and other gangs.

I was determined to survive. Gang politics and fighting other gang members was beneath me, no longer on my agenda. Although I showed all Gangster Disciple members respect, my only job was to ensure my safety.

In the state prison system, the gangs ran the prison. In the federal system, the guards and staff ran the prison. People from all over the country, and for that matter, the world, were locked up in the federal system. If one gang got a stronghold in a facility, its members would be sent from state to state and prison to prison, a practice the federal government called "diesel therapy."

I met all kinds of people in Oxford, and went about working the prison, trying to meet everyone, as if I were running for political office. I met East Indians, Italians, Cubans, white and black. Native Americans came to federal prison from reservations, created after the government stole their land. Any crime committed on a reservation is a federal offense. About 100 Native American inmates were in Oxford's prison population. Oxford provided them with a sweat lodge as part of their religious program. I asked all kinds of questions about their heritage and their life and learned they are a proud people. I also met Cubans who had left Cuba because of Castro. I asked them questions, too. I used my federal prison experience to learn as much as I could about other people and their cultures.

I also started lifting weights to get into shape.

Many in federal prison have cooperated with the government, in one way or another, to lessen their sentences. Some prisoners even continued to do so while incarcerated. Stool pigeons and rats were despised by players. I was treated with the highest respect in prison from anybody else who was in *the game,* because I chose not to sell out my family, my friends, and my soul to the government.

Most prisoners were locked up for drug-related charges. Fellow inmates were fascinated that I had imprinted Visa Gold credit cards, and successfully used them. My social status made my way easier and I used it to meet fascinating, intelligent characters: a dentist who ran a multimillion-dollar drug ring; a Puerto Rican freedom fighter who had been locked up for fifteen years for bombing a police station in Chicago; Noah Robinson, Jesse Jackson's half brother, a multimillion-aire, found guilty on conspiracy charges ranging from murder-for-hire to aiding and abetting the El Rukins, and attempting to legitimize their lucrative drug business. He vehemently denied all the charges against him. From what I knew about Noah, he was a brilliant man, much like his half brother, the two-time presidential candidate, Reverend Jesse L. Jackson. Prior to Noah's sentence to prison, he owned several Wendy's restaurants and other businesses in Chicago.

Noah carried himself with dignity and class. We became friends and he often shared advice, and expressed the need for me to reach my potential. He treated me like a little brother. Noah also had a life sentence.

I was most impressed with the fact that he was working on his appeal, completely without the assistance of legal counsel. He had so much legal work stacked up, there was no room in his cell for a cellmate. I watched Noah work day and night on his appeal, as he fought and struggled to get back to his family.

One of the wiser, more intelligent brothers that I met in Oxford was Mr. Dixon. I called him Dix. Although he had been down fifteen years, he was in tremendous physical shape and a good-looking brother. But more importantly, he was in better mental condition. After fifteen years, Dix hadn't missed a beat. If you talked to him, you wouldn't know that he had been locked up that long. Most people who have done that much time show signs of mental collapse.

I hung around Dix and asked him a lot of questions about how he survived fifteen years in prison. I figured if Dix could survive all those years and look the way he did, then I could follow his example and surely survive my six and a half years. He was careful about what he ate, and stayed away from the drugs and alcohol that were readily available in prison. I learned a lot from Dix. He became a mentor for me.

The most interesting brother I met in Oxford was a guy named Joseph Blair, nicknamed Big Money, who was about forty years old, six-six, and weighed about 250 pounds. He knew Mike Tyson, Muhammad Ali, Naomi Campbell, Michael Jordan, and Magic Johnson, and showed me pictures of himself with Steve Wyn, the owner of the Mirage hotel in Las Vegas, eating dinner with Muhammad Ali at the house of The Greatest's mother in Chicago, and lounging with Tina Marie.

One weekend, my parents were visiting me, at the same time Money's mother was visiting him. We sat at a table together and talked. His mother told my parents how, one weekend, Money flew her to Las Vegas to meet Diana Ross. Money took her to Caesar's Palace to see the diva perform. During the show, Diana Ross walked to their table and sang to Money. After the show, Money took his mother backstage, and they all went to dinner. Big Money said the day he met Diana Ross, she stumbled when they met, because he looked so good.

In federal prison, everybody had to work. Money and I were both sent to the kitchen for our first prison jobs. We both hated it. To pass the time away, we both began doing destructive things. We spent our time trying to outdo each other's pranks. If he flooded the bathroom, I would set a fire. If they assigned us to clean and we had to use the vacuum, we would cut the cord. You name it, we did it.

There was an occasion when some big shots from the federal government were scheduled to tour Oxford with the warden. Money and I had decided that we were going to put a dead rat in the soup. We knew that would cause a disturbance in the chow hall during the official visit. When the day arrived, we had our rats in hand as the soup preparation began. After several pots were ready for the meat phase of the recipe, we reluctantly decided against the rats. We didn't want our fellow inmates to have to eat that mess.

CHAPTER 32

Sex, Alcohol, Depression and Prison Profits

The average sentence in Oxford was fifteen to twenty years, and there was a lot of tension, especially from guys with life sentences. Inmates were always fighting, and getting stabbed over nothing. Occasionally someone was killed. There were a lot of homosexuals. Many were in the closet, but many more were out of the closet and actively seeking partners.

There was one Cuban homosexual named Jorge—who went by the name Diana—who even had breasts. He could often be seen holding hands and kissing his man. I had seen that before. It was nothing new, just part of what some guys do in prison. I don't care how feminine a guy acts—a hairy behind, a penis, and a pair of testicles don't turn me on. Many guys with long sentences get weak. The saying was, "There ain't no joy like a big butt boy." Same-sex activity is a matter of convenience.

One of the more creative aspects of prison life was a drink called "hooch." It is an alcoholic drink whose making would put Ernest and Julio Gallo to shame. Hooch was made with fruit and sugar. Some inmates would bury hooch in containers underground to allow it to age and then sell it for a profit. Some guys were drunk every day; they were alcoholics. And of course, inmates dealt drugs.

I was determined to keep my mind and body clear, and face being in prison clean and sober. Although I was still very angry and had a bad attitude, I didn't resort to any substances or sex to get me through. I knew the only thing I still controlled in my life was my mind. I didn't dare pollute that.

Mr. McQueen had filed an appeal on my behalf in the appellate court. I was hoping that my sentence would be cut in half. In the meantime, I continued to defy the prison administration every way I could, every step of the way.

A factory, Unicor, that made cables and other items for the military, employed at least 90 percent of the prison population. Inmates had to work from 9:00 A.M. to 5:00 P.M. five days a week. Starting pay was nineteen cents an hour. After working there for years, a lucky few made a dollar an hour, or more.

After working for such meager wages, many would then buy candy, snacks, cigarettes and gym shoes, giving the money right back to the prison commissary. Unicor sold the goods for profit. In October 1996, *60 Minutes* aired a piece on Unicor, and showed how it was putting its competitors out of business. Prisoners don't receive health insurance, profit-sharing, or a bonus for a job well done. There's no need for Unicor to export jobs to a Third World country because they have the prison population as its almost free labor force.

They should have at least paid the inmates minimum wage. Nevertheless, I had sense enough not to work in Unicor. The last thing I wanted to do was make a profit for the government.

The hundreds of prison staff at Oxford were basically poor farmers, and people who couldn't do anything else. There were only two black officers—one man and one woman. My fate lay in the hands of those redneck farmers turned prison guards, lieutenants, and captains.

One day in the chow hall, a white officer said, "As bad as it is here in prison, at least you get to eat three meals a day. I bet you didn't eat this well out there on welfare." He, and many other ignorant prison staff, believed Oxford had rescued the black inmates. I would look at the scruffy clothes the officers and prison staff wore and laugh to myself. I would have thrown away their best suits and shoes.

As a result of my attitude and behavior, I was sent at least eight times to the hole for breaking the rules.

Earl was traveling back and forth to Africa, and working a lot. He sent me postcards from Africa and he always let me know that no matter how far he traveled, his thoughts were with me. I often called him at work and at home. But it was hard to stay close, and I missed Earl's positive energy. Despite his constant reassurances, it became increasingly difficult for me to remain strong and upbeat.

Prison life was depressing and lonely. My parents were halfway across the country; I only saw them once a year. Eve and I were divorced, and she was dating. That meant I rarely saw my children. The negativity of prison life consumed me. I became depressed.

I stopped going to Juma prayer. I stopped combing my hair and started wearing a bandanna on my head all the time. I stopped shaving and grew a ragged beard. I had so many years in front of me, I couldn't see straight.

I had been there for close to two years when I finally got word from Mr. McQueen regarding my appeal. I was desperately hoping that somehow I would get lifted out of that hell called prison life. I ripped open my letter and read, "I regret to inform you that the appellate court denied your appeal." I was crushed.

The cold, hard reality set in: I would spend four more years in prison. I fell into a daze, playing basketball and lifting weights every day, while cursing Delilah, Flex, and the rest of my codefendants. I became bitter, and spent my days devising plots to exact revenge on everybody who had crossed me. Some nights, I lay awake, imagining my release and how I would avenge all those I hated. The lantern Earl tried to keep lit grew dim, as pure loathing began to fill my heart. He tried to be a beacon of light during those dark days, but I couldn't see the light at the end of the tunnel.

I missed women so much; it was almost unbearable. My only relief was to masturbate. While many brothers adopted the big-butt-boy philosophy, my theory was, what five fingers can't do, won't get done. Women in pornographic magazines became my sexual outlets. It wasn't uncommon for me to masturbate a few times a day.

Years without sexual contact with a woman took its toll on me mentally. One day walking outdoors on the prison grounds, I noticed two beetles copulating. I stopped to look with voyeuristic pleasure. I'd watched countless other inmates lose their minds. It was painfully clear to me that I was seeing signs of my own mental breakdown.

Life at Oxford became more bizarre each day. Gloria, a black homosexual in my housing unit, had smooth skin and a behind that rivaled some sisters'. He acted like a woman, and on Saturday nights, some brothers would get drunk on hooch and crowd around Gloria's cell. He would grease up with baby oil and put on a freak show, inserting shampoo bottles and other objects into his ass for the perverse pleasure of the drunks, hooting and hollering inside his cell.

Many inmates gave up and flushed down the toilet the morals and values they came to prison with. Witnessing that kind of behavior by my fellow inmates, I knew I hadn't completely lost my mind. For the same reason I refused to cooperate with the federal government, my character and integrity wouldn't allow me to forget who I was and where I came from, even in prison. Just because I was locked up like an animal, didn't mean I had to act like one.

One night after I had showered, I was in my cell with my robe on, combing my hair. Gloria walked into my cell, and dropped to his knees and said, "You're so fine. Can I please just suck your dick? You know I won't tell anybody. Nobody's gonna know."

I looked down at Gloria and said, "*I* will know. No thank you."

Gloria was always after me to have sex with him. I would smile and politely refuse. Gloria was eventually transferred for disciplinary reasons. Months later, word came from one of the federal prison hospitals back to a counselor at Oxford that Gloria had AIDS. I never saw so many long, sick faces.

Men having sex with each other is a part of prison life. Either one engages in the activity, or one does not. People on the outside think everyone who goes to prison gets raped. It happens, but usually to a young kid who doesn't know the ropes and is new to the prison system. The truth is, more than enough men in prison are willing to provide a sexual outlet for other inmates. There isn't as much a need to rape people in prison as people think. No matter how sexually frustrated I was, having sex with men was simply not an option for me.

Some brothers gambled, betting on everything from pool games to professional sports. Prison gambling debts were paid off by a family member on the outside. A money order would be sent into prison and placed on an inmate's account. That account allowed inmates to buy gym shoes, jogging suits, watches, snacks and cosmetic items from the commissary. It wasn't uncommon to hear of guys winning or losing tens of thousands of dollars, since some inmates were wealthy.

Of approximately a thousand inmates, the majority were black, then Hispanic, then white. The prison officials segregated the races. Blacks and whites were never assigned to the same cell. Whites ate on one side of the chow hall, while the blacks ate on the opposite end. Some blacks called the whites "devils," and some whites called the blacks "niggers." The Hispanics and Indians thought they were better than everyone else. One Indian almost beat a brother to death for calling him "Chief." Some of the whites were nazi's and skinheads. Many of the brothers were in the Nation of Islam. Add to the mix gang members from the Bloods and Crips from Los Angeles, and Gangster Disciples and Vice Lords from around the country, as well as the Latin and Cuban gangs. Needless to say, the racial tension was high.

The environment that I called home was like an active volcano. It always smoked, could provide a little fire from time to time, or it could erupt with a deadly riot, seeking to destroy all that stood in its way. It was never safe to relax. That could cost you your life.

While my cousin, who was involved with me in the credit card conspiracy, continued in law school, and my family and friends led normal lives, I was fighting daily to maintain a semblance of mental sanity.

My small part in the drama of prison life at Oxford was to steal all the food I could get from the kitchen, and sell or exchange it for the things I needed. I stole sugar for the brothers making hooch. I stole meat, canned goods, and pies for those with a voracious appetite.

I had the biggest collection of pornographic magazines on the compound. I bought, sold and traded in those magazines. I could get a guy a magazine with the woman of his choice: black, white, Asian, you name it, I could provide it. Because I could talk with anybody, I had access to everyone's magazines. My ability to communicate transcended race, gangs, and petty prison politics. As months slowly turned into years in that place of madness, I etched my own place in the landscape.

I often watched with envy as birds and butterflies freely flew in and out of the prison walls. Even the flies and mosquitoes had more freedom than me. Outside the cell house, two robins always flew together, as if they were protecting each other. Several days of close observation revealed their place of residence was in a tree on the side of the housing unit. When I examined the tree that the robins called home, I saw among the branches a nest that contained four eggs. I decided to check the nest each day until the eggs hatched. I had to carefully avoid the eyes of the guards in the watchtowers.

Waiting for the eggs to hatch, feeling the mounting loneliness of prison, I decided to take one of the baby birds as a pet, once they hatched. A pet was a sorely needed diversion from prison life. I spent the next few weeks watching and waiting for the eggs to hatch.

When the eggs finally hatched, the tiny birds had no feathers, and their eyes were shut. They were quite ugly. Robins grow up fast, and within a month, I took the one that I wanted from the nest, carefully placed the bird in my pocket and brought it back to my cell to a shoe box full of grass and leaves. I wanted my pet to be comfortable in its new home. Every day I would collect worms, as its mother would, and feed it. After a few months, my bird Hawk and I got along famously. He would sit on my shoulder and lay on my chest as I went to sleep at night. I kept Hawk a secret from everyone, except my closest friends, for if the prison staff found him, they would take the bird and put me in the hole.

Evidently I held Hawk too tightly as I slept one night and broke his leg. He couldn't stand up the next day. I tried to make a cast for his leg, but it didn't work. Hawk died.

I was miserably sad, thinking that if I had left the little robin alone, he would still be living. And again, I was desperately lonely.

About a month after Hawk's death, I was walking the prison grounds and noticed a small green tree frog on the leaf of a flower. I almost couldn't see the frog because its color blended so well with the flower. I caught the frog, brought him to my cell and put him in a jar.

I had caught many frogs for pets when I was a child, so I was familiar with their care and upkeep. Frogs will only eat food that is moving, so I would kill flies, tie them to a piece of dental floss, and dangle it in front of me. The frog would watch for a second, open his mouth, spring out his tongue, and snap up the fly. I would show that trick to my city-boy friends. They were amazed; most had never seen a frog, let alone watched one eat.

Somebody had asked a friend if I was crazy because every day he would see me running around the cell house searching for flies and killing them. He thought I had lost my mind.

My frog turned out to be a more ideal pet than my dearly departed bird. Depending on the colors of the leaves I put in the jar, my frog would turn the color of those leaves. He would change from shades of brown to shades of green. By changing colors to adapt to his new environment, my frog brought a sense of sanity to my insane world.

CHAPTER 33

Rock Bottom

The prison administration and staff members, especially the ones who worked in the kitchen, began to watch me closely, hoping to catch me stealing something. During this surveillance period, I woke up one morning feeling that something was in my left eye. I looked into the mirror to see if, perhaps, there was an eyelash in my eye. There wasn't, and nothing else foreign was there. Yet it felt like something was lodged in it, and my eye was red and swollen, with an unusual amount of the "sleep" around the upper and lower lids. I had the early signs of pinkeye.

The officer in my housing unit came by my cell, as he did every day, to make sure I was ready for my work detail in the kitchen. "I'm sick," I said. "I want to see a doctor before I go to work." The officer threatened me. "I'm not going to the kitchen, with my eye infected." He said if I refused to go to work, he would send me to the hole.

I wasn't looking for a confrontation. But I said, "I don't give a fuck what you do."

Ten minutes later, two more officers appeared at my cell. They put handcuffs on me, and walked me to the segregation unit, better known as the hole. The officers who ran it were sick of seeing my face. As a result of constantly getting into trouble, I had to go before a discipline board.

My hearing wasn't scheduled for almost two weeks. With time on my hands, I began to act a fool, throwing food outside of my cell, tossing cartons of milk against the outside wall, hurling insults at every officer within earshot.

While in the hole, a prisoner was only allowed to make one phone call a week. I chose to call my father, who warned me to control my temper at the disciplinary hearing. I called my father because in spite of our many disagreements, I knew he was strong and I respected his wisdom and intelligence. I knew he would advise me well. I told my father I would control my temper, but I intended to give the disciplinary board a piece of my mind.

The disciplinary board consisted of lieutenants, prison staff, and the chairman. The chairman sat as judge, jury and executioner. Prisoners basically have no rights. I knew it would be a waste of time to explain why I didn't go to work, so I decided to go to the hearing and show my ass.

On the morning of the hearing, two guards escorted me, still handcuffed, to the room where the disciplinary board was waiting. My eye was visibly infected.

The disciplinary board was run by Rick Gerski, an older, straitlaced, rules-and-regulations guy.

Mr. Gerski said, "Good morning."

"What the hell is good about it?" I responded.

"Why haven't you gone to work?" Gerski asked.

"I don't give a damn about working in prison."

The lieutenant tried to say something, but I started talking again.

Mr. Gerski said, "Shut up."

That was the excuse I was looking for. I stared at Mr. Gerski and said, "What did you say to me, motherfucker?"

He became red-faced and yelled for the guards to remove me from the room. I was dragged from the room, but not before I told them all to go straight to hell. Just like my yelling in the courtroom, that outburst would cost me, too.

The disciplinary board hit me with everything they could. I lost ninety days of commissary privileges; I lost fourteen days of good time, meaning I would have to spend fourteen more days in prison than my original sentence called for because of my behavior; and I received ninety days in the hole. I was escorted back to my cell a very angry man, alone and apart from the world and everything in it.

The hole is more than a jail within the prison. It is a place where you are truly cut off, almost entirely, from human contact and interaction. In the regular prison population, I could talk on the phone, listen to the radio, and watch TV. In the hole, there is none of that. Except for a shower, and a minimal amount of exercise time every other day, you are locked up in a very small space every single minute. Meals were brought by the guards and served through a mail slot in the door. The cell was cold, dark, dirty, and dreary.

I didn't care what happened to me. I paced my cell like a caged animal.

People lose their minds in the hole. People think of prison in terms of physical survival, but it's a harder feat to survive prison without losing your mind.

The infection in my left eye had gotten worse and spread to my right eye. Both eyes were almost closed shut with mucus. The guards ignored my requests for medical attention. Each morning I had to pull my eyes open in order to see. By the time they sent for a doctor to examine me, I had been in the hole for three weeks. The doctor determined that the infection was too advanced for him to treat; he would have to call an eye specialist from outside the prison to come in and treat me. Perhaps the prison administration feared a lawsuit, because the next day the eye specialist arrived.

After a battery of tests, the optometrist said the infection hadn't moved to any vital parts of my eyes. He gave me some drops that stung like pure alcohol to use several times a day. He said that had the infection been allowed to expand much further, I would have gone blind. I was relieved and grateful for the doctor.

When I returned to my cell, I was shaken. I reflected on how close I came to losing my eyesight. That angel who had been watching me all of my life had again arrived just in the nick of time. As I sat there in my cell, listening to the hollering and screaming of the other convicts, I realized how far I had fallen in life. I got up to put some more medicine into my eyes. Gazing into the mirror for the first time in weeks, I was frightened by what I saw. My hair was a mess, my eyes swollen shut with mucus, and my skin badly broken out. I barely recognized the man looking back. I looked ugly. I stared into the mirror trying to find myself; the ugly person in the mirror was who I had become. The horrible truth was, I was even uglier on the inside. I had fallen lower than I ever imagined I could.

As I stood there, transfixed by the image in front of me, in midst of the deafening noise that emanated throughout the hole, in that cell, in Oxford Maximum Security Prison, having fallen to my lowest point, I heard my grandmother's soft voice telling me: "You can make it." I heard her voice say, "Victor, you can make it. Don't give up, I love you." At that moment, I realized I would never survive prison the way I was going about it. Even if I did, I would be insane when I got out. I would be no good to myself, and more important, no good to my children.

I stayed up all night thinking and praying, and asking God to help me. With puss oozing through the narrow slits of my eyes, I could finally see myself clearly. I realized I had brought all my problems on myself. I had been mad at the world and everybody in it. I was mad at Flex, Delilah, the judge, the prosecutor, the Secret Service, and the Department of Probation. But I was to blame. It was all my fault. I was the reason I was in prison. If I had just thrown all the Visa Gold credit cards into Lake Michigan, none of what was going on would have happened. I alone chose to counterfeit those credit cards, and I chose who would help me to do it.

I looked at all the crimes I had committed since I was released from prison in 1986. I was lucky to have received only the time I was given. I had committed armed robberies and any number of illegal activities. All around me were other men, many of them younger, with twenty-five years or more. Most of them couldn't boast of doing a quarter of the crimes I had committed. All in all, I was blessed. Lots of inmates in Oxford had codefendants who told on them, and those brothers were doing life sentences. Flex, Delilah, and the rest of my codefendants were wrong for what they did, but in order for me to survive and move on, I needed to let that anger go. Informants and stool pigeons are a part of *the game*. I played with the fire and got burned.

I realized that I was doing exactly what the Secret Service agents, the prosecutor, Suzie Simpleton, Flex, and Delilah would want me to do—waste away in prison, and perhaps go crazy or die. If that occurred, then no one would ever know what my so-called friends had done to me. Moreover, I would never reach my true potential in life.

I lay in bed with a strange sense that God must have some purpose for me in my life, other than to rot in prison.

Mary Louise Martin's encouraging words, "You can make it," continued to echo in my head. I fell asleep that night recounting the many things my grandmother had told me as a boy. Of those many things, nothing stood out more than when she told me that I would grow up and minister to people, and follow in the footsteps of my grandfather—Reverend A. M. Martin. For the first time, my grandmother's words took on a different tone in my mind. Her words became a guide and a light to follow . . . out of the hole and the madness that had become my life.

I let go of most of my anger that night, although I was still disturbed about my cousin's conduct. For the life of me, I still couldn't understand how someone in my own family would do that to me. That would be something I would pray on and continue to struggle with for a long, long time.

Prison destroys people. It makes a bad person worse. I was caught up in a vicious cycle of being angry and blaming others. I was full of self-pity. I knew that I had to get hold of myself quickly, before I totally self-destructed. In order for me to truly evolve as a person, I would have to look deep within. There was no one else for me to turn to for help.

CHAPTER 34

The Road to Redemption

There is no such thing as prison rehabilitation. The individual has to rehabilitate himself. When they finally let me out of the hole, the season had changed from winter to spring. I had been in the hole for six months. Along with the changing seasons, there was born a change in me.

I realized that I had to address what was inside me that allowed me to commit armed robberies, credit card fraud, and a host of other illegal activities. What was it about me that made me have a blatant disregard for the rights of everyday people? I had to address whatever was inside me that was causing my negative behavior. That self-destructive behavior had cost me more than eight years of my life—years I could have spent with my family and friends, years I could have lived productively.

I had about three and a half years left on my sentence. I began to explore my inner self, hoping to find answers to questions that I had about my life. As I began to study my behavior and seek ways to change it, I recognized that, first, I had to take a more positive approach toward my remaining time in prison. My actions on a day-to-day basis had to reflect the changes taking place in my heart. Slowly, I began to embody my grandmother's words: "You can make it."

My grandfather died on the pulpit preaching the Gospel. My grandmother spoke the Gospel, and walked in the way of the Lord all of her life. In order to become more spiritually balanced, I began reading and studying the Bible. And I resumed my reading of the Koran. I incorporated both religions as I searched for knowledge and understanding.

My grandmother taught me well the power and spiritual strength that lies in the Bible. Although I realized that there was also a great deal to learn from the Koran, I never strayed far from the conventional teachings of my grandmother. There is only one God. You can call him Allah, Jehovah, or the Supreme Being, if you like. Learning how other cultures manifest their roads to God was of interest to me and, in many ways, brought me closer to God.

In the hole, I had gained weight. I put myself on a strict diet of fish and chicken. I gave up eating all red meat. I stopped drinking pop and eating candy. I no longer ate late at night. I then began jogging a few miles and lifting weights, on even and odd days respectively. I was managing my time. I was doing the time instead of the time doing me. My body took on that buffed look of someone who spent hours in the gym.

Having addressed my spirit and body, it was time to address my mind. I signed up for some college courses. I read everything available. Three books were particularly moving.

The first was Les Brown's *Live Your Dreams*. It showed me that you can change your life by believing in yourself. Regardless of your circumstances, you can achieve success. I found his philosophy of achieving success, in spite of life's circumstances, particularly challenging, because I was in prison. However, I believed that I was up to the challenge, and I readily embraced his philosophy of self-empowerment. The second was Nathan McCall's *Makes You Want to Holler*. McCall came from a good home, yet found himself in prison, and somehow he had found the strength to resurrect his life.

The third was *The Autobiography of Malcolm X*. Malcolm X had been immersed in a life of crime, and then imprisoned. During his period of incarceration, he was spiritually enriched. He changed his life, and went on to do great things. I found myself identifying with his struggle to reach his true potential in life. I realized that if Malcolm X could turn his life around and use his diverse experience in life to help and reach people, then so could I.

I have always admired Oprah Winfrey. What she has accomplished professionally and personally, has been nothing short of remarkable. One day while watching her show, Oprah said something that really touched me: "Just because you fall in the mud, doesn't mean that you have to wallow in it." Those words forced me to consider my predicament in prison. Oprah's words encouraged me to continue, to keep that fire in my heart, to maintain my positive upward rise. I became determined not to wallow in my own mistakes. I was beginning to understand I could survive prison. But, more important, I realized I could achieve anything if I believed in myself.

I had talent. I only needed to channel it in a positive direction for positive results. I had applied my talent in a negative direction, and I was rewarded with two prison sentences.

I began to approach day-to-day life in prison with a positive disposition, even putting my best foot forward with the prison staff. I had always been at war with authority, as a child, with my teachers; as a teenager, with my parents; and as an adult, with the judge, the Secret Service, the prosecutor, and prison staff. Nobody on staff in Oxford was responsible for my incarceration, nobody just reached into my penthouse apartment and locked me up. My behavior, my disregard for people and the law put me in prison for a second time. I began treating the prison staff with respect. I was accorded the same.

The captain at Oxford was Mr. James, a nice-looking man in his forties, who always carried himself with dignity and class. He was from the East Coast and was a sharp dresser. The second most powerful man at Oxford, only the warden had more clout than Mr. James.

During the first half of my prison sentence, I occasionally bumped heads with Mr. James. However, he began to notice the significant change in my behavior, and we began to talk from time to time. I explained the circumstances that led me to Oxford. Mr. James respected me for not becoming an informant. We became friends, and would spend hours talking in his office.

Mr. James told me that in his twenty-plus years of working in corrections, he had never met a prisoner who had more potential to succeed in life. I had heard that throughout my life. However, after three years in prison, to hear someone say that meant a lot to me. I spent so much time talking to him that many inmates thought I was in his office providing him with information about illegal activities going on in Oxford. Mr. James never asked me to give him any information. He gave me another chance, fostered my belief that I could do well in life. He even let my mother send me a tape of her singing and playing the piano during the Christmas holidays and allowed me to listen to it in his office.

Then Eve started bringing my children to see me again. We fell in love again. I was vulnerable. I would have fallen in love with E.T., the Extra-Terrestrial, if it came to visit, but still my relationship with Eve was refreshing. Everybody in prison wants somebody to talk with, to love them. We had phone sex frequently. She would send love letters and sexy pictures in lingerie. We talked about putting our family back together.

Eventually, Eve and I started arguing about the usual things couples argue about when one of them is in prison. I questioned where she was when she wasn't at home; she reiterated what I did to her when we were married. The pressure of raising two children on her own, with no man to love her physically, took its toll, as did our distance from each other.

During a visit, she told me that she was in love with another man and getting married. I was shocked and angry. I couldn't respond. I was devastated. I enjoyed our visits. I looked forward to seeing her and my daughters once a month.

Once she moved in with her fiancé, I called him and said, "I love my daughters. I don't want my children taken advantage of in any way. If my daughters need to be disciplined, let their mother do it. I have never hit them, and don't you."

Her fiancé had children, too; when people try to play *The Brady Bunch,* things usually go awry. I told Eve her new relationship wouldn't work out, and sure enough, about a month later, she was living at home with her parents. Then, because of the distance, it would be almost two years before I would see her and my children again.

Despite my breakup with Eve, I continued to try to be the best that I could be. I often talked with Earl, as well as a few old girlfriends. I regularly phoned my children and tried to maintain a presence in their life. I started to see some of those rays of light at the end of the tunnel that Earl was always talking about. I talked to my parents at least once a week. However, after nine years in prison, it was evident in our conversations that my mother and father, although they loved me, had given up hope of my ever really changing my life.

I was becoming known in the prison compound as a brother who had a positive approach toward life. Many brothers sought me out to talk with me about their problems. Others were interested in hearing about how I made the credit cards so when they were released, they could use that knowledge to continue their life of crime. I would refuse to discuss it. No matter how glamorous my credit card conspiracy sounded, I was locked up because of it. The last thing I wanted to do was encourage anybody to do what I did. I understood that encouraging someone to commit a crime was not only wrong, but more important, it was damaging to my spirit. I believe that once we obtain true knowledge of who we are, and what part we play in the universe, we begin a new life. Consequently, to dwell on past negative activities would destroy the new life I was beginning to enjoy in my enlightened state of consciousness.

One day I was putting my tray back into the rack in the chow hall. As I turned around I felt as if I had been drawn into the twilight zone. Right in front of me stood Cool Breeze. I couldn't believe my eyes. He was standing before me in his prison uniform, as if we were standing in a dream. Momentarily stunned, I halfheartedly extended my hand to shake his. Then, when I realized that it wasn't a dream, I grabbed him and we hugged. We left the chow hall and walked around the prison grounds.

CB was the only person at Oxford who I actually knew before I came there. And as happy as I was to see my old associate, it was depressing to see him locked up in a cage, just like me. But the most overwhelming feeling I had was one of pity and horror. CB received a fresh 14 years. CB would have to serve at least 11 years, 10 months, and 24 days. He could expect to get released somewhere around 2006.

CB was thirty-two years old when he began that sentence. The real tragedy was that he left his longtime girlfriend, now his beautiful wife, and a one-year-old baby boy behind. CB played *the game* again, with his eyes wide open. Everybody who plays *the game* has to pay one way or the other. The old saying "crime does not pay" is false. Crime does pay, but there is a price—all who play, must pay.

At that time, I didn't have a roommate, so I arranged with a counselor to have CB move in with me. I had really begun to throw myself into helping other people, and it felt good to do so. In helping CB, I was also helping myself on my quest for spiritual evolution.

I had a zeal to help other people. I spent a lot of time talking with a young brother named Deuce. He was about twenty-five years old, and reminded me of myself when I was younger. The last thing that I wanted Deuce to do was get out of prison, only to return years later, as I had done. I wanted to make sure that he didn't pass through his prison sentence in a daze. I encouraged him to look around the prison compound, and understand what had happened to his life. Deuce needed to understand he could overcome his tragedy and create a prosperous life—legally. I encouraged Deuce to read and enroll in some college courses. Physically, he was in great shape. But I impressed upon him that the most important thing to work out was his mind.

I did not know it, but I was beginning to do what my grandmother had always said I would do. I was beginning to speak to people. My grandmother's vision had truly begun. I was growing into the man I was supposed to be. I no longer had the outlook that life is forever and nothing could ever happen to me. I looked around at brothers doing life sentences and realized that if I didn't continue to change my life, I would grow old and die in prison. I had been good to *the game,* and it had been good to me. I loved *the game,* but it was time to retire.

I had grown too much as a person to commit crimes anymore. I no longer had the desire in my heart to do the things I had done in the past. I knew there were other things in life that would lead me to fulfill my potential.

Meanwhile, every week a new busload of prisoners would enter Oxford Federal Prison. The largest number were black, then Hispanic, and the least, white. Some were as young as eighteen and faced life sentences. I wondered why somebody wasn't warning young brothers about prison.

I committed myself; I would make it my business upon my release from prison to speak to people, especially young black boys and girls, and warn them about the criminal justice system. Black people are the most represented group in prisons across the country. I hoped my words and experiences might keep others from suffering in this hell.

CHAPTER 35

The Speech

A round 1994, Congress put a clause in the crime bill that gave federal prisoners up to a year off on their sentences if they completed a drug treatment program. I didn't have a drug problem, but for a year off, I was determined to participate in the program. I was one of hundreds of inmates who wanted to be admitted into the program. I met with the head of the program, Dr. Cramdon, who reviewed my record, saw I had not been arrested for drugs and had no drug use in my record, then told me he could not approve me for the program. "If Mr. James recommended me, would that make a difference?" I asked.

Dr. Cramdon looked up and said, "A recommendation from Mr. James would definitely make a difference."

Shortly after I had joined the drug treatment program, I discovered that only prisoners who *hadn't* committed a violent felony were eligible. Since I had armed robbery convictions, I wasn't entitled to a year off.

I was so angry, I couldn't see straight. Those armed robberies I had committed a decade before were still haunting me. I was punished for those crimes; I paid for them in the 1980s; my debt to society for them should have been terminated. I contemplated dropping out of the program.

But the drug program had other things to offer, for example, examining criminal thinking. The program director, Ron Knecht, and I became friends. He asked the participants to tell stories about their lives. Most of the other inmates were afraid; however, I was in my element. I gave speeches to the class on everything from getting a job with a prison record to avoiding negative influences in your life.

Many in the drug program class were jealous and hated to hear my presentations, but I didn't care. I was on a mission. I was preparing for my life after I left prison. The program lasted six months. During that time, I tried to speak at least once a week. My presentations would come from related topics on television news, newspapers, or magazine articles, as well as my own personal experiences.

I was sitting in my cell one day, taking it easy, with less than two years left on my sentence, as happy as someone in prison could possibly be. With most of my prison sentence behind me, I felt fortunate. I was reading a magazine and came across an article about Larry Hoover, the head of the Gangster Disciples. It talked about his life and his recent indictment in federal court for a drug charge. I was surprised, because Mr. Hoover had already been in prison for more than twenty years. As far as I knew, he was due for parole. I had also read that he was trying to get young people registered to vote and involved in politics through a political organization in Chicago, called 21st Century Vote. I knew that powerful people in politics wouldn't want him to do that. His troubles disheartened me. He was wise and I felt that he would come out of prison and help put a stop to the gang wars on Chicago's inner-city streets. I suspected he had been entrapped in a conspiracy.

I had met his codefendant in East Moline years ago. He had since been released, and I had hoped that Mr. Hoover would be, too. I looked forward to meeting him one day. So many people who knew him told me that he would like me. Now, I might never get a chance to meet him.

I completed the drug program in July 1995. I was asked to give a graduation speech on behalf of my class before 150 to 200 people. That was something new for me.

I worked long and hard in my cell at night, practicing my diction and studying my facial expressions in the mirror. I had been watching the O. J. Simpson trial, like everyone else, and I was impressed with Johnnie Cochran's speaking skills and eloquence. I also liked the easy, relaxed manner in which President Bill Clinton speaks. I really began analyzing speaking styles, as I created and honed my own.

I concluded that if I was going to be serious about making a living speaking when I got out of prison, I had better start challenging myself. I decided not to use any notes and memorize my whole speech. If Johnnie Cochran could speak without notes, so could I.

I had always spoken behind a podium, but I would leave the protection of the podium and walk out in front of it and interact with my audience. In my cell, I practiced day and night in front of the mirror to prepare for the event.

My hard work paid off. When the big day came, I was extremely well prepared. Dr. Cramdon brought in a professional speaker from the University of Wisconsin to be the keynote and two others in the class were going to speak. As I sat there waiting my turn, I was nervous. My heart raced, and I was sweating. It was the same way I felt before I did an armed robbery. I knew how to handle my nervousness. I sat there and harnessed the fear, for the first time in my adult life, for something positive.

The keynote speaker was paid $1,000, and he read his speech while standing behind the podium. The warden, Mr. James, most of the important staff at Oxford, and invited guests were in the audience.

I wondered if I had made a mistake; the professional speaker was using notes and standing behind a podium. Nevertheless, I decided to stay with my game plan and push myself to another level. My grandmother's words "You can make it" and her prophecy that I would one day speak to large crowds of people encouraged me. I knew that she was smiling on me.

The keynote speaker finished his fifteen-minute talk. Then my two classmates took the podium and read from their notes for five minutes each. They basically stood up and praised the program. The prison staff didn't really expect any of us to give a decent speech. As far as they were concerned, it was an amazing feat for a convict to stand up and say anything at all. I was determined to show everyone in that room that I wasn't a fool. Suddenly, the time was at hand.

Ron Knecht went to the podium and said, "And now, Mr. Victor Woods." I stood up and everybody clapped and cheered.

When I walked to the podium, to my surprise, my nervousness evaporated. I stood before the audience as if I were born to be there. The only thing I carried was my black leather folder, with good old-fashioned inspiration inside: a picture of my mother and father, one of my grandmother and me holding hands, and one of my children. The ones I loved the most were present, so that if I needed a boost in confidence, I could look at them for support.

I began in front of the podium, but as I continued speaking, I began to walk out in front of it, and then from side to side, like many of the great speakers I had seen on TV. After about ten minutes of cracking jokes and praising the program, Dr. Cramdon gave me a look like "OK now, little monkey, get off the stage." I had told the other inmates that I was going to address the issue of not getting a year off because of past criminal behavior.

I could feel the spirit of my grandfather with each word that I spoke. It felt as if I had been speaking all my life. I slipped easily into the role. I walked into another dimension, as I preached that while the program was good, it wasn't *that* good. The graduation ceremony was a showcase for everybody but the prisoners. The prison staff needed to highlight their trained monkeys, so they could continue to receive their fat paychecks from the federal government. While I may have been one of those monkeys that day, I was far from a trained one. I was a revolutionary monkey, and I was about to rock the boat.

I told the audience that I was the voice of many. Dr. Cramdon was sitting up front, his face turning beet-red; he braced himself for what I might say in front of the other prison officials.

I said Congress had set aside good time for graduates from the program. I gave several examples of participants who should have received it, but did not, because of past violent felonies. It was one thing to exclude a prisoner from receiving the year off if he had been convicted of a violent felony for his current case, however, to go back, in some cases as much as ten years, to a felony that disqualified him, was unjust.

As I walked all around the room making my point, many wore shocked looks on their faces, especially the prison staff members. Some prison officials looked appalled. I spoke more than half an hour without notes. When I finished my speech, almost everybody started clapping, and many stood.

The keynote speaker asked to be introduced to me. People lined up to shake my hand, so the keynote speaker had to wait his turn. He told me I did a fantastic job, and asked where I learned to speak. "My grandfather died while preaching in the pulpit. My father is a great public speaker," I said. "It's in my blood."

Mr. James told me afterward, "If you don't do something with all that talent when you get out of prison, then shame on you!" After that, everybody treated me differently. I was already well liked and accepted by most of the prisoners, but after my speech, even the staff treated me with more respect.

That drug program graduation speech marked the first time I used my talents toward something good. It had been a long time since anyone had been impressed and praised me for anything positive. It really felt good. No, it felt great. I never knew I could feel that good. I was fulfilling the prophecy of my grandmother. I determined to continue to be the best that I could be.

After my graduation speech made its way through the prison grapevine, many of the prison organizations wanted me to speak to their groups. A minister from the Nation of Islam asked me to speak and I graciously accepted. My speech was about using one's time in prison for productive purposes, and preparing for eventual release.

On the day I spoke, I followed three other speakers with reputations as leaders in prison. The brothers before me had left the crowd restless, and in order to recapture their attention, when I took the podium, I put my hand over my eyes, and pretended to cry. "I have AIDS," I said. "I didn't get it through a drug transfusion, but from homosexual activity." A few brothers said, "It's OK, brother, speak." Others offered words of encouragement.

I let the gravity of the situation sink in, then lifted my head, smiled and said, "I don't have AIDS. I was making sure I had everybody's attention." Everybody laughed, almost falling out of their chairs.

Now that I had their attention, I said there were no Mike Tysons or Michael Jordans in the room. Instead of constantly building their bodies with weights, or playing cards, dominoes, and sports all day, they should read books and begin to educate themselves. I clarified for them how prisons are a billion-dollar business.

I reached into my bag and pulled out a copy of the Federal Sentencing Guidelines. I told them that many black people feel the federal government has a conspiracy to lock up black men. But I explained that if the federal government *is* engaging in a conspiracy to lock up black men, that conspiracy has been outlined for all to see in the sentencing guidelines. I said we have to take responsibility for ourselves not to go to prison. No matter how wrong the United States government has been and might continue to be, only a fool would continue to do crimes.

"If you were walking on a bridge and saw a sign that said the bridge was out, would you continue to walk down that bridge to your death, or turn around to life? We must all turn our lives around, initially for ourselves, but most important, for the sake of our children."

I reached in my bag again, and pulled out the jar that had held my pet frog. That was dramatic because prisoners weren't allowed to have pets. I had debated whether I wanted to let everybody see that I had a frog, but my tree frog made a good point. I knew that the benefit of my point outweighed the risk of losing my pet. I opened the jar and took out my little frog. "Even though my tree frog is brown, it wasn't always." I showed them the inside of the jar, filled with brown leaves and bark. "When I caught my frog, it was green, sitting on a green leaf of a flower. When I brought my frog inside, it changed its color to brown. My tree frog changed its color to blend in with his new environment. Can't we be like this frog and change our colors to get ready for the world? Don't we, as human beings, have as much sense as that frog?"

I had about a year left in prison, and I was quietly waiting to get out. With the average sentence in Oxford so long, I didn't brag that I was getting out. That year, 1995, I received some surprises. The first was seeing Harry Aleman again. He had been sentenced to twelve years in prison and sent to Oxford with the rest of the men accused of running the Chicago Mafia, including Rocky Infelice, who had received a life sentence.

Harry and I renewed our friendship and often walked the yard, engaged in lengthy dialogue. Harry continued to hammer home to me that I had a lot of talent and potential. He constantly encouraged me to use those gifts in a positive way.

One evening, Harry showed me an article from *The Wall Street Journal* that said Harry had been acquitted of killing a Teamster in 1972. A former Mafia attorney turned government informant said he had paid off the judge who later acquitted Harry. The state's attorney in Chicago wanted to have a second trial against Harry for that murder, despite the law known as "double jeopardy," based on the Fifth Amendment of the Constitution that prohibits retrials of acquitted defendants.

"I am worried for you, Harry," I said.

Harry looked at me, nonchalantly smiled and said, "The state can never get around double jeopardy."

The state's attorney in Chicago argued before the Illinois Supreme Court that since the judge sitting on the case had been bribed, Harry was not in jeopardy. The Illinois Supreme Court ruled in favor of the state's attorney. For the first time in the history of Illinois, and perhaps of the United States of America, someone was tried again for a crime of which they were previously acquitted.

When Harry and I had that conversation, I knew he couldn't fathom that on November 25, 1997, he would be sentenced to between 100 and 300 years in prison for that 1972 murder of the Teamster. The FBI described Harry as the most feared organized crime hit man in Chicago at one time. To me, Harry will always be the guy who set me straight on not being a gangster for the rest of my life.

After I was released from prison, I had the opportunity to go to court and see Harry one last time. As he looked over at me from the defense table, we both smiled. I held up my book jacket so he could see it. The look in his eyes said it all. I know he knew, as he saw me sitting there in my suit and tie and holding my book jacket, that I had taken his advice.

My second surprise came from seeing someone I had not seen since my days in state prison in East Moline. While strolling in the yard one day, I saw KeKe. It had been eight years since he and Tops had taken me under their wings. He was in Oxford for a fraud case.

After we embraced, I joked that if it hadn't been for his tutelage in *the game,* I might not have been in federal prison. I explained to him that I was in an ongoing process to change my life. KeKe was in his forties, and I knew that if he didn't change his life, he would die in prison. I wanted to help KeKe change his life, as I had changed mine. A few months later, he was transferred.

As I looked around at the broken lives of fellow human beings, I wanted more than ever to leave prison and be the best that I could possibly be. One of the biggest injustices I encountered during my prison experience was the many young black men in prison with long sentences for selling crack cocaine. Many young brothers were hoping that Congress would change the crack sentencing laws.

During the time this book was written, the sentencing laws between powder cocaine and crack cocaine were vastly different. Young men and women need to know that of the people arrested for drug possession; three out of four are black, even though 12 percent of both the white and black population use drugs.

My last surprise occurred one day when I called Eve's house to speak to my children. Eve asked if I had heard about Tony Pappas, who had opened a small flower shop in a suburb. I had not. Eve read from an article in *The Chicago Tribune.* The article described how my friend had run a man and woman off the road and down a sixty-foot embankment because of a traffic dispute on the expressway. The woman was killed, the man survived and would detail the incident in open court and recount how his sister had died. I stood at that pay phone in shock.

WGN, the Chicago television superstation, broadcast the story. I learned that Tony had been released on a million-dollar bond. As his defense, he claimed the traffic dispute was caused by the people in the other vehicle. Tony's attorney sought to reduce the charge to manslaughter.

After I was released from prison, I had an opportunity to see Tony one last time . . . in court. The judge sentenced him to forty-five years in state prison. I was saddened for my friend. Tony was an angry man, a result of his father's murder, and further agitated because the murderers have never been brought to justice. He never healed from that travesty.

CHAPTER 36

Leaving Oxford

On December 5, 1995, Mr. James assigned me to six months in a halfway house. That meant that I would get out of prison in July 1996. In a halfway house a prisoner still has strict rules and regulations to follow: be in at 9:00 P.M., random checks for drug and alcohol use; and if a halfway resident failed to follow the rules and regulations, he would immediately be sent back to prison. But you could hold a job and interact with the community. If you complied with the rules, you could eventually earn a weekend pass to go home. So literally, you had one foot in and one foot out. I was fortunate to receive six months of halfway house time: most guys got two to four months.

Halfway house affords former inmates a period of transition from their incarceration, yet there is an economic motive. They are part of the billion-dollar prison industry. Residents pay rent; 25 percent of their paychecks, regardless of the amount. Therefore, a halfway house has a financial interest in their residents securing jobs, and if you are unable to find work, the halfway house provides one. At the halfway house where I stayed, we removed asbestos from buildings, a job that could kill you.

I called my mother and father, and Earl, who were all very happy. They brought me up on a current family affair involving my sisters and their friends and children. My father is a tennis player and he would often talk to me about the many duels he would have on the courts at the country club he belonged to. I never counted the years when I was doing time; I counted months, because that was more bearable. I had six months left, and would be back in Chicago for the Fourth of July weekend. I was excited and thankful to God that I could finally see the light at the end of the tunnel that Earl had talked about for the past five and a half years.

Then, on December 17, 1995, I was informed that the Bureau of

Prisons had lowered my custody level from maximum to minimum; I could no longer be imprisoned at Oxford and had a choice between a minimum security prison in Duluth, Minnesota; Rochester, New York, or the MCC in Chicago. I was shocked. For five years, I envisioned meeting my parents, children, and Earl outside the gates of Oxford, Wisconsin. Mr. James sent a letter to prison officials to persuade them to allow me to stay in Oxford, but the letter was not enough; I was going to be shipped out on December 22, 1995.

I knew not to get upset about the sudden change. Almost six years in prison had taught me that nothing in prison was stable. At any time, you could be shipped away or killed. You always had to expect the unexpected. I chose to be sent to Chicago, to be close to home.

I immediately started thinking about the upside of it. I would be able to see or talk to Earl every day. I called Earl and told him I was coming back to the MCC. Whatever hesitation I might have felt about being transferred was quickly washed away by the excitement in his voice.

I was a little nervous around some of the other prisoners who still had decades left on their sentences. A guy with a long sentence can't help but be jealous when he sees someone getting ready to leave. I spent my last days in Oxford shaking hands and taking pictures with friends. I exchanged addresses with some of the brothers I was close with, one of them the alleged leader of the El Rukins, Jeff Fort. We had no idea that he would be dead less than a year later. Little Fort's body was found in a lake in Indiana. He was shot. Authorities suspected that it was gang related. The reality of violence in our urban streets means a young black man is sometimes safer in prison than his own neighborhood. Anthony Fort might be alive today if he were still in prison.

The evening before I left, Mr. James came to my cell. After we recapped my years at Oxford, he grabbed and hugged me. We shared a warm embrace. "In all my years working in the Bureau of Prisons, I have never hugged an inmate before," Mr. James told me. "You have so much potential; I believe in you."

"I won't let you down," I replied.

"I know you won't," he said.

My final order of business was to find a way to send my tree frog home to my children. There was no way I could smuggle it into the

MCC. But neither could I put him in an envelope and mail him home. I talked a prison counselor into helping me find my frog a safe passage home. I gave the counselor the tree frog prepackaged to be mailed to my children. I was concerned about it traveling in the cold, but that was a risk I had to take.

I spent my final night in Oxford wide awake. I didn't sleep a minute. I wanted to stay up and remember my last five and a half years in there. A few brothers stayed up with me. We watched TV and talked. One by one, everybody went to bed, and I sat alone for a few hours, realizing that I was actually going to make it out of Oxford alive.

At around 4:30 A.M., an officer called me out of the unit. I walked with him to the chow hall for breakfast. The compound seemed so peaceful. Usually, hundreds of people come and go through the prison, but at that hour it was quite tranquil.

I had only juice. There were about seven other prisoners who would be traveling. I watched the other brothers stuff themselves with all the food they could get. I prefer to travel on an empty stomach; it keeps me alert.

After the other inmates finished eating, the guards took us to the receiving area. I saw brothers who participated in the riot when Congress failed to lower the crack sentencing guidelines. They had been in the hole for a few months, and looked and acted that way, refusing to be handcuffed, and cursing at the marshals. They were headed to the worst maximum security prisons the federal government had to offer, probably either Lewisburg, Pennsylvania, or Marion, Illinois. They had nothing to lose by showing their ass.

I understood their anger. But breaking windows and starting riots in federal prison will change nothing. I felt sorry for those brothers, caught in a perpetual state of madness. I spoke with a couple of them as I waited to get fingerprinted, have my picture taken, and then be handcuffed in preparation for my journey. Because my security clearance had been lowered to minimum, I was spared the shackles on my ankles. It felt strange to receive special treatment.

We walked out of the prison gates. The morning air was cold. I could feel the chill as we walked to the bus. Two prison guards stood outside—in front and in back of the bus—with shotguns. If any prisoner made a false move, we might all be shot. My life was in someone else's hands. I resolved it would be my last time to get on a bus handcuffed.

It would be a four-hour ride to Chicago. There was plenty of room on the bus, so I sat by myself. I tried to put the last five and a half years of my life in perspective. As the bus moved along the highway, I thought of what might lie ahead for me at the MCC with only six months left. Whatever I would face, I could deal with.

The brothers slept on the bus, but I stayed awake and watched the faces of the people driving alongside us on the roadway. As they looked up into the bus, their faces showed a twisted mixture of curiosity, fear, and disgust. I hated being looked at that way. I saw a woman nudge her husband or boyfriend who was driving the car, as she pointed to the bus full of prisoners—me included.

When we were about forty-five minutes from Chicago, in the distance, I could see the suburbs where I grew up. Much had changed in the years I was gone. There were so many new stores and buildings, I could hardly recognize the area. We continued to roll along, and seeing the Chicago skyline, I felt a twinge of excitement.

I wasn't going home, but I knew it was the last stop for me *before* going home. It felt good to be back in Chicago, even if I was only going to another prison. We pulled up to the MCC; it looked exactly as it did almost six years ago. I and another prisoner were unloaded to the MCC receiving department. The rest of the inmates remained on the bus to continue the ride to their new prison.

I was supposed to go to the twenty-fifth floor, where everybody had already been sentenced, and whose inmates helped to run the MCC. Those inmates had either informed on too many people to go to a real prison, or been sentenced to a year or less in prison. But the twenty-fifth floor was full, so I was temporarily placed on the twenty-third floor, a dorm floor, which meant there were no cells, just sections of beds. I hated being in dorms; there was no privacy, germs flew freely, and there was constant noise. I got on the elevator, and resigned myself to my fate.

I was eager to get upstairs and call Earl. He would come right down to see me. The officer buzzed me in. I checked in with the officer by giving him my picture ID card. Everybody was looking to see the new guy. Years ago, walking into a new jail scared me; now I was a veteran. But I was ending my journey as opposed to starting it. It was noisy as hell, and there was confusion everywhere, just as I imagined it would be; the prisoners were out of control.

While the officer was giving me my bed assignment, a voice called out, "Hey, Billy Dee." It was somebody from the old school, because I no longer used a nickname. I turned and to my surprise, KeKe was smiling at me. I was sad to see him; it meant he had been indicted on another criminal case. I thought I wouldn't see him again after we both had been released from prison.

We approached each other with our arms extended, and hugged. KeKe told the officer to put me in his section. I got a bed on the top bunk, right over KeKe's. He told me some of my old friends were also in the MCC, and on our floor—Noah Robinson, Jesse Jackson's half brother, and Big, the El Rukin general I met in 1991, who had given me a Koran. I greeted them all. Big was given a life sentence, and he went to Leavenworth with a smile on his face. He was prepared to do the rest of his life in prison, rather than cooperate with the federal government and inform on his friends to get a lesser sentence. They and a host of other El Rukins were given a new trial because of prosecution misconduct on their last trial.

I called Earl and within an hour, the officer was calling my name for an attorney visit. It had been six months since he had last seen me. We had tears of joy in our eyes as we hugged and greeted each other. We sat in the attorneys' visiting room and got caught up on everything that was happening in our lives. He stayed until visiting hours were over.

Back upstairs, I called my parents and Eve. My mother was glad I had been transferred. She felt I was one step closer to home. Eve told me she and the children thought the tree frog was dead when they received it; it wasn't moving and was so cold. But they blew on the tree frog, and it woke up from its hibernation. Eve was happy to talk to me, and asked me to call her later. I could tell she still loved me. She kept telling me to call and check on the frog. But I knew she wanted to talk to me.

KeKe and I stayed awake all night getting caught up. KeKe was about six months short of being released on his current federal prison sentence, and now the federal government had charged him with an old case for fraud. They were trying to give him four more years.

KeKe looked tired and worried. He had a headful of gray hair. I felt sorry for my good friend. All the stuff he taught me at East Moline, about having to pay back *the game,* had caught up with him.

I asked him about my buddies who were transferred to Pekin prison with him, especially my good friend Deuce, the good-looking younger brother with tons of potential, who reminded me of myself when I was his age. I had encouraged him to change his life while we were at Oxford. His ten-year sentence was his first, and unlike KeKe's counsel to me, I didn't want him going back into *the game* when he was released. I had believed that I could make a living committing crime and Deuce had the same gleam in his eyes that I had in my early years in *the game*. KeKe told me everybody was fine.

The next day, Earl came to see me at around noon as he did almost every day, like clockwork. It was just like old times, only better, because five years ago when he was coming, my future was uncertain. Now, I was only six months short of getting out, and the future looked bright.

The downside of being locked up at the MCC was that there were no weights, and you only got fresh air once a week. It sounds terrible to say you miss any kind of prison, but I had it made in Oxford. I missed my single room, the big gym and fresh air. I was in the MCC only four days before I caught a cold that was circulating around the unit.

That weekend, Eve brought the children to see me. She wanted to be more than friends, since I was getting out soon. Tragedy hit when I had been in the MCC for about a week. I called home and my mother told me that my father's mother had died. For five years, nobody had been seriously ill in my family. I had always felt sorry for prisoners whose family members passed away. The Bureau of Prisons refused to let inmates attend the funerals. I found myself in the same position. My mother told me Father had cried and was very upset. I had never been very close to my grandmother on my father's side. I never got a chance to know her. I mourned her passing, but I most wanted to be there for my father. My sister told me that she had never heard my father cry as he did when news of his mother's death reached him.

All my life, my father was a pillar of strength for us all. For once, he needed his family's support. I wanted so badly to be there for him, the same way he had been there for me in my life, despite our many problems. My father is a good man and his heart has always been in the right place. I went to talk to my counselor about the possibility of attending the funeral. But, even as I asked, I knew they were not going to let me go. I had seen that drill too many times before. With my record, I knew that even though I had only six months left, I still stood little chance of going.

I filled out the necessary request forms, but as expected, I was denied based on my previous armed robbery convictions. I was cited as a security risk. Those robberies still haunted me. All my father's sisters would be present with their husbands and children, and would wonder where my father's oldest son was. (My family kept my situation secret.) They might conclude that I didn't care to be there when nothing in the world, except being incarcerated, could keep me from supporting my father in his time of need.

I had hoped to be out of prison before anyone in my family died. I was in prison one too many times; I was paying for *the game* I chose to play. I looked for solace in the fact that it wasn't my parents, or one of my sisters or their ornery children who had died.

I remember a man at Oxford whose two sons were shot. One died and the other was in critical condition. Because of his security level, he was unable to attend his son's funeral.

I called my father and gave him all the support I could. Father tried to sound strong, but I could hear pain in his voice. I hurt for him. My grandmother was buried on a Friday at noon. I got on my knees and prayed for her and my family. It was all I could do.

My mother sent me pictures from the funeral. There was a group picture of all the grandchildren, except me. I already knew how horrible prison could be. But as I looked at the picture of all my relatives together without me at my grandmother's funeral, I hated life in prison even more. That solidified my quest for continued spiritual growth and personal improvement, so that once I was released from prison, I would never be locked up again.

Life in the MCC was particularly irritating. The lights on the twenty-third floor stayed on all night. Noise was constant. The bathrooms and toilets were completely filthy. KeKe smoked, so our bunks were in the smoking section, which I hated. I despised working in the kitchen; it is the hardest prison job you can have. Imagine a restaurant that serves 1,000 people breakfast, lunch and dinner seven days a week, where you earn nineteen cents an hour, working from 12:00 P.M. to 7:30 P.M., every day. But I had only six months left.

CHAPTER 37

Earl Losing It All

Earl came to see me daily. I would leave work to go to the visiting room which, of course, I loved. I always thanked him for coming, especially on those days when I was really dogging it. Hearing them say "Woods, you have an attorney visit" was sweet music to my ears.

Unbeknownst to me, Earl was having his own problems. One and a half years before, he had left the law firm and with Gerald, his roommate and good friend from Morehouse, and two women, started a business that promoted networking in different venues in Chicago. By the time I arrived at the MCC, something drastic had happened with the business, but Earl keeps his problems to himself and rarely talked about them. After much prodding and prying, I learned that the four of them collectively built the business to the point where the gatherings became the premier after-work event to attend in Chicago. Even in prison, I had heard about its popularity from other friends who attended their events. On some occasions, more than 1,000 brothers and sisters participated in the networking and socializing affairs.

Earl never gave me all of the specifics, but mentioned that dissension had grown between the men and women, who held different views on how the business should expand and its future direction. Since October 1992, Gerald, Earl, and the two ladies hosted an event called "First Friday's," and the four of them formed a corporation, First Friday's, Inc. In September 1995, without Gerald and Earl's consent or knowledge, First Friday's, Inc. hosted its last event.

In September 1995, the ladies said they no longer wanted to be in business with Earl and Gerald and suggested liquidating the company. Earl and Gerald objected, and because of the dispute, the ladies suggested the October "First Friday's" be postponed.

The ladies then used the goodwill and resources created by all four, to host their own event—also called "First Friday's"—without Gerald and Earl, and formed a corporation called Original First Friday's, Inc. Earl and Gerald had been "taken."

Earl had stopped practicing law to pursue his dreams and First Friday's was his main source of income. The business upset left Earl in complete financial disarray. It didn't affect Gerald in the same way; he was still an intern.

Earl threw some promotional events on his own, but he was losing money. He spent all of his savings, was all borrowed-out from family and friends, and had reached the limits of his credit cards. He couldn't pay his bills, including rent and telephone. Gerald was in medical school and wasn't in a position to help him.

Earl kept a smile on his face throughout, and even continued to do legal work for brothers and sisters in need, sometimes for free, during his period of adversity. His hot water and heat were cut off; he had to take showers at a gym where he worked out. At night he slept in the kitchen on the floor, with the oven turned on, to put a bite in the Chicago Hawk. Eventually, his telephone was turned off for nonpayment, and he was evicted from his apartment. Despite it all, he continued to visit me every day and offer me encouragement, although he could hardly afford public transportation. One day he had to choose between buying the local newspaper or having bus fare to come to see me. It hurt me to see him that way. But I was proud of the way he handled his situation, glad to see Earl could smile in both good times and bad. Earl's upbeat attitude in the face of disaster brought us closer. I was particularly impressed with Earl's attitude, because he had grown up in the affluent North Shore suburban area. His father was a doctor; he had it all. He graduated from Morehouse College, where he pledged Alpha Phi Alpha, like his grandfather, father, and uncle; went into commercial banking; graduated from Washington University School of Law. Earl's young life had been charmed.

Losing everything is tough for anybody. But for people who have had everything and lost it, it is particularly hard. Earl left the prestigious law firm to pursue his dreams and now had to face everybody after publicly losing First Friday's. He faced people with his head bloodied, but unbowed.

As we sat in the attorneys' visiting room, I told my best friend, the man who had been my spiritual adviser for the last six years, "What you are going through is your test to see if you are worthy to be on top. I believe in you, as much as you believe in me. You have fallen, and now is the time to show your integrity, character and potential. Down is not necessarily out," I said, as I elaborated on my commitment to survive the years I had been in prison. "I challenged you to be the best you can be. Every great person has had to overcome obstacles: surpassing them was what made them great."

Earl had shown me many lessons in life; now he got a lesson from me. "Never forget what it felt like to not have heat and to sleep by the kitchen stove in the dead of Chicago's winter. Never forget the humiliation of being in eviction court, not as an attorney, but as a defendant. Remember the feeling of an empty stomach, those times you had no money and felt too proud to ask for more help, so you fasted. And, most of all, never forget what it feels like to get screwed by people you trusted, because to forget is to allow it to happen again." Earl was much too proud to go back home and ask his parents for help, although eventually he did have to move back home after I was released from prison.

I said, "I will never forget why I have been in prison the last six years." I told him there was no shame in falling down, the shame lies in not getting up. Earl sat in the attorneys' visiting room, not in his usual authoritative, teaching position. Instead, he was my student and I his teacher, explaining the facts of life as I had come to learn them.

Earl was getting a hard lesson in life. The lesson was: money will make people do some strange things—rob, kill, and even forget your friends and business partners. It doesn't matter which side of the fence you're on. If you're out in *the game* or working at IBM, there are people out there who are looking to rip you off.

Lastly, what was perhaps most impressive about my best friend during that period of madness was his vision. As Earl was unsuccessfully trying to avoid being evicted; hosting social events that lost money; dealing with the ladies from First Friday's; actively seeking legal cases to make money; helping other people with their projects for free; and being a best friend to me, he suggested and got me to start writing this book. I always knew my best friend was special, but handling everything and everyone the way he did, with character and integrity, is part of the reason why Earl is also a breed apart.

CHAPTER 38

The Meetings

Islamic prayer was held on Friday's on the twenty-first floor. I had intended not to go to Juma prayer for a while. I wanted to stay to myself. Religious services in prison were ripe with gossip, backbiting, and competition to get elected to various offices. However, Big wanted me to go with him, and I couldn't refuse my friend.

Another El Rukin general, whose Islamic name was Raheem, acted as Imam during Juma prayers. The twenty-first floor was where Larry Hoover was being housed. That was the closest I had ever been to the man for whom my admiration had continued to grow throughout the years. I wanted to meet him. With all the trouble Earl was having with money, I could introduce Earl and Mr. Hoover, and maybe Earl could be hired to do some legal work.

Larry Hoover was not the kind of man you just walked up to. His lawyer probably told him not to talk to anybody he didn't already know. He was on the news daily, and appeared regularly in the Chicago newspapers. The federal government had charged Mr. Hoover as being the head of a hundred-million-dollar-a-year drug business, although Mr. Hoover had been in prison for more than twenty years.

Big had already met Mr. Hoover. He used to carry messages from Jeff Fort to Larry Hoover, when Jeff was imprisoned. Big agreed to set up the meeting. By introducing me to Mr. Hoover, Big was putting his reputation on the line. I couldn't wait until Friday. I talked to Earl, and told him that I was going to, at long last, meet Mr. Hoover. I explained to Earl that I wanted him to meet Mr. Hoover and perhaps do some legal work for him.

I was excited as we took the elevator to the twenty-first floor to attend Juma prayer. Everybody went into the back room to pray, except Big and me. I followed him out to the dorm—identical to the floor I was on, including the backdrop of noise and smoke. Mr. Hoover started walking toward us when he saw Big.

Mr. Hoover was about five-nine, with light brown skin, and had a dignified manner. He had a relaxed confidence in his walk, not arrogance. I stood behind Big as he whispered something to Mr. Hoover, and then said, "Victor, this is Mr. Hoover." It felt good to be finally standing next to someone I had heard so much about. It was unfortunate our meeting had to be in jail.

I extended my arm to Mr. Hoover, and he shook my hand. I gave him that hard, firm handshake Father had taught me as a teenager. I said, "Mr. Hoover, I am sorry to hear about your present problems. I admire you."

He looked at me and said, "Don't worry about it," in such a sincere way that he almost made me feel, for a minute, that I *didn't* need to worry about it. But I knew he was in very serious trouble.

I thanked Big again for introducing me. I planned to talk with Mr. Hoover more the following week, and spent a few hours imagining exactly what I wanted to say. The next Friday when I went to Juma prayer, men lined up to talk to him—like he was the president of the United States.

I waited patiently and when my turn came, I asked him if I could talk to him in private. He said "Yes" and we walked away from everybody else. Then I told him about Earl.

Mr. Hoover listened carefully to what I was saying. I knew he would be leery of me, and I certainly didn't blame him. I had written my birth date and Social Security number on a piece of paper. I gave it to him and told him to have me checked out.

He smiled and said, "You must have known what I was thinking."

"A man in your position can't be too careful," I replied. He shook my hand and told me we would get to know each other. I left with the feeling that I had made some headway, although Mr. Hoover didn't know quite what to think of me, yet.

I continued to think of ways to get closer to him. KeKe had done some time with Mr. Hoover at Stateville prison. KeKe had said that they were good friends. I asked KeKe to go down to the twenty-first floor with me and get me a little closer to Mr. Hoover, and he was excited to help me.

"Bring pictures of some of your old girlfriends to show Mr. Hoover," he said.

"I want to keep my meetings with Mr. Hoover on a serious note," I said, but KeKe insisted, saying, "Mr. Hoover likes looking at pretty women. He will appreciate seeing the flicks."

If I was going to show him pictures, I might as well show him Earl and my family, as well.

Getting KeKe to Juma was like getting a dog to take a bath. KeKe wanted to go up with me to see Mr. Hoover, but he hated participating in anything religious. KeKe accompanied me to Juma prayer, but once it was over, he dashed over to Mr. Hoover; they embraced and talked with the ease of old friends. KeKe's relationship with Mr. Hoover was much more relaxed than Big's. He respected and liked Big, but he had hung out with KeKe, playing cards and basketball when they were younger.

KeKe handed Mr. Hoover the pictures of Lanette and a few other old girlfriends. I apologized to Mr. Hoover; confessing to him that KeKe had insisted we show them to him. I was relieved when Mr. Hoover laughed and said he liked the pictures. He asked me who the girls were and seemed impressed with the pictures of my family.

When Earl came to visit me that night, I told him he had a date to meet with Larry Hoover.

I knew Mr. Hoover had a clothing line called Ghetto Prisoner and thought perhaps Earl could work with Mr. Hoover on that.

I wrote a letter and sent it through the "system" to Mr. Hoover; it was to be opened and read when the two met, and explained how honored I was that we had had a chance to meet, and if he was reading the letter, it meant he was sitting across from my best friend in the world—someone who could be trusted to help him with his impending legal problems.

I couldn't wait to see Earl and hear the news about the meeting the next day. After we hugged, I excitedly asked, "What happened?"

He said, "Mr. Hoover read the letter, and then destroyed it. Our meeting went well. He wants me to look into the clothing line business."

"When are you going over there?"

"I've already been there and talked to Mr. Hoover's wife. She's running the clothing business."

I was delighted at how well the meeting had gone, and so proud of and happy for Earl.

In the end, Earl was not retained, and nothing materialized, but it was my way of trying to help Mr. Hoover and my best friend.

It was March 1996, and another series of meetings helped me come to grips with the fact that I had less than 120 days left on my prison sentence. Eve was coming to see me every other weekend. Being *short* had gotten me some "act right." Among prisoners, when a guy gets close to coming home, his wife or girlfriend starts acting right.

I couldn't think of any woman I knew who would have waited for me for six years. I couldn't think of any woman I would have waited for, for six years either. While I had stayed in touch with a few of my old girlfriends, they all went on with their lives. I still loved Eve and enjoyed her company. Six years was a long time to be alone.

I hadn't put much into any relationship with a woman, and therefore, I didn't get much back. I had to accept that. I had started cheating on Eve a month after we were married. I hadn't been much of a husband or father.

I was in *the game,* and it isn't conducive to a healthy marriage. You can't set your house on fire, and get mad when your pictures burn. I couldn't stay mad at Eve because she had relationships with other men while I was gone.

Part of growing up and being a man is to look at yourself. Every man in prison has to find his own road to peace. Looking at my relationship with Eve honestly was part of that road for me.

Over the years, I told Earl that when I got out of prison, I wanted to do public speaking in the schools. I wanted to share my experience and give some real information to unsuspecting teenagers—about gangs, drugs and prison. Now that time was short, we prepared to go into schools and talk to students. Earl wanted me to write down topics that I planned to discuss. Those would serve as outlines for subject matter and content for potential speeches.

I pretty much dismissed the thought as fast as Earl had suggested it. I was never a good student, and writing a book was never something I remotely thought I could do. Of course, Earl prodded and pestered me about it every chance he got. He constantly challenged

me with, "Why can't you write a book?" and "Why don't you do it?"
One day I would say maybe, which is what one would expect from me,
the king of procrastination. However, Earl stood steadfast, and tried
to make me see that my life and my story would make a worthy book.

Earl even took to reading some of the pages to his friends. He then
would rush back and tell me how fascinated people were, and how
much they liked it. Eventually, Earl's excitement and enthusiasm in
my life story, and how it might help people, bit me. I began churning
out chapters, writing day and night.

I was working in the warehouse located in the prison basement.
Other prisoners would see me writing and jokingly say, "What are you
doing, Woods, writing a book?" Then they would laugh. I kept that
information to myself. Many times, brothers weren't supportive of
different endeavors, especially when they see a brother trying to be
positive. When people laughed at me, that only fueled my fire to
achieve even more.

In fact, most of the black officers and staff who worked at the
MCC were negative. They seemed to carry themselves with an attitude
that they were better than the prisoners. The truth is, I think that
most of the people working in prisons across the country don't have
much themselves. It makes them feel good to be able to look down on
somebody.

Most of those young brothers in the conversation could hardly
speak proper English, let alone fill out a job application. I wondered
why those free black men would spend so much time talking to the
young brothers about millionaire sports figures. Instead, why not tell
them about how to prepare for, and get a job, when they were released.

I got so disgusted that one day I actually pulled one of the warehouse managers aside, and asked him why he didn't spend more time
talking about positive things. The guard really didn't have an answer,
he just looked kind of stupid. I know as black people, we tolerate and
accept too little of ourselves, especially our young black men.

That black man was seemingly in the know, since he had a job and
collected a paycheck. I just wondered why he wasn't sharing his
knowledge with the brothers who were incarcerated and in desperate
need of knowledge. I have always been, and still am, a proud man. I
didn't act or behave or carry myself like a prisoner.

In prison, the correctional officers and prison staff wanted the inmates to be subservient and meek. I never forgot who I was, or where I came from. I knew that even though I was a prisoner, I still had potential. I knew that I was a human being, and that I deserved respect. Once a prisoner forgets those things, and unfortunately many of them do, then they are destined for failure and ultimate destruction of the worst kind—destruction of the spirit.

CHAPTER 39

Preamble to Freedom

On a day close to my release a prisoner had a bowel movement all over the bathroom floor and toilet seat. Then he stopped up the toilet with garbage. I was told to clean it up. I was now at a crossroad in my life. If I refused, I would be put in the hole and surely lose my halfway house time.

With less than 100 days left, and six months of halfway house weighing in the balance, my new attitude on life was now put to the ultimate test. The decision was surprisingly easy to make. With Earl and my family waiting, I had to get home. Nothing was going to stop me, not even something as degrading as cleaning up human excrement.

With that ruling my mind, and amid the jeers and cackles of the other prisoners saying, "I know you're not going to clean up that shit," I put on rubber gloves and a mask and got on my hands and knees and did exactly that. It was the most degrading incident I'd ever had to face in prison, and probably my life. But my eyes were on the prize of freedom. I was thirty-one years old. I had become wise enough to know that there is a time to be strong and unbending, like when the government wanted me to become an informant, and a time to yield. What doesn't destroy you or make you crazy, will make you stronger.

My last birthday in prison was March 23, 1996. I was only twenty-seven years old when I went to prison. Now, at thirty-two, I reminisced about the years that had passed. I thanked God for watching over me and keeping me healthy during my years of incarceration. I called my parents, Eve, and my daughters. They all wished me a happy birthday. Earl came by to see me, and we reveled in the thought that next year on my birthday, I would be free. That night, I had nachos and cheese, with pop. I invited a couple of brothers I had become cool with to my cell. My cellmate at the time was from India, in prison for trying to bribe an immigration officer so he could stay in this country and work. We all sat back and ate, and they wished me a happy birthday.

In late April, my case manager told me that my custody level had dropped from minimum in, to minimum out—I could work outside the MCC. I would be working in the prison lobby.

When I first arrived, I had asked that my custody level be dropped, but I was refused because of my history of armed robberies. Seventy days short of release, I was now a good candidate, and one of the brothers who worked down there was leaving to go home.

Working outside was the next best thing to going home. I was excited, and I immediately called Earl and my family to relay the news.

Working in the lobby was a night job from 10:00 P.M. to 3:00 A.M. It was the perfect job. I could sleep late, and when I did get up, most of the other inmates would be at work. The unit was quiet.

The lobby was where visitors and employees first walked in. I was told that when I took out the rubbish or just wanted some fresh air, I could just walk outside. After almost six years in prison, I could step right out of the front doors of the prison. It almost didn't seem possible. I started work on a Thursday. I couldn't wait for that night. Thinking about being outside, right in the heart of downtown Chicago and not being hand-cuffed, was exhilarating.

I was assigned to work in the lobby with an old man named Mr. Towson. When they called our names to go to work, I quickly got up and left the unit. We got on the elevator, and were dropped off on the floor where the captains' and lieutenants' offices were located. I had never been on that floor before. Then we went to the employee lounge and got sack lunches out of the refrigerator. We watched TV for about ten minutes. Then another officer took us to another elevator, which would take us downstairs to the lobby.

One of the lieutenants looked at me and said, "Oh, you must be the new lobby orderly." I half expected him to say, "Oh, hell no, we can't let Woods go down to the lobby," but he just smiled and went about his business.

Another officer came and said, "It's time to go." We went to an intercom with a camera in front of it. There, under the eyes of the camera, I was asked my name and number. I said "Victor Woods 04946-424." The doors were electronically opened. Then we went into an elevator and downstairs to the lobby. My heart was racing. We got off the elevator, went through metal gates where an officer looked down at us from the control booth. He checked our faces against a picture, then he opened the first gate. After we entered and it closed, the other mechanical gate opened.

After several steps, there I stood, in the lobby Eve and Earl walked through to see me. I saw the blue lockers where personal belongings were kept and the check-in desk where all visitors have to show some identification to be admitted. I looked out the window. Clark Street intersected with Van Buren, underneath the "El" tracks. I saw cars and people walking from here to there. I stared hard at the two glass doors that separated me from the outside world. I could walk outside without handcuffs or leg irons. My heart sped up.

Mr. Towson took me around and showed me my various duties. We had to mop and buff the floors and keep the bathrooms clean. All I could think about was going out of that front door without handcuffs. After the tour, Mr. Towson said he wanted to take a break and go smoke a cigarette.

I had brought a cigar with me, so I could light up once I got outside. For six years I could not go outside without looking through a fence, or seeing a guard with a shotgun in the tower. Smoking a cigar was in order, even a thirty-cent stogie. As we headed toward the door, I followed closely behind Mr. Towson.

He pushed the door open. I stood staring out. Finally, I walked through. No words can articulate the feeling that I had after being locked in a cage for half a decade. It was a deeply satisfying, indescribable sense of exhilaration and joy.

Taxicabs, buses and passenger cars drove by in the refreshing evening air. I could have walked away; there were no guards to stop me. I could have simply flagged a cab or got on a bus. Instead, I stood intoxicated by simply standing in the open air. Mr. Towson looked at me in a way that let me know that he knew what I was feeling. Only another person who has been locked up could understand.

I listened to the sounds of the street. I had a fleeting urge to catch one of those buses. But, with less than sixty days left to do, that would be foolish. Knowing I *could* have walked away, had I chosen to, was an unbelievably freeing feeling.

I took my cigar out of my pocket and said a silent prayer. I thanked

God for letting me live to see that day. Then I unwrapped my cigar and lit it. As I stood there smoking, I looked out at the little park in front of the MCC. Benches were surrounded by neatly manicured trees.

A man sat in the dark, on a bench. I had told Earl I was going to start my new job in the lobby. He never mentioned he might stop by; it was against the rules. Doing so would be a very bold thing, considering he was a lawyer. I looked closer: it was Earl.

Mr. Towson smoked his cigarette and paid Earl no attention. I wanted to wave or give Earl a sign to let him know how excited I was to see him, but all I could do was casually look in his direction and puff on my cigar. Our eyes locked, we gave each other a hard look, and that was all the communication we needed.

Earl had been with me for the entire six years, never failing once to be there for me when I needed him. I guess that after all the years of seeing me in a cage, he needed to see me outside of a prison. Earl's presence there on that night told me that the two of us, together, were a part of something bigger than ourselves. Earl looked at me as if to say, "Can you finally see the light?"

It was a cool crisp May night, about fifty-five degrees, with clear skies. The night had a dreamlike quality. I scanned the streets and watched the people moving along. I once thought I had owned the Chicago streets; I no longer even felt a part of it all. I had been gone too long.

There was a lot of work to be done in the lobby. The warden, as well as the rest of the staff members, had to go through the lobby every morning to get to their jobs. The lobby was a showplace for the prison and had to be well maintained.

We finished up our work around 2:00 A.M. When the officer came down to the lobby to escort us back to our cells, I *chose* to go upstairs. It meant the world to me that I had a choice.

Locked back in my cell, I relaxed on my bunk and thought about how far I had come. I thought of my many good friends at Oxford, who would never have the opportunities ahead of me. Again, I thanked God for keeping me healthy. It had been a hard fight during the last six years. During my incarceration, I had been preparing for my success in the outside world. I had learned too much about life to be a criminal any longer.

I lay in that bunk that night and silently thanked God for giving me the strength to forbear. I tried so hard over my six years in prison to maintain my sanity. I knew many of the other prisoners locked up with me had lost their minds. I had made it my business not to fall into the same kind of destructive pattern that other prisoners got caught up with.

You see, in prison, the attitude is "Hey, if I'm in prison, I'm going to act a certain way, because of where I am." Some of the guys I knew had sex with other men while in prison, simply because there were no women around. Ordinarily, I don't think most of those guys were what you would consider gay, out in the free world. But, because so many other people were having sex with men, or getting high, or fighting like animals, they just followed suit. In their minds, it was all in the name of survival.

If I had spent my last six years in prison having sex with men, just because I was horny, I might have gotten HIV or AIDS. If I had spent my six years in prison getting drunk or smoking dope, what good would I be now? Sure, there were times I felt so low that I wanted to get high or drunk simply to escape. In fact, there were *many* times when I wanted to get high, but I knew better. I thank God that I found the strength and didn't get involved in those all-consuming activities.

To become involved with those activities would end any real chance I would have had to be successful when I was released. Not successful as a criminal, but successful in mainstream America.

I will be the first person to say that you have to be tough to make it through the prison system. But you also have to be tough in life on the outside. The key is to be tough when you have to, but maintain a sense of balance wherever you are. That behavior would help me to better acclimate myself once I returned to society. I had believed in a brighter day, and it was coming, I thought, as I drifted off to sleep.

When I woke up I couldn't wait to call my family and tell them what it felt like to stand outside in the free world again. After talking to my parents and Eve, and sharing all my excitement, I wanted to talk to Earl. I wanted to call him in the morning, but the telephones were monitored. Since I couldn't talk privately, I had to wait until he came to see me. True to form, Earl was there at noon. When they called me for an attorney visit, I quickly got up, and rode the elevator down to the visiting room. They pat-searched me, and I walked through the open visiting area, back to the attorneys' visiting room. As I entered the room, Earl jumped up and we hugged. We looked at each other, had a silent conversation with our eyes, and began to laugh with the excitement of children.

We reminisced about how far we had come. Not how far *I* had come. We had become so close that my struggle had become *his* struggle and his struggle mine.

My time at the MCC was far less stressful, because I knew I could go outside every night. Earl, Eve, and my daughters continued to see me regularly.

Earl had made a point of showing up at interesting times. After 12:30 A.M., an officer, called a perimeter man, walked around the building to make sure nobody was trying to break in or out. Between rounds, he usually stood in the lobby, or out in front. Sometimes I would stand out front with him and talk, and one night, I noticed a man walking briskly toward us wearing a jogging suit and carrying a black leather bag. I couldn't believe it was Earl. I didn't know he had guts like that. He walked right up to the officer, who was wearing a bulletproof vest, and asked if he had listened to the basketball playoffs that evening. That was the first whole year Michael Jordan had returned to the Chicago Bulls from baseball, so playoff fever was high, but the officer was a little startled at Earl's approach. I pretended that I didn't know him, and stood there in amazement as the officer told him that he hadn't heard what the score was. Earl was risking a lot. He came to visit me almost every day and could easily have been recognized by many officers. I discovered Earl occasionally liked to play with fire.

On another occasion, he got Eve involved with the act. Mr. Lopez, a Spanish inmate who had also been given a job in the lobby, came up to me while I was mopping the lobby floor, and told me to look out the window. Two people, apparently a couple, were out in front having a heated argument, in the area near the benches. The brother sported a giant Sly Stone afro. He was really going at it with the woman. A closer look revealed that the man was Earl, and the woman was Eve.

With a big smile on my face, I pretended I didn't know them. I did, however, grab my broom and go outside to sweep the stairs in front. They both made eye contact with me. They sat on the bench, watched me work for about fifteen minutes, and then left. I was touched that they went so far to surprise me. I was also glad that after six years, Eve had a chance to see me outside of the prison walls.

Late in May, I got the official word from my counselor that my last day would be June 30, 1996. I prayed and praised God. I had hoped I would get the full six months of halfway house time and now it was official. I called my parents and Earl.

Life in the MCC took on a different feel. Everything looked different to me after I received my release date. All the other inmates seemed to move in slow motion. The days took on a more mellow tone. I kept news of my release to myself. I only told Mr. Hoover, Noah Robinson, Big, and KeKe—people I could trust. Those brothers were the true players. A player wasn't going to be jealous when you leave. A player celebrates when another player does his time, and leaves. I planned to tell the rest of the guys on my way out, to prevent a jealous fool from planting drugs or a shank in my locker.

I had collected letters and paperwork in six years. Ordinarily, you put your stuff in a big box and send it home. But in prison, everybody sees everything. Someone was bound to discover I was getting ready to leave if I did that. I gave Earl some and I mailed some a little at a time to Valerie to avoid suspicion that I was being released.

June was not without drama. Rumor was that Raheem, the Imam for Friday's Juma prayers and a general for the El Rukins, had become a government informant and would testify against Jesse Jackson's half brother, Noah Robinson, and Big.

I refused to believe it. Raheem seemed so strong. We had often spoken about *the game*, about all the people who didn't do the right thing by taking it on the chin when they got caught. Raheem had already been locked up for ten years because of an informant. Rumors in prison spread like wildfire, and the MCC was abuzz with talk. I waited to talk to Big before I believed it.

I sat next to Big during Juma prayer session. Big rarely showed emotion, but that day I could see his stress on his face.

I whispered, "Is it true?" He nodded his head vertically.

I was sick to my stomach. Like Larry Hoover, who was also facing life, Big's concern was for his family. After Juma, Big made an emotional plea to me to look after his children. Big was a brave, strong man looking a life sentence straight in the eye, without blinking. We hugged each other with tears in our eyes.

I had chosen to sit in prison for six years, rather than try to live with what Raheem was doing. But everybody was trying to cut a deal and pass the buck rather than take responsibility for what they had done. The best example is Salvatore "Sammy the Bull" Gravano, a man who admitted killing nineteen people. But because he agreed to testify against his best friend, John Gotti, and helped to put him in prison, Gravano was set free.

Some family members of the victims he murdered were outraged that the federal government was more concerned with cutting deals with informants who have bloodied hands, than the pursuit of justice.

Mr. Gravano is now a celebrity of sorts, whose book was published; he was on the cover of the Sunday pullout section of many newspapers; and a made-for-TV movie about his life, *Witness to the Mob,* premiered in May of 1998. He was once again jailed in 2000.

The seconds turned into minutes, the minutes into hours, the hours into days. I was nine days short of being released. It felt as if I had been walking on a cloud. Yet I was grounded with the understanding that I was one of the lucky ones, one of the blessed ones. I had been true to *the game,* and I was getting a chance to get out with my life intact. I had so much more to do with my life and was eager to get started.

Earl continued coming to see me every day, and sent me inspirational cards that began and ended: My Friend, My Brother.

June 22, 1996
Take time to reflect the long hard journey.
Never forget that journey, the people, the triumphs,
the pain, the loss, the embarrassment, the smiles,
the lessons, and the evolution.
The light at the end of the tunnel is before us.
When we cross into the light, let us be true to our
friendship, ourselves, our family, and our spirits.

June 23, 1996

I want you to know and understand that our dynamic
transcends time and space.
Please know that no matter where our paths and travels
take us, I will always be there for you.
If ever I am not physically with you, know that you can
always, and I do mean always, tap into my energy.

June 24, 1996

These last few days are particularly good for introspection.
Now is a good time to talk less, and listen to what you are
saying to yourself.
In the coming days of transition, it will be important that
you heed your spirits calling for nourishment, in all of
its forms and manifestations.
Close your eyes, and talk with yourself.

June 25, 1996

We must always maintain our positive energy.
We must always utilize our talents, and our resources, for
our families' futures.
We have to create an environment for evolution and growth.
Remember, For whom much is given, Much is expected.

June 26, 1996

EXCELLENCE!!!
We must always strive for, and seek to attain excellence.
We must create situations, and work with people,
who seek that too.

June 27, 1996

You are truly in a unique position—you're in a
place and time to completely re-create yourself.
What you create is up to you.
But the tools and resources are available for greatness.
Patience and perspective will assist you in creating
your new self.

Allow yourself to carefully weave your new web of life,
with diligence, faith, wisdom, intelligence and spirit.
Enjoy the evolution.
I look forward to it.

June 28, 1996

The road before you will offer many trials
and tribulations.
It will be during these times that you will know within if
your spirit has grown, evolved.
The bad times will challenge you to manifest your
re-created self.
However, if you meet those tests, and pass, you will
forever be able to look within, and feel that inner
security, strength, and wisdom.
You will have found—your balance and harmony.

June 29, 1996

Several years ago, when we were in the bowels of Cook
County jail, I asked you if you could see the light at
the end of the tunnel.
During those dark days, I think you had some doubt about
that light, but you followed me through the muck and the mire.
Today, less than 48 hours away, that light now shines.
That light was so distant previously, now needs sunglasses
to be dimmed.
That light and the new day are yours.
May you honor the new day, the way you honored
yourself, when you sat for six years.

I spent my final days sorting out my thoughts. It was hard to believe that I had only three days left. After six years of watching other people getting ready to leave, it was finally my turn. I was never jealous of other prisoners when they left, because I always knew my time would come.

As guys huddled around the TV set, or waited in a line to take a shower, or use the phone, I thought with peacefulness that in a few short days, all that madness would be behind me. Eve's parents had already made reservations for her and my children to spend a week in Wisconsin. She was leaving on the Friday before my release. Therefore, she wouldn't be there on Monday when I was released. She was upset about it and disappointed.

In prison, the biggest topic was probably women. Guys were always talking about what they were going to do with a woman when they got out. I was no different. However, the fact that I didn't have a woman waiting for me when I got out didn't bother me much. I had a woman waiting for me the first time I got out of prison, and we headed straight for the hotel. However, my mental state in 1986 was light-years apart, compared to 1996. I had more important things on my mind than women.

My mind was on thanking God for protecting me and keeping me safe for six years. Most importantly, my mind was on my continuing journey into my spiritual development. I wanted to be the best I could be so that my grandmother, parents, sisters, children and Earl could be proud of me. But most of all, I needed to be proud of myself.

CHAPTER 40

Free at Last

I told Earl that when I was released, I wanted to lay my prayer rug out in the area where the benches were, facing the east toward the holy city of Mecca. I wanted to thank Allah for my release from bondage. I asked Earl if he would make salat with me.

Friday, June 28, 1996, was my last prison Juma prayer. I said my good-byes to Big. It was truly difficult to see my friend in such a horrible situation. After Juma prayer, I walked down to find Mr. Hoover, who was watching TV. We went to a corner, and with tears in my eyes, I told him how much it had meant to me to have finally met him. I wished him luck with his case. I hugged him, sadly realizing that I might never see him again, because he will probably never get out of prison.

I left Mr. Hoover and Big in the MCC, vowing never to come back, determined to prove to myself that I could turn my life around. I knew and understood that how much money a man had in his pocket didn't determine how successful that man was. To leave prison and secure a job, raise my daughters, and live the kind of life my grandmother and family envisioned for me—had nothing to do with money. Mr. Hoover and Big never told me not to come back. They could look in my eyes and see that I never would.

Eve and my daughters came to see me that Friday night. At the close of the visit, we all held hands, prayed, and thanked God that in less than seventy-two hours, I would no longer be in the MCC.

I was sleeping well through the nights. I had always envisioned my final days as filled with so much excitement that I wouldn't be able to contain myself, or sleep. However, a new peaceful calm over my body, and my final days were in perfect balance.

Earl came to visit on Saturday. We spent the whole day remembering all the courtrooms, judges, and prisons we had seen during the past six years.

That evening, after lockup, I told my cellmate that I would be leaving Monday morning. He was surprised, yet happy for me.

As I've said before, in prison, there's always something happening, and my last days were no different. It had been rumored that a couple was having sex in the parking lot across the street. The lot was a multileveled parking garage. An enclosed lit stairwell with glass windows connected each level. If you looked out of your cell windows, you could see people clearly as they walked to their cars.

There was a rumor that some guy was bringing a woman to the parking garage and having sex with her there. Several people had told me about it, so I suspected that it must have been true. I had stayed up late that night, writing this book. My cellmate had already fallen asleep.

Around 2:00 A.M., I noticed a new Cadillac had pulled up to the very top level of the parking garage. This was strange, because all the other levels were empty. So why bother to drive up to the top level?

Then a man, and a woman wearing a short dress, walked into the stairwell. Immediately they began kissing. At that moment, I knew the rumor was based on fact. In minutes she was performing oral sex. I then woke up my cellmate to participate in the early morning entertainment.

My cellmate was shocked and excited, and he kept swearing. It sounded funny because of his accent. Several other brothers were up, and I could hear the men hollering and yelling. Shortly thereafter, the couple was having sex in the doggy-style position.

It was all very sexy and frustrating all at once. The building was filled with horny men who wouldn't be able to love a woman again for many years, if at all. I'm sure after the initial excitement wore off, many of the brothers were left with the thought of someone else doing exactly what they saw being done to that woman, to their wives, fiancés, or girlfriends.

For me, the feeling was less intense. I was leaving in thirty-two hours. I knew that I would be free to one day make love again to a woman. I was thankful. That morning the floor was abuzz with everyone's version of what occurred earlier in the morning.

The next day, I called my parents, and we discussed my plans for my release. My mother spoke to me intently about staying out of trouble, and what would happen to me if I ever got into trouble again. I had told her over the years that I had changed, but there was no way I could put her mind at ease, except to come out of prison and show her. I had been involved in so much negative activity in my life, it was hard for people who once knew me to believe that I intended to make my life better.

I often wonder if perhaps those very same people who can't seem to bring themselves to fathom that I have changed, somehow lack the ability to change themselves and grow in their lives. Perhaps they simply cannot grasp the concept of the essence of change itself. Because I know some people have limited perspectives, I tried not to take negative attitudes personally. This would be something I would continue to deal with as I made my way through the world.

On Sunday, visiting hours were only from 12:00 P.M. to 3:00 P.M. Earl came to see me at noon for our last prison visit. I hugged and thanked him for being a true friend. With tears in my eyes, I said that he was an angel God had sent to watch over me. Earl saw the vision of my grandmother.

I continued to let tears flow as he told me what our friendship meant to him. We agreed God had brought us together for a reason, and we committed to go in whatever direction that spirit, that energy that God created, leads us.

That night, I went around and let a few of the brothers I was cool with, know that I was leaving in the morning. I told them to keep it on the down-low. Most of them could keep a secret for my last twelve hours.

After lockdown, I packed up all of my stuff. I was told by the counselor that an officer would call me around 8:30 A.M. to leave the unit. I would go down to the receiving unit, where I would be released.

That night as I lay in my bed, I thought about when I was first offered the deal of five years' probation. I thought about Delilah and Flex. I thought about my cousin who was about to graduate from law school. I remembered how quick they all were to use those credit cards, the big smiles on their faces and the joy of the new things they had purchased.

After six years in prison, I was sorry I had ever seen a blank Visa Gold credit card. I was leaving in the morning, and coming back into the world a wiser man. My character and integrity were in place. I had taken responsibility for my actions and not blamed others to prevent owning up to what I did. I was going to regain my freedom with my head held high.

We all make mistakes. We are all human. What you do after you make a mistake will determine your true character. If you can handle a good day, that's great. If you can stand up and face triumph and disaster, and treat those two impostors just the same, you have evolved. That's what life is all about.

I always knew that ultimately, there was a price to pay for everything that we do in life. My friends were unwilling to pay the price for their actions, so they shifted the blame to me. They lessened their burden, and increased mine. However, their actions are not without consequence. Remember, nobody cheats *the game*. Somewhere along the road of life, it will have its way with them. I, on the other hand, faced my negative behavior, and took responsibility not only for myself, but for others, too. I had made peace with myself, and I was looking forward to a new day, my independence day.

I came into prison a complete fool. I was selfish, dishonest, out of touch with my spirituality, and did not know what I was meant to do with my time on earth. I was leaving prison with a sense of self, with a purpose, and a clear conscience. I had balance and some wisdom. I had learned important lessons about myself and life.

Victor Woods faced his calamity head-on, with no excuses. In my confusion, I looked to God for guidance and God had watched over me during my days and nights and sent an angel to encourage and comfort me.

My participation in the Visa Gold credit card conspiracy was wrong. What I did after I was arrested was a step in the right direction—I took responsibility. After six years I was healthy and wise, with a renewed attitude. It was better for me to go to prison for six years and change my life than to have remained in society a lost, greedy, and selfish person. My feet used to be lazy, and my mind was devious. I closed my eyes on my last night in prison in total peace. I had truly laid the foundation to become what my grandmother always had envisioned.

On Monday July 1, 1996, I woke up around 5:00 A.M. I combed my hair and washed up. I sat down and waited for them to open my cell door at 6:00 A.M. for breakfast. I praised and thanked God again, as I readied myself for freedom. When the doors opened, only a few people knew I was leaving. It felt strange to be among the other inmates, knowing that I wouldn't be there with them in a few hours.

Earl had brought to the receiving department the only suit left from my previous life, along with a starched white shirt and tie, and polished shoes. It was one of my favorite Hugo Boss suits and it still looked new and in style.

I went up to thank Mr. McWhorter and Mr. Warrior, my case manager and counselor, who both treated me like a human being, not a prisoner.

Earl was going to meet me in the lobby at 10:00 A.M. I sat nervously watching the clock. With my moment hours away, I feared someone, somewhere, would stop my release, or, that President Clinton would sign a bill to keep all criminals in prison forever. I worried as if these unlikely events were possibilities.

At approximately 8:30 A.M., they finally called me from my unit. When I walked down to the main floor, carrying a small box filled with my belongings, other inmates knew that I was leaving. Some gathered around to shake my hand. If anyone was jealous, they didn't have enough time to take advantage of it. I got on the elevator, and the officer took me downstairs for my last fingerprinting and photograph session. They took their time. Releasing a prisoner from prison is serious business. The Bureau of Prisons takes strong measures to ensure they are releasing the right inmate.

The next phase of my release was to receive my clothes. I could finally take off that ugly orange jumpsuit. In all the morning's excitement, I forgot to put on underwear. So, I sat there with my suit on, and no "drawers."

I had to call Mrs. Strickland, the beautiful black woman who was the officer in charge of the receiving department, and ask her to please get me some underwear. I felt like a fool. She came back laughing as she handed me some boxers.

I was ready to go by 9:15 A.M. But they couldn't release me until 10:00 A.M. I then had an hour to get from the MCC to the halfway house. I sat in a little room and waited for 10:00 A.M. That period from 9:20 A.M. to 10:00 A.M. was the longest forty minutes of my life. I kept thinking the warden, or somebody, would stop my release.

I had asked Earl to bring a duffel bag with him so I wouldn't have to carry my stuff in a box. I asked Mrs. Strickland if she wouldn't mind calling downstairs to the lobby and have the officers send up the duffel bag. When it arrived, I knew Earl was waiting.

At 10:00 A.M., the officer came and got me. They took me out of the jail through a side exit. Before I left, I had to say my name and number to the man in the control booth, one last time. The door popped open, and I walked back into the world after six years, two months, and four days.

I stepped out into a beautiful sunlit morning, the temperature around eighty degrees. I walked around the side of the building to the front lobby where Earl was waiting. I approached the door, walking fast with excitement, I saw Earl through the glass doors, sitting on a bench reading. We hugged. We both had big Cheshire cat grins on our faces. Earl handed me a pair of sunglasses; I had told him my eyes were sensitive to sunlight. He then pressed into my palm a card dated July 1, 1996. The front read *Congratulations*. Its design was a multicolored intricate knot from Ethiopia, whose endless strings symbolized infinity. Inside were the following words from Rudyard Kipling.

IF
If you can keep your head when all about you
Are losing theirs and blaming it on you;
If you can trust yourself when all men doubt you,
But make allowance for their doubting too;
If you can wait and not be tired by waiting;
Or being lied about, don't deal in lies,
Or, being hated, don't give way to hating,
And yet don't look too good, nor talk too wise;

If you can dream—and not make dreams your master;
If you can think—and not make thoughts your aim;
If you can meet with triumph and disaster
And treat those two impostors just the same;
If you can bear to hear the truth you've spoken
Twisted by knaves to make a trap for fools,
Or watch the things you gave your life to, broken,
And stoop and build 'em up with worn-out tools;

If you can make one heap of all your winnings
And risk it in one turn of pitch-and-toss,
And lose, and start again at your beginnings
And never breathe a word about your loss;
If you can force your heart and nerve and sinew
To serve your turn long after they are gone,
And so hold on when there is nothing in you
Except the Will which says to them: "Hold on";

If you can talk with crowds and keep your virtue,
Or walk with kings—nor lose the common touch;
If neither foes nor loving friends can hurt you;
If all men count with you, but none too much;
If you can fill the unforgiving minute
With sixty seconds' worth of distance run—
Yours is the earth and everything that's in it,
And—which is more—you'll be a Man, my son!

We then walked out to the middle of the park. I laid down my prayer rug. We faced the east, and I thanked Allah for giving me that day. I promised to live the way I was meant to live. I also recited some Muslim prayers, as Earl and I were kneeling, in our suits, in front of the MCC.

After we prayed, I handed Earl an envelope with his name on it. I told him that inside were some words to explain how I felt about our friendship, and what he had done for me. He opened it, and discovered that there was nothing written inside. He looked puzzled, and I told him there were no words to describe how I felt, and what his friendship meant to me.

Earl then handed me a surprise—a Visa credit card with my name on it.

He pulled out two Dunhill cigars, we lit them, and walked into our destiny!

Growing up in the suburbs has many advantages, such as superior school systems, and generally a safer environment in which to live and

raise children. I spent my childhood in the blanket of suburban security. I didn't experience what many urban people of color experienced.
I never had to go to school in fear of my life because somebody might
take out a gun and shoot me, simply because I had on what was perceived as the wrong color hat or shirt.

I did not know what it was like to come home from school to a
refrigerator with no food. Or live in a house without running water. In
my early years, I thought that everybody had the basic means for survival. I did not know anyone personally who was without those things.
In my reality, I thought all was well for just about everyone. My
mother told me not to waste food because people were starving in the
world, but I really failed to grasp what that meant.

However, knowing, and really feeling and seeing people who were
without, was not a part of my upbringing. I remember listening to a
group of mostly white adults talk at a neighborhood gathering about
crime. One of the men said, very matter-of-factly, that when a person
commits a crime, they should be put in jail, and the key thrown away.
As far as I was concerned back then, I concurred wholeheartedly. I did
not know any criminals. I had not broken the law as of yet, and more
importantly, I was not living in an environment where I needed to
steal to survive.

In my own arrogance and ignorance, I could not possibly imagine
why people would commit crimes. So the only sensible thing I could
think of was to lock people up who broke the law. Like my neighbor, I
lacked compassion and understanding.

In my twelve years of going in and out of jails and prison, I never
met any young black man similar to myself—someone who came from
a privileged background, and then went to prison. In fact, I met very
few white people in prison who came from the background that I did.

Having gone through the federal and state prison systems, I have a
much different perspective on why the majority of people commit
crimes. What should be done to those people who commit crimes?
The majority of people I met in prison did not choose a life of crime
like I did. I had many examples of successful professionals to give me
perspective of what a black person could achieve in this country. I
needed only to look at my own parents to see two college graduates
and professionals.

When I looked further at my aunts, uncles and parents' friends, I was surrounded by doctors, lawyers and business executives. I clearly *chose* my path of crime. I had to seek out the criminal life; it didn't come looking for me. The majority of brothers, and people of color I met in prison, came from broken homes. Many had one parent, while others had none. The only professional people they came into contact with were on television or at the doctor's office.

Most of the brothers in prison grew up without having the basic skills for survival in a competitive world. The only people they saw driving nice cars, wearing nice clothes and having money were the drug dealers, hustlers and players. Just like when I was a small boy, I could not understand their reality and what their life was like, no more than they could really understand or believe my reality in the suburbs.

I know many black and white successful people who scoff at the notion that one's environment may dictate one's outcome in life. Of course, this thought process is based on the many black people who have successfully completed college, and perhaps graduate school, and made it into corporate America. Moreover, white America and some successful blacks are quick to hold up those precious few who have made it, as if to say, "Look, the rest of you black folks can make it, too."

I think that many people look at a black person who may not have made it, and assume that he didn't try, or that he chose not to make it. The truth of the matter is, it is easier for the average black person to get through the eye of the needle, than to be successful in this country.

They say when a man and woman make love and his sperm enters her womb, that only the strongest and most determined sperm gets close to fertilizing the egg, and only one sperm actually does. Now, that doesn't mean that all the rest of the sperm are trifling, and didn't try to reach the egg. Of course not, all of them simply could not get through the obstacles facing them. They were too great. Similarly, the obstacles facing the average black child growing up in urban cities and in housing projects across America, are just sometimes too great for success.

The truth: In all the jails and prisons across the country, a significant percentage of black men in this country are in prison, and women of color are catching up at an alarming rate. Too many black families, and 40 percent of black children are living in poverty. Something is very much awry in the black community, and this country. Unfortunately, it has been for a very long time.

We often talk of slavery in the past tense. However, slavery is alive and well in this country. Just like they used to pack men and women on slave ships hundreds of years ago; this country now packs black people on top of one another in jails and prisons throughout the United States.

We still have plantations in this country. Now, we call them prisons.

A person can easily trace back the plight of black people in this country, and understand the predicament that we are in today. I say "we" because even if you, personally, are well-off, the majority of black people are not. Therefore, if your people are suffering, then you should also feel that suffering as well, and try to do something about it.

However, we as a people are not helping one another generally, and black people specifically are not concerned about our brothers' and sisters' suffering. Thus, the cycle of poverty and hopelessness continues. Black people continue to look for, and depend upon, organizations or other people for help. Black people need to first look within for improvement. Then, black people, individually, one person at a time, must take a brother or a sister who is in need of help, and put in time and, yes, some resources to assist in improving one's circumstances.

My parents have told me of all the prejudices they had personally endured, which were not unlike the experiences of millions of blacks in this country. However, it was also a beautiful time because most black people came together, dark- and light-skinned, working-class and professional, and rich and poor folks. If you were black in America, you did not have any rights. All blacks were in search of justice and equality, and came together in that quest.

It was a time when we called each other "brother" and "sister" and genuinely meant it. We were all in the struggle together, primarily because segregation kept us that way. After we gained the theoretical right for equal opportunity and to be treated fairly, without discrimination, many fortunate blacks moved forward, and out of the once segregated community. For the most part, the black masses were unable to overcome the decades and centuries of poverty, hopelessness and discrimination. The majority of black people remained in ghettos across America, where they remain today.

There was a time when "brother" and "sister" was an expression of peace and true brotherhood. Now, when we hear those words, they're used to put you at ease before you get robbed. We are feeding off of ourselves in our communities like piranhas. Not only do many of us not know our history, but some do not even want to know it.

In midst of all the confusion, some of our race have excelled. Many of us who have "made it" are doing nothing at all to help others, except, perhaps, giving to a social organization to ease their conscience, instead of getting into the muck and the mire. Some of us have become too bourgeois to get next to a brother or sister who needs help. The real shame is that many of us have turned our backs on the black communities' most precious resource—our children. It is so much easier to send money than roll up your sleeves, and stand with one in need. It looks and smells too bad.

The funny thing those blacks in the suburbs fail to recognize is some whites hate you solely because of your skin color. It does not matter that you are a doctor or a lawyer or have a Ph.D. Because at 11:00 o'clock at night in an outdoor parking lot, or while trying to hail a taxi, with all your degrees, from the white and even some non-white perspectives: you are still a "nigger" to those ignorant and unenlightened. It is also frightening because there are many silent voices who are influential in politics and corporate America, who share those very same sentiments.

Meanwhile, black folks continue to perpetuate the madness among ourselves, while ignoring the fact that the criminal justice system is a multibillion-dollar industry. In 1995, the government spent $23.2 billion for prisons and law enforcement, yet it only spent $6.9 billion for prevention.

You can find businesses like Corrections Corporation of America (CCA) that manage correctional facilities for the government. At the time of this writing, CCA has 41,594 of prisoner capacity for prison facilities under contract. Within twelve to eighteen months, they will open sixteen new prison facilities. CCA's millions of dollars in profit continue to increase at rates palatable to the money seekers on Wall Street.

In 1996 and 1997 prison management company stocks had increasing profits, and look to continue in years to come—mostly at the expense of young black men and women, and other people of color.

As a society, I think we need to be concerned about prison privatization. Prisons are already in a state of disarray, and the situation will only worsen if there is a profit margin in the equation. There will be many shortcomings to prison privatization, similar to what happened with the proposed change in the health care industry. The only difference is, most people do not care about those incarcerated. Therefore, the outcry will not reach a fever pitch until it's too late.

We can really see the business side of prisons with this example. Since 1980 California has built eighteen prisons. Prisoners have increased from 24,000 to 134,000. Guards have increased from 5,000 to 23,000. A guard's salary has increased from $14,400 in 1980 to $44,676 in 1995, the latter being more than $10,000 more than the average state teacher's salary. The CCPOA has benefited enormously by the increased incarceration rate, in part provided by the "Three Strikes" law.

Inside the prison system, there are lost generations of mostly black men and women, and other people of color. As far as the prison system is concerned, as it relates to corrections, blacks have more to be concerned about than any other group. Rehabilitation, if you look historically as well as today, never really existed. The prison system in this country is nothing more than a breeding mechanism for future criminals, to ensure future profitability.

Society is breeding criminals in ghettos all over this country, for consumption in the criminal justice system. In small dilapidated towns like the one I was incarcerated in at Oxford, the primary business that maintained the community was the prison. It is happening all over the United States in small rural towns. When the local industry fails, the government will build a prison to help the economy. There are even some communities actively bidding to have a prison built in their town—all in the name of additional tax revenues and jobs.

Understand the process here. Someone will be paid for the land where the government will build the prison. Someone will be paid to survey the land. Someone will be paid to draft the prison plans. Someone will be paid for the construction of the prison. Someone will be paid for the materials to build the prison. Someone will be paid to run and maintain the prison. People will be paid to work as guards and staff in the prison. Someone will be paid to provide the security system for the prison. Someone will be paid for the computers in the prison. Someone will be paid to furnish Bureau of Prisons uniforms that all prisoners must wear. Some company will be paid to provide the food for the prisoners. Someone will be paid to provide all the necessary equipment to run the prison. Someone will be paid to be a social worker, case worker, doctor, dentist, and vending machine person.

This country is planting significant numbers of black men in prison, where they depreciate mentally and physically. Then, they are released with no skills, training, or support, and told to survive. With no other alternative, most resort to what they know best, which is, unfortunately, criminal activity.

Upon my release from prison, my probation officer flat-out told me that she didn't believe in rehabilitation. The real shame of it is that my probation officer is a black woman. Black women have the most to gain if black men leave prison to return to their communities and families rehabilitated, with a renewed sense of purpose.

It seems to me that my probation officer should have embraced my new state of consciousness. When I was in federal prison, the administration from the warden on down wouldn't hesitate to tell you that their job was not to rehabilitate, but to keep inmates incarcerated, and nothing more. That position was encouraged and enforced by the Federal Bureau of Prisons.

The goal is to maintain crime. All of the jobs on some level mentioned above, and more, would be lost or severely affected with the reduction of crime. That reduction would have an adverse effect on the economy. Misery, hopelessness and broken homes and families, coupled with inequity in educational resources, fuels the criminal justice system in this country. In some places, it is more economically viable for black men to be incarcerated, than working a nine-to-five job.

Each time a crime is committed in this country, it means job security for millions of people across the United States.

Brothers and sisters (and all people in this country) have got to wake up right now, this minute. Tomorrow is too late. Everyone in this country needs to honestly sit down and examine where we are headed with regard to prisons and prisoners in this country.

The time is coming when we all will be affected by this circumstance, directly or indirectly. We can deal with this now, or we can deal with this when tens of thousands of angry individuals are released from prison. After ten-, twenty-, and thirty-plus year sentences, with no skills or realistic prospect for being integrated into mainstream society—they are very, very mad. Where are they going to go? What are they going to do? What are *we* going to do? But, most importantly, what are *you* going to do?

Of the Spirit

I believe that life is a series of moments: good ones that bring us joy and fond memories; bad ones that bring us pain and hopefully a lesson learned. I believe that at least one of the keys to a good life is to try to have more good moments than bad. As we move through life from birth, we experience multitudes of moments before we eventually pass on. I believe this process is a long journey through life that provides opportunities to evolve along the way. I believe every human being has something good to offer the world.

As a young boy, moving through my journey, my grandmother often told me that I would follow my grandfather's footsteps and preach. She said I would speak before large crowds of people. At the time of my grandmother's prophecy, I laughed at the very notion. The thought that I would be speaking to a crowd of people about anything was not something I could fathom. There was an assured and knowing tone in my grandmother's voice. With all of her wisdom and divine sense of spirituality, she knew what I was destined to do, as sure as she knew there was a God in heaven.

The fact that you are reading this book is proof of my grandmother's prophecy, because through this book, I am reaching crowds of people. As I struggle to make sense of my life, I realize that without having gone on my journey in life, I would not have been enriched by the experiences and knowledge that I possess. My insights and perspectives are generally more diverse than the average person. My experiences and moments have given me a unique message, without which I would not have this story to share.

I do not regret my path in life, except for the people I have hurt along the way.

Often I am asked for advice on how to change a loved one's behavior. If I could bottle it and create a home remedy, I would make a fortune. However, there is no clear-cut way to change from living a life of crime to one within mainstream society.

While I do not have a definite formula to succeed, I do know that working toward balance, harmony, and spirituality is a good place for all human beings to start. I believe that we all inherently possess a conscience. However, many people, like myself, choose to turn it off, in their quest for personal satisfaction.

For me, expensive cars, clothes, and money were more important than the people I hurt with my illegal activities. By turning off my conscience, I also altered my balance, thus causing disharmony. Moreover, my sense of spirituality was misguided, because in order to continue my behavior, I had to ignore my spirit.

When one truly understands how they fit into the universe and everything in it, then they can begin to reach their potential. A manifestation of life is energy. We decide if we create and develop energy that is positive or negative.

There was no positive energy within my past behavior. The energy was negative and powerful and infected my life in a detrimental way. Many people live within negative energy for so long, that they cannot distinguish between the positive and negative. Those who choose to participate and thrive in negative activities cannot grow. They can only spread the infection it creates onto others.

You will change the problems in your life when you get sick and tired of being sick and tired. I was sick and tired of being in prison. I was sick and tired of being away from my family. I was sick and tired of bending over and spreading my buttock cheeks so a correctional officer could look up my behind to see if I was sneaking in drugs after a visit. I was sick and tired of being humiliated and locked up like an animal.

I knew I could not change that situation. However, I knew if I could change my thinking and behavior, then I could change my life. Instead of praying to get out of prison, I accepted my situation, and I prayed for wisdom, knowledge, understanding, and health.

Wisdom, knowledge, and understanding are three key elements to life. Wisdom allows us to be prudent in our decision making. Without wisdom, a person continues to make foolish mistakes throughout his or her life. We are destined to repeat the same mistakes, until we learn our lesson. I have definitely gained wisdom. Finding it is an ongoing process that began my second time in prison.

Knowledge, I believe, is what makes the difference between an intelligent person and an ignorant person. Early in life, I believed I knew everything, and had all the answers. Because I lacked wisdom and knowledge, experiences became my teacher. Instead of going through life seeking enlightenment, I was learning as I moved alone during my journey in life.

Life is often cruel and harsh. If one has to experience all the good and bad life has to offer, because one lacks wisdom and fails to seek and acquire knowledge, then that person is headed on a long, hard, and painful path in life—the same long path I set out on, at fifteen years old.

Understanding allows us to interpret wisdom and knowledge. Understanding allows us to grasp the many experiences and nuances in life, and use them to create balance, within ourselves, other people, and our environment. There is an energy, a force that emanates and radiates through us. We all have the ability to be in harmony with it.

My grandmother probably had the greatest impact on my life— more than any other person I have ever met. Her words and constant reassurances during my troubled childhood, saying "You can make it," rang out when I was in the hole in prison. Often a vision of her beautiful face was all that I had to focus on, during all of the madness in prison. Her undying and unyielding belief, that God had a calling for me to do something meaningful with my life was, and forever will be, indelibly embedded in my mind and my soul.

My grandmother knew what I would eventually become before I or anybody else had a clue. I know that even today, I am still living on the prayers of my departed grandmother. I know her spirit watches over me every day. I wish my grandmother were still alive to watch and hear me speak. Tears well up in my eyes just thinking about how proud she would be.

I can hear her now making comparisons of me to my late grandfather.

Ultimately, God is behind all the success in my life. He is responsible for who I am, and what I hope to become. God put people in my life to protect me, and help me along the way. Most of all, and above everything else, I thank God.

When people ask me how I changed my life, without hesitation, I say that God is responsible. I humble myself before him, for I am clear, that without him, I would be nothing.

Afterword

The date is October 3, 2009, exactly thirteen years after my release from Oxford. Wisconsin's maximum security federal prison. As I sat in the back of a black limousine, dressed in an Armani suit, on my way to my first national appearance on CNN, I gazed out the window at the faces of people strolling down Chicago's Magnificent Mile, the same famous street where I had charged millions of dollars on counterfeit Visa Gold Cards twenty years earlier. I reflected on just how I had arrived at this moment and how much things had changed. In fact, the irony was unmistakable. Think about it for a moment: Victor Woods, wearing an expensive suit and riding in a nice car in downtown Chicago, was not that unusual given my past experiences. However, riding in a car on my way to being interviewed on CNN before a national audience was anything but usual for me. Was it luck? Perhaps a game of chance that would soon broadcast my face, my voice, and my published book across the world? Or was it a carefully crafted plan, a vision fueled by the relentless drive and determination I had always had since I was two years old? To be clear, luck had nothing to do with it. I've always resented it when someone wishes me luck. It's been said that the harder you work the luckier you get. Those are the words I live by. Contrary to the wishes of some who had forgotten about me, or thought they had heard the last of Victor Woods—those so-called friends, informants, family members, and law-enforcement officers who celebrated my incarceration and left me to rot in prison.

As I gazed at these familiar buildings, sidewalks, and streets, my mind drifted back to the federal halfway house on Chicago's West Side, my first "home" after being released from prison. It was exactly what you would imagine: dark, dirty, dreary, and depressing. Most of the staff didn't want to be there at all, and among the residents there were only a few familiar faces who were grossly unprepared for life after prison. I checked in at the front desk and was given my rule book and room assignment. Cheap drapes and a wooden desk decorated my room. It wasn't the Ritz Carlton, on the other hand, it wasn't a prison cell either. I was halfway to freedom and grateful for it.

The energy at the halfway house was negative, and I pretty much stayed to myself. Almost everyone had a scam, a hustle, or a get-rich-quick scheme. Many of the residents couldn't even finish a few months there, and quite a few were sent back to prison for drinking or curfew issues. Most hadn't spent their time in prison wisely nor considered life beyond having sex and getting back to their respective drug of choice. I, however, was on a carefully crafted, well-thought-out mission. If you don't plan, then you plan to fail, and I was determined and ready to succeed.

I had contacted Project Build when I was in prison, after reading a newspaper article about it. It's an organization that works with inner-city kids in an effort to direct them away from drugs and gang violence. Now that I was out, I interviewed with its executive director and staff, and they unleashed me on the Chicago public school system, where, ironically, the thing that had always gotten me in trouble my whole life—talking—was now the very thing that would prove my greatest gift. My mother and father had always said I had a big mouth, but they had failed to realize that that was my biggest asset. I had been talking to people all my life. Finally I understood my unique gift and purpose. In fact, unbeknownst to me, I had begun honing my professional speaking skills as a criminal and had continued in prison. I knew if I could influence and motivate convicts I could talk to anyone. When inmates saw me speak they were moved and uplifted. All I needed was a microphone and an audience. My skill set as a speaker was as good as or better than anybody else's out there on the lecture circuit. There's a saying that the two things people fear the most are dying and public speaking. People say they'd rather die than have to speak in front of an audience. But I was doing armed robberies at fifteen years old and was fearless even then. There has never been, nor will there ever be, an audience that could scare me. If I'm able to get to heaven—and I hope I can—I'll be in heaven giving speeches.

The truth is that success escapes some because they live with imaginary iron bars, much like the bars I saw while locked away. They are trapped inside a prison of their own making. A universal principle of success is to understand that it begins with your mind-set. I've applied these success principles to everything I do, and I articulate them to others. The audience for the success ideologies is endless.

I've met many people who aspire to be professional speakers. Almost without exception, they have a snowball's chance in hell of achieving success. To be a professional speaker means somebody is paying you. It's just like being a singer, an actor, or a professional athlete: without question, you have to be damned talented, period. If you are one of those rare people with that kind of talent, then you have to be able to promote yourself, run a business, and deal with all sorts of issues that have nothing to do with your talent at all. In fact, you have to be prepared to make all kinds of sacrifices for years and years, all the while being relentless no matter what you aspire to be. You can never ask yourself, What if it doesn't work? Failure is not an option for me, and the part of me that is fearless and determined—whether as a criminal or a motivational speaker—has served me well.

When I was released from federal prison, my parents gave me money for a used car, and I settled into a small apartment with rented furniture and my first new suit, which cost $90 used. Gone were the days of $2,000 suits and a penthouse apartment. It wasn't that I didn't care about money anymore—after all, money is up there with air and water—but I knew that helping people by giving them hope was more important than how much money I had in my pocket. And of course I knew that if I worked hard, I would regain all those material things I had lost. I never ever thought even once—even when things got tough—about revisiting a life of crime. I knew with every ounce of my being that I was going to make it, which was the quintessential message my grandmother burned into my psyche. I used the negative comments from all kinds of people to fuel my success and determination. I even welcomed their negativity. Like 50 Cent says, "I need you to hate me so I can use it."

I was hired to speak at the largest juvenile detention center in the world, in Chicago. It holds thousands of children (unfortunately, almost all black). I had a way with teenagers, especially those who had lost their way and gotten into trouble. I could see things in them that other people—especially those who just studied and read books about at-risk youth—could not see. Those teenagers knew I used to be just like them, and that's just something you can't fake. I was able to reach the most incorrigible young boys and girls because of my experiences. Most of the kids who get into trouble have most, if not all the tools, they need to make it. They just need someone like me to show them how.

If I couldn't get paid speaking engagements, I would speak for free, knowing that my success would be calculated in being seen and heard. I knew that, once people heard me, they would either pay me to come back or recommended me to someone who would pay me. Either way it worked out. Maya Angelou once said, "Do what you love and the money will follow." It's just like the baseball or football player who gets paid to play the game that he always loved as a child. What could possibly be better than that?

I soon found myself on a plane, flying out of town for the first time for a speaking engagement. That was truly a significant moment. It had been a long time since I had been proud of myself, and it felt good. Of course, the more success I achieved, the more haters I attracted. I took that as a testament to how good I was. Sammy Davis, Jr., used to say that as long as people are talking about you, even if it's bad, it's good. When they stop talking about you, your career is dead. I had people talking, and my story resonated, especially my refusal to cooperate with the government and inform on people to lessen my time and save my own skin. I've been speaking for eighteen years now, and I have never had to submit a job application and suffer the indignity of being refused a position because of prior mistakes in my life. Truly God has blessed me and rewarded me for being faithful.

Every speaking engagement led me to another opportunity. I continued to practice and work hard and hone my skills to be the best. I spoke everywhere and anywhere, from Morehouse College Business School and New York's Fordham University, to Disney World and the United States Environmental Protection Agency, as well as conferences for criminal justice, business, and entrepreneurship to audiences of politicians, professors, doctors, students, and athletes. In fact, one of the public relations people for the St. Louis Rams once approached me about speaking to their rookies, in view of the league's behavioral and decision-making challenges regarding a number of their players. Some people couldn't relate to my criminal behavior, although most found it fascinating. I often refer to myself as the black "Catch Me If You Can"—the true story turned movie about Frank

Abagnale, who counterfeited checks and was portrayed in the movie by Leonardo DiCaprio. I had the opportunity to meet with Drake's CFO about the possibility of him portraying me in the movie of my life story, as well as Bow Wow, who would make a compelling leading man. To be certain, whoever does take on the role of Victor Woods will have to embody a high level of range able to go from A to Z in an instant as an actor. As it turns out, just about every successful person I met has enthusiastically embraced my relentless nature and not taking no for an answer. My message has always been clearly this: it's not where you start it's where you finish. Some of the people I admire the most and have tried to emulate in my own life embody that quote: Bill Clinton, Malcolm X, Gandhi, Muhammad Ali, Larry Flint, Barack Obama, Teddy Roosevelt, Harriet Tubman, Rosa Parks, Oprah Winfrey, Johnnie Cochran, Ambassador Andrew Young, Martin Luther King, Jr., Jay Z, Sean Combs, Quincy Jones, Mary J. Blige, Joel Osteen, Bruce Lee, Frank Sinatra, Dean Martin, Sammy Davis, Jr., Tony Bennett, Jimi Hendrix, Eric Clapton, the Beatles, Michael Jackson, Steve Jobs, Bill Gates, James Dean, Donald Trump, and Adam Clayton Powell, Jr. These are some of the people whose stories drive me to be the best I can be no matter what negative circumstances life might throw in my direction. After God, nothing was more important to me than being a successful speaker. I have sacrificed a lot to accomplish my goals: any successful person can concur with that statement. My journey also afforded me the opportunity to expand my horizons. I have been privileged to visit Africa and Brazil and Holland. I have traveled all over the United States. Most important, I have been able to use my success and life lessons in prisons across the country to uplift those lost souls who have been mistreated in life. I have been able to speak out on political injustice and unrest in places like Ferguson, Missouri, where the tragic and controversial death of Michael Brown occurred, and I've advocated for change leading a march against violence in downtown Chicago in response to the multitudes of children who have been senselessly murdered. I've also worked with law enforcement officials all over the country on matters from public safety to diversity. I was even able to reconnect with Chief Lester Aradi, who had a shotgun trained at my head years earlier. We have spoken at conferences together and formed an unlikely friendship. He is now one of my biggest supporters. In fact, he once told a national audience attending a criminal justice conference that by supporting me he has done more to curb violence and crime than he had in thirty-five years of law enforcement.

Rest assured it has not been missed by this writer: how fortunate I am. I want all those who read my book to know that I am eternally thankful to God for all that He has blessed me with. In no way, shape, or form is my life perfect, nor am I. However, I am finally at peace with myself, knowing I have given my all to rewrite my wrongs and be worthy of my many gifts God has blessed me with. To be clear, no one said it would be easy in getting to the top. In life, one's chosen profession is going to be a dogfight crowded with a parade of people who will be leading the band to keep you down or in a place they prefer. When you think things are so bad and you feel you can't go on, allow me to share these words my grandmother bestowed upon me through all my trials and tribulations. She simply said, "You can make it." I encourage all who read this book to dare to believe in that wisdom.

—Victor Woods

To my literary agent and friend, Claudia Menza: words can never express the gratitude that I have for you for believing in me and loving me and being one of my most dearest and treasured friends. I appreciate everything you have done for me and continue to do for me to help me on my journey. May your life continue to be filled with happiness and joy: you deserve it.

Judith Curr: thank you for believing in me and publishing me and helping me bring my story to the next level. You gave me an opportunity when no one else would. I am eternally and forever grateful to you for that. I will make sure that your substance and greatness is known for the rest of my life.

Kimberle O'Sullivan, my executive director and very special friend: you are a wonderful, intelligent, talented, and very beautiful woman both inside and out. You, without question, are one of the most treasured and closest friends I have in my life. You have been there for me and worked tirelessly every step of the way to ensure that we continue to move our vision forward. Your belief in God and willingness to help others makes you a magnificent person to be around. May your spirit and light always shine bright and illuminate for all those in your presence.

Ambassador Andrew Young: meeting you has been one of the great privileges of my life. Your friendship, wisdom, and advice have been invaluable. Your stand on civil rights and your commitment to public service has made you a beacon of light and an example of excellence for all of humanity for now and evermore. I will continue to live a life worthy of my association.

Bill Clinton: thanks for the inspiration.

Earl Caldwell: thank you for all the love and encouragement you gave me. I appreciate you nurturing my spirit and believing in me when few else did. You and your family always will have a special place in my heart.

Chaka Khan: thank you for your time and advice: I will never forget your kindness and support.

Malcolm X's daughter, Ilyasah Shabazz: thank you for your friendship and unconditional love and all that you do to help people around the world.

Todd Hunter: thank you for your kind and special attention to my life story. You are excellent and outstanding at what you do. I look forward to our continued friendship.

To the late Bernie Mac: thank you for your friendship, wisdom, and guidance. Your presence in the world is missed.

Mama Simmons: thank you for always being in my corner and praying for me and telling me the truth even when I didn't want to hear it. I will always love you.

Asa Powell: I love you and I am so proud of all your achievements. I challenged you to greatness and you had the courage and tenacity to reach it. Thank you for always loving and supporting me and taking care of me when I've needed it.

Larry Hoover: thank you for the time you spent with me and the long talks we had. Your words of wisdom that you shared with me were not given in vain. I listened to every word and have applied them to my life. May you be free one day soon be free: until then, I'll be thinking of you.

Bill O'Reilly: thank you for your interest in my story and having me on your show.

Don Lemon: thanks for your friendship and putting me on the air. I appreciate it.

Police Chief Lester Aradi, formerly of the Buffalo Grove, Illinois, and Largo, Illinois, police departments: thanks for your friendship, forgiveness, and belief and what I'm all about and what I'm doing. Your support has been invaluable.

The late Harry Aleman: the advice you gave me in our cell helped transform my life. The lessons you taught me are invaluable.

The late Rocky and Felice: I will always remember walking the yard with you and the wisdom you bestowed on me: it altered my life. Thank you.

Attorney Tom McQueen: thank you for fighting for me. You are a superb and masterful attorney.

Attorney Horberg: thank you for fighting for my children and your high level of representation. It is appreciated.

Colonel Rick Wells, Manatee County Sheriff's Department: thank you for your friendship and always saying yes to me and helping me in every way you can. You are one of the finest law enforcement officers in the world.

Police Chief Frank Giammarese, Bloomingdale Police Department: I've enjoyed working with your department.

Police Chief Gregg Hall, Hazelwood Police Department: I appreciate your support and belief in me.

Police Chief Robert Marshall, Naperville Police Department: I've enjoyed working with you and your department.

Owez Nanjee: you are one of the sharpest and smartest guys that I know. I appreciate our friendship and wish you all the best.

Captain Jim Wayman: thank you for believing in me and saving my eyesight in prison.

Sophia Jennings: you are a breath of fresh air and a talented, smart, and ambitious woman, and most important, you are my friend and one of my biggest supporters. Thank you for all you do for me.

Christopher Perry, my friend and warrior: you've always protected me and loved me and my children. You are an incredible friend. May you find true happiness and joy in your life.

Jeffery Wank, agent, Hollywood, California: thanks for your vision and effort and belief in my story.

Adam Troy: thank you for your friendship, time, and being an excellent example of what it takes to make it.

Zackary Larson: I appreciate our friendship and your belief and support in my vision. You are an ambitious young man who has a bright future.

Attorney John David Simpson: thank you for never giving up on me and remaining my friend when hypocrites turned their back on me: you have stood by me, supported me, and believed in me. Your character, substance, and commitment to excellence has no equal. Know that I believe in you also and that I am your friend and will always be here for you whenever you call. You are truly my brother.

Attorney Londell McMillan, super lawyer and owner/CEO of Source magazine: thanks for spending time with me and sharing your valuable knowledge of what it takes to get the job done.

Dr. Robert Reidy, Jr.: thanks for believing in me and opening doors and giving me opportunities to share my message. You are a great man of vision and integrity.

Pastor Corey Brooks: thank you for believing in me, marching with me, and standing with me: you are my friend.

Pastor Jamal Bryant: thank you for your friendship and opening the door to your church for me to speak and touch so many lives.

Fred Karam: thank you for the advice you've given me throughout the years. You have cared about me and my family and friends. You welcomed me into your life and have been a tremendous influence on me. Please know that I respect you and honor our friendship at all times. I know that you are a man of honor, and I am privileged to call you my brother.

John Gailer: thanks to you and all your staff at National Dropout Prevention for your support.

Superintendent Rosario Agostaro: thank you for your leadership and your vision and commitment to education. The world is a better place with you in it.

Superintendent Constance Evelyn: thank you for your wit, courage, and tenacity, and for bringing me into your district.

Dr. Reginald Williams: thank you for your support and friendship.

Dr. Allene Gold: thank you for your belief in me and your commitment to education.

Principal Kirk Reinhardt and Assistant Principal Debra Fitzgerald, Kingston High School, Kingston, New York: thank you for all the work that you do for children and your community and bringing me in to speak in your district.

Assistant Superintendent Bonville, Kingston, New York: thank you for your vision and belief in me and your commitment in making schools a better place for children.

Assistant Principal Karmen La'Shaun Miller, Desert Oasis High School: what a blessing you have been to me and the students and staff within your midst. God bless.

Eric Vanzant and Lee Brannon: thank you for your time and leadership: you both exemplify what education is all about.

Pamela Matthis, lecture agent: thanks for your commitment and professionalism. I look forward to further collaboration and success together.

Assistant Principal Payne and Mr. Peoples, Hazelwood East School District: thank you for all that you do and your belief in me and your commitment to seeing that all children get a fair shot at the prize.

Missy Weld, Worldwide Speakers Agency: thank you for your belief in my message.

Bishop Bates: you are a great man of integrity and vision. Thank you for your friendship.

Jason Mimms: thanks for always being there and helping me when I needed you. Nothing but great things for you, my friend.

Printed in the United States
By Bookmasters